SPORT MANAGEMENT IN SCHOOLS AND COLLEGES

SPORT MANAGEMENT IN SCHOOLS AND COLLEGES

HAROLD J. VANDERZWAAG

University of Massachusetts

JOHN WILEY & SONS

NEW YORK • CHICHESTER • BRISBANE • TORONTO

Library of Congress Cataloging in Publication Data:

VanderZwaag, Harold J.
    Sport management in schools and colleges.

    Includes bibliographical references and index.
    1. School sports—Management. 2. Sports—Organiza-
tion and administration. 3. School sports—United States—
Management. 4. Sports—Organization and administra-
tion—United States I. Title.
GV346.V36 1984   796'.07'1173   83-14783
ISBN 0-471-87135-4

41,903

Preface

It is important to understand the frame of reference that characterizes this book. The primary thrust is on future possibilities—what could be—rather than on an assessment of the status quo. Of course, we invariably have to begin with the current situation. Seldom do we have the opportunity to start from scratch. Therefore, it will be evident that a considerable amount of attention has been given to an analysis of the present structure of, and functions in, school and college sport programs. However, it is equally important to recognize that things are changing, and the need for further change is increasingly evident. The field of physical education is in transition, and athletic programs are also experiencing many new challenges. In the meantime, sport management is an emerging concept although the truth of the matter is that the management of sport programs in the schools and colleges is far from being something new. It has been there and continues to be there in what could be called a disjointed form. What is needed is an integrated sport management program that proceeds from a systematic approach to management.

Two considerations underlie the entire discussion. The first is sport, and the second is management. In simplest terms, sport is conceived as including all physical games as well as the skills that lead up to those games. Thus, we are able to identify a long listing of sports that comprise the collective notion of sport. Basketball is a sport, and dribbling is a sport skill that leads to, or is part of, the sport of basketball. Likewise, tennis is a sport, and the serve in tennis is a counterpart to dribbling in basketball. There are many other such examples that one could give to identify the collective realm of sport.

At any rate, that is the kind of activity that is to be managed. Right now it is easy to note that we have sport in physical education, in athletics (interscholastic or intercollegiate sport), and in what we already label as sport, namely, intramural sport. What we need to do is to tie all this together from a management perspective. The focus is on an integrated sport program that would include instructional, intramural, and interscholastic or intercollegiate components.

The other consideration, management, provides the basis of the five middle chapters of this book. Basically, to manage is to plan, organize, staff, direct, and control. Although each of these functions is already being carried out in school and college sport programs, there is good reason to believe that each could also be handled much more effectively.

PLANNING

At least two aspects of planning stand out as being relatively weak. Program objectives and policy development are major areas for concern. Much more could be done in terms of setting meaningul objectives for the program and then carefully communicating those objectives to the other segments of the educational community as well as the public at large. No longer can sport administrators can get by with saying that their programs contribute to the educational goals of the institution. Someone is almost certain to want to know how that takes place. Also there is a need for a more straightforward, external presentation of the objectives. Throughout the book, an attempt has been made to stress the potential importance of solid and meaningful objectives. One cannot hope for much when they are treated in a light-hearted manner.

Policy development frequently lags behind other components of planning owing to the fact that it is not necessarily essential to the immediate action: It may be necessary to establish certain procedures, but we can continue to operate in a fairly ad hoc manner without a firm foundation for the important recurring matters. As indicated in Chapter 2, it seems to me that many schools and colleges need additional and improved policies with respect to athletes and coaches. The latter groups represent the bottom line in the interscholastic and intercollegiate realms. They also are subjects for special attention because they extend beyond the boundaries of institutional policies related to students and teachers. Also, generally speaking, if things are right with the athletes and coaches, the situation is probably a good one. By the same token, difficulties with athletes or coaches or both can quickly lead to deterioration in what might otherwise be a sound program. Those who manage school or college sport programs should give more attention to policy development as it relates to athletes and coaches.

ORGANIZING

The function of organizing actually points to the major limitation in existing school and college sport programs. In fact, this limitation is one of the principal reasons for the particular approach that has been taken in this book. The essence of the limitation is found in the continued attmpt to preserve the intercollegiate (or interscholastic), intramural, and physical education units as completely separate entities. Even putting these units under an umbrella title with an umbrella director will not solve the problem. The need for an integrated sport program is paramount. This cannot be accomplished unless some definite organizational changes are made. These, in turn, can be accomplished by beginning with what is already the built-in organizational base for school or college sport—namely, organization according to sports. We already have the basketball program, the field hockey program, and the like. From there we only need to go to a recognition that each of these programs has its intercollegiate, intramural, and instructional components. This is the fundamental reason why it is so important to have a sport coordinator for each sport. The need for integration is particularly evident in terms of the intramural and instructional components. In the larger programs, it will always be necessary to employ coaches who only coach as well as have an athletic director (A.D.) who is involved only with the intercollegiate operation. However, even there, the coach should be organizationally tied in with the total basketball program (or whatever sport is involved), and the A.D. should function under a director of the total sport program.

Obviously, none of this will materialize if sport is not also organizationally separated out from the other components of physical education. If the latter unit continues to comprise programs in sport, dance, and all other forms of exercise, the goal of an integrated sport program in the schools and colleges will never become a reality.

STAFFING

It is somewhat more difficult to pinpoint the deficiencies related to the staffing function in school and college sport. I suspect that, in general, the administrators of programs have done a better job with staffing than they have with planning or organizing. However, a few points are worthy of attention. To begin with, there is always room for sharpening the actual selection process. This is heightened in school and college sport owing to the relatively large number of applicants for any given position. Although contacts are important in any line of work, some effort should be made to reduce the reliance on the "old boy" network in hiring people for the various positions in the sport programs. Also it would appear that in many cases the interview procedure could be considerably improved in an effort to determine better the fit between the candidate's qualifications and the particular needs in the position that is to be filled.

In many cases, there is probably also room for improvement in the orientation phase of staffing. Policy orientation represents a particularly acute area. The staff should be thoroughly informed about those policies that affect athletes, coaches, and other staff personnel. However, it does seem that any deficiency here is just as much related to policy development as to policy orientation. In fact, such a deficiency may be even more related to policy development than to policy orientation.

Development tends to be one of the more frequently neglected aspects of staffing. In the context of school and college sport, the deficiency is particularly evident in the development of coaches for work in the sport program after they are no longer involved in coaching. It is somewhat difficult to be precise about suggesting what can be done to facilitate the development of coaches beyond the coaching situation. Certainly, advanced degree work will help, but that is not the whole answer. In general, coaches must be exposed as far as possible to the broader parameters of sport management so that they are better prepared to focus their attention beyond the coaching realm whenever a change in assignment is considered to be the most appropriate course of action.

Directing

Reading Chapter 5 should make it clear that directing is the most diverse of the five managerial functions. Considerable territory is involved in delegation, motivation, coordination, managing differences, and managing change. Obviously, there is always some room for improvement with respect to each of these aspects. Coordination will always remain a particular challenge in school or college sport owing to the disjunctive nature of the work in the various sports. However, I suspect that the management of difference and the management of change signal the areas of particular concern at the present time.

Although much progress has been made, there continues to be a primary need to manage any differences between the men's and women's programs as related to background, abilities, attitudes, and tasks. Basically, these differences are much like those that are found whenever an established program is compared with a newly developed program. Depending on the particular stage of development, every situation will be different. But, in general, administrators have to be sensitive to which procedures are applicable to women's sports programs as well to the men's program and which have to be altered to meet current needs. Much the same situation exists in noting the differences among the various sports. For example, if an institution has a relatively high-powered spectator sport program involving intercollegiate football or basketball or both, there is no way in which the directing function can be equally applied to all units or personnel within the total department. In essence, within any given institution, collegiate sport is not necessarily collegiate sport, and high school sport is not necessarily high school sport. Built-in priorities will determine differences in various kinds of support services in the daily process of directing. It is impossible to begin to manage differences without that kind of recognition.

Aside from the situation surrounding women's sports (which reflects the need to manage both differences and change), there is one change factor that is pervasive in all school and college sport programs. This is the economic factor. The control theme here is that very few, if any, of these programs can afford to do their financial planning and subsequent directing within the limitation of institutional resources and gate receipts. Exactly how each sport program copes with this change factor will be determined locally. For some programs, the management of change may be manifested in the employment of a special fund raiser. In others, it may mean extended booster club involvement. Selected colleges may seek added television revenue. Still others may be in a position to benefit from various combinations of external revenue support. At any rate, the directing function in school and college sport today necessitates a continuous exploration of all possible funding sources. It's no longer a simple matter of institutional funds plus gate receipts.

Controlling

The concept of control has been more or less stressed from the beginning of this book through the remainder of the body of the text. In the first chapter, the thoughts of Edwin Cady kenote the need for more control in college sport. Although possibly not as dramatically as college sport does, high school sport also reveals certain deficiencies in this regard.

To be more specific, the performance standards for athletic directors and coaches represent the critical control areas. Obviously, responsibilities for control of the athletic situation do not rest solely with the A.D. and the coaches. Cady makes that point very clearly. One might say that it is first and foremost an institutional responsibility, headed by the college president or high school principal. But that responsibility will never be completely carried out unless the athletic directors and coaches are provided with performance standards that are consistent with the objectives of the program and that are realistic. Basically what this amounts to is that school and college sport programs might be improved considerably if administrators would at least begin to utilize some of the principal tenets of management by objectives (MBO). As a start, it would help if programs were to identify their key result areas and then proceed to develop some routine, problem-solving and innovative objectives. Another control step would be to determine how well these objectives are met. Without these basics, it is rather unlikely that we will see much improvement in the control of school or college sport programs.

Harold J. VanderZwaag

Acknowledgments

I wish to thank those people who have made special contributions to the production of this publication. Two graduate students, Laura Canfield and Peter Hart, provided considerable assistance in the preparation of the original manuscript. The departmental secretary, Caroline Gouin, facilitated the steady flow of correspondence with John Wiley & Sons. Special thanks go to the three of them for their ground floor assistance.

The book would be far short the present quality if it were not for the careful and perceptive review of Dr. Herbert Appenzeller. The significance of his contribution far exceeds that which is found in the typical review process. His expertise as an athletic director and prolific author provided a special dimension in assessing the work.

It has been a pleasure to work with the editor, Raymond O'Connell, and other members of Wiley. I appreciate their patience and advice.

Finally, this book would not be a reality if it were not for the unfailing support and encouragement of my wife, Jane Barker VanderZwaag, and other members of my family. They also deserve a most grateful "thank you."

H.J.V.

Contents

CHAPTER 1

The Parameters of Sport Management

CONCEPTS AND PROBLEMS

Theoretical Support for Policy Development in Sport
The Pursuit of Excellence—A Solid Rationale for Elite Sport Programs
Significance of "The Game" in Sport
Relationship Between Training and the "Ideal" Coach
Records and Standardization
The Sport Fan as a Special Kind of Spectator
Key Questions in the Management of School or College Sport Programs
"The Big Game"
Relative Importance of Control in College Sport
The Common Denominator Between Sport and Management
The Continuous Flow Among the Managerial Functions

Before managerial guidelines for sport programs in the schools and colleges are discussed, it seems desirable to set forth a theoretical framework for sport management. Although the management of sport programs is readily identifiable, there is good reason to believe that people have various conceptions about the nature of management. Any differences in conception are probably compounded when we focus on the specifics of sport management. What are the parameters of sport? What are the components of effective management? How do these lead us to a more systematic understanding of sport management?

THE NATURE OF SPORT

From one standpoint, sport is perhaps better understood through experience than through any attempt to analyze the nature of the activity externally. Each of us has our own experiences in sport and with sport, and such experiences are probably

1

essential in our understanding of sport. But a fuller understanding is restricted through the very limitation of personal experience. It is impossible for anyone to generalize accurately only from what represents our experiential background. For example, someone may have had minimal or no involvement, either as a participant or a spectator, with the "trinity" of American sports (football, basketball, and baseball), as identified by Michael Novak in *The Joy of Sports*. Likewise another person may not have even seen a game of lacrosse or field hockey and yet be an avid football fan. In such cases, the difference in experiential backgrounds would likely yield contrasting conclusions regarding the nature of sport. So, in spite of the importance of the sport experience in gaining a partial understanding of sport, it seems desirable to enhance that perspective within the framework of a broader theoretical structure. I have selected three works that seem to offer a potential source of theoretical support for sport managers who are seeking a basis for policy development. In each case, a summary of the work is presented within the context of the management implication for those working in school or college programs.

Paul Weiss, Sport: A Philosophic Inquiry

Paul Weiss's *Sport: A Philsophic Inquiry* was published in 1969. In the ensuing years it has been the most widely discussed publication in the area of sport philosophy. That is not to say that everyone concurs with Weiss's line of thinking about sport, but it can safely be said that he has provided a stimulus for the development of other position statements with regard to sport.

The book is fairly unique in the extent to which it is structured around a single theme—the pursuit of excellence in sport. Weiss advances the dual hypothesis that the athlete is atttracted to sport owing to a desire to pursue excellence through the medium of sport and that the spectator is attracted as a result of an identification need with the athlete's pursuit of excellence. The athlete clearly occupies the center of the stage in Weiss's account of the sport enterprise in which he provides a rather detailed account of what makes an athlete an athlete. Weiss also draws several comparisons between athletes and others who are leaders or people of distinction in such fields as art, religion, government, and scholarship.

The most obvious managerial implication is that *Sport: A Philosophic Inquiry* offers a solid rationale for anyone involved with the management of an elite sport program. Coaches of professional sport teams and most athletic directors and college coaches would have to like what Weiss says about athletes and coaches. The athlete and the coach are both placed on a pedestal within the framework of an ideal perspective. The only real limitation would be that some elite sport programs would operate at cross-purposes with a few particulars in Weiss's treatise. For example, he states: "If scholarships are given as a payment for engaging in athletic contests, especially those which bring in large gate receipts or strong alumni support, the aims of education are perverted" (p 31) Clearly a fairly large segment of intercollegiate athletic programs in the United States would have to put aside that particular point while searching for a basis for policy development. Nevertheless, the general temper of the book offers much in the way of a firm foundation for intercollegiate athletics or any other elite sport program.

How does Weiss assess sport? In his conception, the essence of sport is to be found in "the game" of sport. This is also why the athlete occupies the center of the stage because it is the athlete who will make the game what it is or is not. Nothing really counts until the whistle blows. After that it is up to the athletes to demonstrate what they can do as athletes. Of course, others, such as officials, coaches, and spectators, have considerable effect on what happens in the game. "But only the players play, and thereby make both themselves and a game" (p. 165).

The stress on "the game" has important implications for the management of sport programs in schools and colleges. Everything possible must be done to maximize the potential for the well-played game. Suitable scheduling, selection of competent officials, provisions for adequate facilities and equipment, attraction of spectators, crowd accommodation, and (most importantly) the proper preparation of athletes are all aimed in one direction—to facilitate the "good game." If the game is all right, generally speaking, everything else is all right in sport. If it is not, there is good reason to believe that something is amiss from a management perspective. Only the athletes can assure that it will be a well-played game. However, they must have the support services to possess the opportunity to demonstrate what they can do as athletes. Judgment of the well-played game is not necessarily made on the basis of winning and losing because obviously there have to be a winner and a loser. As Weiss indicates, the athlete should want to win and should strive to win. Such desire and action are consistent with the very nature of sport. Even though the urge to win is the very essence of the well-played game, that is different from placing the premium on the end result, the victory or the loss. This idea would seem to have particular significance for the management of sport programs in the majority of schools and colleges, perhaps exclusive of Division I university level teams where financial considerations will inevitably result in a focus on the victory. Of course, it could also be argued that all college and university teams should approach the topic of winning and losing from the same philosophical stance.

Weiss also focuses on two other ideas that relate inextricably to the preparation for "the game." Proper training and competent coaching are central ideas in his analysis of what must precede the real test of the athlete in the game situation. These certainly are not new ideas for those who are on the "firing line" or "in the trenches" in the sport enterprise. However, Weiss approaches these ideas with certain dimensions that have considerable import for those who aspire to the effective management of sport programs in the school or college setting.

Training is viewed as the process of both satisfying and dissatisfying the athlete at the same time. It is also the process by which the mind is adjusted to meet the challenges of the body. In relatively unskilled performances, there appears to be an inherent disequilibrium between the mind and the body. It can be readily understood why training emerges as a key concept in any attempt to understand the nature of sport. Physical performance vividly dramatizes the need for strengthening the union between mind and body. From a management perspective everything possible must be done to plan, organize, direct, and control an effective training program.

Here is where Weiss's "ideal" coach comes into the picture. The word *ideal* is used because there is also a recognition that many coaches fall short in the process of totally preparing the athlete. He implies that all too frequently coaches proceed from a supervisorlike mode of operation in which there is insufficient attention to the total training needs of the individual athlete.

At least two other managerial concerns emerge from *Sport: A Philosophic Inquiry*. Records and standardization are key points in the development of the total treatise. The two are obviously related, and each is an integral factor in Weiss's development of the pursuit of excellence theme.

Records are not viewed as ends but, instead, as instrumental symbols of what can be accomplished. They serve as a motivational force for all athletes who would strive to be excellent in their sport. One has little difficulty in recognizing that record keeping is an important element in highly organized sport programs. Records are used as constant points of comparison among athletes and teams. Yet there may also be times when too much stress is placed on the record although those who make the various managerial decisions within the sport enterprise must, of course, consider the significance of records in the total program. This is particularly true when it comes to evaluating individual and team contributions.

Standardization is a logical extension of the emphasis on records in sport. Basically, standardization is an attempt to minimize differences in playing conditions so as to validate the record. At least two general types of record keeping can be noted within the context of the various sport programs. One of these is the notation of the highest level of achievement among any group of sport participants. The other is a notation of relative standing within the group. Based on these general conditions for record keeping, we find a great variety of individual and team records that are used as repeated points of comparison. Regardless of the specific form of record keeping, the need for some type of standardization remains evident.

Paul Weiss leaves the reader with the impression that everything possible must be done to increase the degree of standardization in sport. In expressing that idea, he is being entirely consistent with the development of his major theme. At the same time, it must be recognized that complete standardization may be an unattainable goal. It would seem that there will invariably be differences in the playing conditions that cannot be accounted for through any predetermined effort to provide for equal competitive circumstances. Nevertheless, the basic idea of standardization remains an important consideration for all those who have the responsibility for planning and organizing the various modes of competition in sport. At the school or college level, this factor becomes particularly critical when decisions have to be made relative to the selection of athletes or teams or both for postseason competition or postseason awards. Numerous other examples could be cited regarding the need for attempts toward standardization within the context of school and college sport programs. However, all the postseason considerations more or less epitomize the problem that can result from managerial ineffectiveness in attempting to meet the needs for standardization.

In summary, Paul Weiss provides the following reference points that can serve as key considerations in policy development for a school or college sport program: the pursuit of excellence, focus on the athlete, significance of "the game," proper training, competent coaching, records, and standardization. These certainly are not new ideas within the context of sport. Anyone who has ever been extensively involved with sport would probably recognize the significance of each element. However, when considered within the framework of the Gestalt relationship provided by Weiss, they offer fine potential as a theoretical launching pad for effective decision making.

Michael Novak, The Joy of Sports

In his book on sport, Michael Novak shares at least one common denominator with Paul Weiss. That is, Novak also offers a sound rationale for the development of elite sport programs. Both of these authors focus their attention on highly organized, highly competitive sport programs that tend to attract a large number of spectators. However, they reach this common ground from different directions. Whereas Weiss places the athlete center stage, Novak procedes from the perspective of the sport fan. It is important to note that Novak's sport fan is not the casual sport spectator who is there merely to be entertained. He conceives of the fan as being a special kind of spectator, one who really cares about the outcome of the contest because of a strong identification with teams or athletes or both. Although Weiss also places emphasis on spectator identification with the athlete's achievements, Novak goes far beyond that point in placing rooting on a pedestal within the sport realm.

There is another major difference of a practical nature between the works of Weiss and Novak. It was noted earlier that Weiss is opposed to athletic scholarships because he feels that they pervert the aims of education. By contrast, Novak feels that universities should proceed even further in the direction of professionalizing the athlete's role in the university environment, suggesting that professional sport teams should subsidize those universities that are preparing professional athletes. The athletic director, football coach, or basketball coach of a Division 1 university would do well to have Novak's book at hand, should someone seek a rationale for the program. The following statement more or less typifies his viewpoint regarding the significance of athletics in the university environment.

But should the universities allow themselves to be used as training grounds for the professionals? Well, there are schools of journalism and television, political science and agriculture, chemistry and engineering, law and medicine, business and accounting, teaching and nursing. Is sports the only profession that ought to be excluded? It is not the least spiritual profession, nor the least mythic, nor the least central to a culture. The athletic programs of certain schools are likely to make as great a contribution to the life, vitality, imagination, and moral unity of a given region as any other school programs. It will pain professors in other fields to admit it (p. 282).

The most direct managerial implications are found in Part Three, which comprises approximately the last half of Novak's book (1976). In the first half of the book, he sets forth his philosophical stance that undergirds the more practical topics that are discussed in the last part. Each of these topics centers around an issue, something about which there are legitimate grounds for debate within the sport sector. In most cases, he also expresses his own viewpoints as to where he stands with regard to the particular issue. Finally, he concludes with a chapter titled "Some Burkean Reforms," his designation for moderate reforms, which are designed to preserve the best in the sport enterprise from his perspective.

For our purposes we may note Novak's analysis of the issues or areas in which serious questions have been raised or should be raised concerning the conduct of sport programs. It seems rather unlikely that anyone who is involved with the management of a school or college sport program can avoid most of these questions.

1. *Women and Sport.* The question of women and sports is not whether sport should be for women as well as for men. Aside from other considerations, Title IX more or less takes care of that question. Differences of opinion center largely around the nature of the sport competition for women. Along with others, Novak recognizes that women have typically been denied opportunities for certain types of sport experience, particularly in sports where there is evidence of considerable physical force (bodily contact) and aggression. Many of the sports, notably football, have clearly been developed as a male model. By contrast, women have often been socially relegated to certain individual sports such as gymnastics, tennis, swimming, and riding. One of the questions is, To what extent should that pattern be preserved?

The larger question involving women and sport also poses many subquestions. Is there need for new sports for women? If so, along what lines should such sports be developed? Men's sports have obviously been assigned a system of priorities, particularly from a revenue-producing perspective. Should there be a priority system among women's sports? Should women's sports be developed within the framework of a revenue-producing potential? If so, what is the potential? Aside from the revenue-producing factor, which sports should be offered for women within the context of any school or college sport program? Who should make such decisions? How should they be made?

Many of these questions extend beyond Novak's discussion of women and sport. However, his general analysis of the basis for differing viewpoints on women and sport points to these questions, which require answers. More importantly, most of the questions will have to be faced by directors of school and college sport programs at one time or another. It is difficult to imagine that an athletic director could plan and organize his or her program without considering such questions.

2. *Relation of Sport to Politics and Morality.* Novak discusses politics, morality, and sports in a chapter entitled "Sports Are Not 'The Game of Life.'"The concept of transfer is the key to the analysis of this particular topic. A large question centers around the extent to which success, achievement, or even mere participation in sport is transferable to other areas of life. It appears that Novak takes a much stronger stand on this particular issue than he does on the previous issue related to women and sport. In general, he supports the proposition that sports should be accepted for what they are and says that we must be extremely careful about making claims as to what happens to the total individual as a result of extensive involvement in sport. Likewise he opposes the efforts to mix sport with politics and to extend the dimensions of sport from that direction. Yet, on the other side of the coin, Novak concludes by pointing out that sport is an area in which one can learn habits of discipline and poise under fire. In addition, it is quite evident that every athlete will also have to face humiliation at some time. The significant question regarding transfer possibilities still looms as a complex consideration. Nevertheless, some possibilities may exist.

It seems that this should be an area of great sensitivity for those who manage school and college sport programs. The relationship between sport and morality looms as a particularly significant topic at the junior and senior high school levels because the years spent in these institutions are formative ones. Typically, coaches have been inclined to make exaggerated statements regarding character building and related ideas at postseason banquets and other formal occasions recognizing team and individual accomplishments. Is any of this to be taken seriously? If not, is it good public relations to continue along those lines? On the other hand, if there are lessons to be learned through the medium of sport participation, this places a considerable responsibility on those who staff a school sport program. Because there is considerable variance among coaches in terms of what they might do to facilitate the learning of desirable habits, the selection of coaches takes on an added dimension even when there is doubt regarding the extent of transfer between habits or lessons learned in sport and the general conduct of a person's life.

3. *Regionalism and Sport.* To what extent is regionalism an important factor in the conduct of sport programs? Anyone who has lived in various sections of the United States knows that there are certain differences in the approach to sport from one region to another. These differences are manifested in various ways. The most obvious one probably involves the relative popularity of sports. Not all sports are equally popular in all regions or sections of the country. Some of this relates to the climate, but this is not the only consideration. Lacrosse is an example of a sport that reflects the differences in regional popularity. Until fairly recently, it was largely a game of the East Coast in the United States.

However, there are also more subtle regional differences in the sport realm. Some of these revolve around styles of play or the way in which the game is played. These are the differences that Novak uses as the focus for his discussion. More specifically, he analyzes the differences in the style of football from one one region to another region. What then is the issue involving such regionalism? It is largely one of deciding whether the apparent differences are as marked as they might seem.

Novak concludes with a discussion of sports in the Ivy League. He points out that things are supposed to be different in the Ivy League with regard to the attitude toward sport and the conduct of sport programs. Nevertheless, he suggests that in the final analysis any differences may be overshadowed by the importance of winning, which is not a regional matter—the Ivies also seek to be number one.

Those who manage sport programs will also have to consider the regional factor. Should any regional difference be perpetuated? To what extent should regional considerations be taken into account in determining program priorities? Is the regional nature of sport a factor in the selection of coaches? Is it a factor in scheduling athletic contests? These are some of the practical questions that emanate from Novak's treatment of the regional topic.

4. *The Press and Sport.* The issue of the press and sport is a fairly extensive one, revolving around the legitimate role of the press in reporting and commenting about the conduct of sport programs. Michael Novak notes that there are various kinds of sportswriters, ranging from the "house writer" to the critic who seems intent on putting down sport. In general, he deplores the fact that sportswriters are a different breed today. They no longer provide accounts of sport events as in the past. According to Novak, television is the culprit. The extensive exposure of the public to sport through the medium of television has caused the writers to redirect their focus from relating the experience of the sport event.

Whether or not one agrees with Novak's opinions about the media and sport, he provides much food for thought for any athletic director or coach. What kinds of information should be furnished to the press? How should the members of an athletic department attempt to relate to the variety of sportswriters who do exist? More specifically, the selection of a sports information director has to be considered as a critical factor in press relations.

5. *Money and Sport.* There are many aspects of the money issue, as it relates to sport. Novak discusses two parts of the large money issue under "The Universities and the Professionals" and "Money Changers" in the Temple." The latter topic deals largely with the extremely high salaries that are paid today to some professional athletes. The former has been referred to earlier in this chapter, so I will not repeat the thrust of that discussion. It should suffice to say that this is undoubtedly the top managerial concern for a college athletic director, particularly at a Division 1 University.

To summarize Novak's overall contribution, I would say that he has offered a splendid model regarding sport management theory. He provides considerable insight into the nature of sport in the United States. In addition, he hits at many everyday concerns that must be faced by those who have the responsibility for the management of school and college sport programs.

Edwin Cady, The Big Game: College Sports and American Life

As indicated by its title, Edwin Cady's work[1] is particularly applicable as a reference here because it centers entirely on college sport. However, in spite of the more restricted scope, Cady, like Weiss and Novak, focuses on elite sport programs. "The Big Game" is just what the title implies. It is not an account of the intramural sport participant or the intercollegiate participant at the level of relatively low-key competition. Nevertheless, the account tells us much about the nature of sport at the college level, and it can serve as an important reference for those who guide these programs.

The work is divided into two parts. In the first, Cady sets forth the theoretical basis on which the "big game" rests. He begins by stressing that college sport is something special in the United States. While recognizing that professional sport has also shared in the extensive American involvement with sport, he contends that we must look to college sport to find the ultimate significance of American sport, which extends beyond the game per se. In his words, the Big Game "is a major form of public art" (p. 4). In the second part, the more practical part, Cady sets forth the realities of college sport as well as presents suggestions for those who have responsibilities for such a program. This part is aptly entitled "What to Tell the New President About . . .''

Various thoughts of Cady have been selected for presentation here because they both shed light on the nature of college sport and can serve as guidelines for the management of college sport programs.

Control. Control is perhaps the key theme in Cady's entire work. He believes there is a need for careful control of college sport programs—both externally and internally. By external control, he is referring to the kind of control that can be provided by a national organization (e.g., National Collegiate Athletic Association) or a conference. However, near the end he does suggest that the NCAA book of rules should be sent to the archives and that the organization should start afresh. Internal control includes those things that can be done within any given institution to regulate the circumstances surrounding the Big Game. If this is not done, "the damn thing will blow up every time" (p. 189).

The stress on the need for control is also manifested in the title for Part Two of

---

[1]Material in this book taken from Edwin H. Cady is reprinted by permission of The University of Tennessee Press. From Edwin H. Cady, *The Big Game: College Sports and American Life*. Copyright © 1978 by The University of Tennessee Press.

the book. The new college president needs to be told certain things so that he or she will recognize the importance of control. That is not to suggest that all the control can or should rest in the hands of the president. But the president is the one who is ultimately responsible for the way in which the Big Game is handled at his or her institution.

Actually, Cady is a firm believer in faculty control of intercollegiate athletic programs. He favors an arrangement whereby faculty representatives are organized in a control by conference; this serves to coordinate both the internal and external components of control. One of the basic needs for faculty involvement stems from the presence of what Cady calls the "Baker Street Irregulars." That is his term for those people who are external to the university but who make it their business to get involved with the conduct of intercollegiate sport. Invariably, they are people who have money or some other form of influence. Their actions are frequently manifested in the recruitment process. They may or may not be alumni. If the president does not establish a firm means of institutional control, headed by faculty and competent administrators, he or she will increasingly yield to the influence of the Baker Street Irregulars. Yet, the scope and significance of the Big Game is such that there will always be external constituencies who have their finger in the pie. That's why the desired control will never be an easy task.

As difficult as control might be, the only real options are to follow either one of two positions, both of which are rejected by Edwin Cady. One procedure is to conduct the college sport programs according to what is now a fairly popular idea (associated with the name of Vince Lombardi)—that "winning isn't everything —it's the only thing!" The other procedure is to follow the lead of the late Robert M. Hutchins in suggesting that there should be no mix between big time sport and the academic community.

Coach. Perhaps no word is more clearly identified with the American sport scene than the word *coach*. Although the athlete, of necessity, will always remain at the heart of the sport enterprise, the athletic coach has emerged as a special kind of person in American culture. The coach is many different things to many different people; under various circumstances the coach is a teacher, trainer, recruiter, public relations director, counselor, motivator, or authoritarian role model. Coaches are both glorified and damned, often both within a short span of time. In almost any setting, be it professional or social, coaches tend to attract special attention. It is perhaps for these reasons that Cady chose to devote an entire chapter to the topic of the coach. Certainly, an analysis of the role of the coach sheds further light on the nature of sport in the United States. Furthermore, that role would appear to be epitomized at the college level.

Cady goes into a rather detailed discussion regarding the desired qualifications for a college coach. He points out that this is a complex matter, involving an array of talents. A certain indefinable element also seems to exist as a common denominator among all successful coaches. The word *class* emerges as a key concept in terms of what one is looking for in a coach. A coach stands out from the crowd with respect to total presentation of self. Some people even suggest that if, through experience, one has seen enough coaches, one can readily identify the real coach.

In spite of this very idealistic picture involving a coach's qualifications, it is also a well-recognized fact that Big Game coaches live in a very tenuous position with regard to job security. They are hired and fired with great regularity. Cady also discusses in detail their precarious position. This leads him to a most practical point with the suggestion that they should have a greater degree of job security alongside the tenured professors of the university. He recognizes that academic tenure may not always be a valid possibility for many coaches but feels there should at least be some guarantee of a staff position on the institutional payroll. Though some may regard this as a most practical point of discussion, Cady's viewpoint may not be viewed as practical by all university administrators. However, what he has done is to point out a problem that is at the heart of practical concerns in the management of collegiate sport programs. In defense of Cady's position, it can be said that he is entirely consistent with his strong emphasis on control. It would not be very realistic to suggest that institutional control of the athletic program can be maintained when the coach is in a position of having to win or get fired.

Student Athletes and Where They Come From. Cady's first point of information for the new president concerns student athletes and where they come from. His approach is distinctive in that he is not concerned with the geographical origins of athletes. Instead, he attempts to present a picture of the nature of student athletes.

Cady begins by pointing out that the student athlete is at the core of any good college sport program. If there are deficiencies in the selection of these athletes, probably everything else will go wrong. This recognition is compounded by the fact that the college athlete is also a special kind of person. He (or she) may not be special in the same way that a coach is special, but the student athlete comes with a different background from that of the typical student. For one thing, the college athlete has emerged from an extended process, beginning in adolescence, in which many boys (and now girls) compete for positions on the various sport teams. This in itself tends to set the college athlete apart from the general population. Cady points out that it is fairly difficult to generalize about that element, which stands out as a common denominator among successful athletes. Nevertheless, he does cite at least one distinguishing characteristic among the vast variety of cases: "they want to make something happen" (p. 148).

What then is the message here for the college president? Basically, it is a message that brings us back once again to the central theme of control. With respect to the students, the control will have to be manifested in at least two forms. First, the academic aspect has to be considered. Probably many of the student athletes will need some form of tutoring. This may be primarily attributed to both past and present dedication to athletic pursuits. The natural distribution of talents may also be a partial factor in the total picture. Cady favors a tutoring program. Though academic standards must be maintained, everything possible should be done to assist the athletes in obtaining college degrees. Second, there is need for control to protect the athlete from those who would prey on the athlete's talents. Owing to the public visibility of the athlete, there are always those people, largely external to the university, who will use the athlete for their own benefit. Quite obviously, that use can manifest itself in any one of several forms.

Cady tends to be particularly cautious about the extent to which college athletes should look toward a professional sport career. For most of them, it is not a realistic possibility. Consequently, they need to be guided, like any student, toward some other career. For the "blue chippers" a possibility of a professional career in sport may exist. In those cases, the faculty, coaches and administrators should take the lead in advising the athlete regarding negotiations with prospective teams.

Special attention is given to the topics of women student athletes and black student athletes. In the case of the former, it is largely a matter of recognizing that things are changing rapidly. Cady states the situation most succinctly: "The true frontier of intercollegiate athletics in our times is sexual" (p. 178). With regard to the women's participation, he takes a position that has also been expressed by others, including Michael Novak. Cady concurs all the way with the need to increase the participation among women. However, they will have to decide what should be involved in the participation. There may be a need for new sports or a change in emphasis among sports. Most importantly, women will have to decide to what extent they would like their program to be highly competitive.

Perhaps the most unusual feature of Cady's position on women's programs is his viewpoint on financial arrangements. He does not go along with the idea that the expansion of women's programs should necessarily create a financial crunch. His answer is that many of the men's coaches could take over additional duties to include the coaching of women's teams. There is evidence that his suggestion has been implemented to some extent. Yet it seems to be a proposal that tends to be opposed by both men and women for different reasons.

Cady's advice regarding black student athletes is fairly simple and straightforward. What it actually amounts to is an extension of the attention that must be given to all student athletes. By virtue of their cultural backgrounds, many black athletes cannot be expected to compete academically on the same basis with other students. Consequently, additional steps must be taken to enhance their status as bona fide students in efforts to complete their degree work.

Recruiting and Financial Aid. At least one other topic in Cady's work is particularly relevant to our purposes in this chapter. The topic concerns recruiting and related considerations. Certainly, it is a subject that tells us much about the nature of contemporary collegiate sport in the United States. It also is a subject that represents a principal area of concern in the management of collegiate programs. Once again, the concept of control appears as the recurring theme in Cady's position. Even though he strongly supports the right kind of recruiting efforts, the element of control must be there.

He begins by pointing out that the recruitment of college students generally is woven into the very fabric of American higher education. Thus, it should be no great surprise that recruitment has also emerged as a most significant factor in college sport. The only real difference is that coaches face some really special problems in their efforts to obtain the top talent. They are involved with the most highly competitive mode of recruiting. Unfortunately, this is one place where the element of control can emerge as a most serious problem.

Cady's strongest suggestion relates to the recruitment of the quality student athlete. He uses the term *ringer* to describe the athlete who is not likely to survive academically. He points out why this is not beneficial to all concerned in the long run. The basic contention is that the intellectually unqualified student athlete is not likely to remain in school that long in most cases. This leads to lack of squad continuity, lack of recruiting continuity, lack of leadership, and general squad problems. Eventually, the college also acquires a reputation that tends to affect all involved.

Is there any answer to the recruiting dilemma? Another one of Cady's stronger suggestions is that the alumni can be used in a positive way to recruit the right kind of student athlete. After all, they are products of the institution, and they should ultimately be concerned about the reputation of their institution. Their use in the recruiting process would appear to be far preferable to the involvement of the "Baker Street Irregulars," even though it was noted earlier that some alumni may fall into the latter grouping as well. The key to the alumni involvement is that they will require education and guidance as to what is desired in the way of the quality student athlete. As Cady stresses throughout his book, the control here will also not be easy. But it is worth the effort if one has the dual interest of preserving the integrity of education and maintaining the cultural significance of the Big Game.

Conclusion Regarding the Nature of Sport

The task in the first part of this chapter has been to delineate a theoretical structure for the nature of sport that might serve as a guideline for those who manage school and college sport programs. I selected three works that seem to be particularly useful in this regard. There are several other fine references that relate to this topic. However, Weiss, Novak, and Cady were chosen because they offer a particularly meaningful launching pad for the application of sport theory within the context of school and college programs.

Each of the three works serves a distinct purpose in providing the total framework. Weiss keynotes the individual who is central in any attempt to understand sport. His analysis of the athlete unlocks the inner door in any attempt to get at the roots of sport. If we don't understand what makes the athlete an athlete, we will never understand sport. Novak lays bare the essence of what is involved in being a sport fan. We all know that sport fans are an important component of modern sport, and Novak offers an appropriate theoretical explanation of this form of human involvement in sport. Cady brings the two together within the context of that aspect of sport that is uniquely American—college sport. For this reason, his analysis is particularly appropriate for our purposes here. Moreover, his focus on college sport is the most valid appraoch in any attempt to understand the nature of American sport. There is good reason to believe that school sport has been developed by following the collegiate model. Also, professional sport is clearly an outgrowth of the collegiate game.

There is still one missing link in terms of attempting to get a grasp on the total sport enterprise. As noted earlier, Weiss, Novak, and Cady all direct their attention to what could be called "elite" sport programs. That is, they are all concerned with highly organized sport, involving the pursuit of excellence and the attraction of spectators. Needless to say, there is considerably more involved in the total sport picture. We still lack an account of the individual who particpates in sport on a recreational basis through the medium of an intramural school or college program, a private club, a service agency, or other community programs. However, it could also be argued that the elite sport programs set the tone for much of the mass sport participation. The reasons for and the manifestations of that participation may be quite different at the recreational level, but the public sport consciousness is generated through the identification with the elite programs.

THE NATURE OF MANAGEMENT

Sport and management share one major common denominator. As was said earlier, the nature of sport may be better understood through experience in sport than through any theoretical explanation. The very same thing can be said about management. The best way to learn about management is to get involved with it. Nevertheless, as with the sport experience, that does not necessarily mean that management experience is the complete story in becoming an effective manager. A colloquial expression says that "we can't see the forest because of the trees." That may be applicable to management and sport. It is often helpful to examine the broader theoretical base for the actions within the management domain, as well as the sport enterprise.

The available literature on the nature of management is rather extensive. In spite of the assortment of ideas on the subject, there tends to be a strong thread of continuity in the approach that is followed. By and large, management is analyzed by considering the functional activities that constitute the management process. Differences can be noted in the functions that are included in the total process of management. However, for the most part, the differences are more superficial than real. For example, one writer may identify five principal functions in management whereas another sets forth seven functions. Closer examination will probably reveal that the only real difference stems from the way in which the categorization and subgroupings are approached.

Following is a listing of the more commonly identified functions of management.

planning

organizing

staffing

directing

controlling

evaluating

communicating

decision making

It would appear that the first five in the preceding listing represents the core functions, as determined by a review of the related literature. The reason for this may be seen by looking at the last three from a somewhat different perspective. Evaluating could be viewed as a subset of controlling. We evaluate in order to control; evaluation is a partial instrument in control. Communicating and decision making are really quite different from the others in one respect because they cut across all the other listed functions. In other words, we communicate in our organizing, and we communicate while we are directing. Similarly, decision making is an integral part of planning, staffing, or any of the other functions. Consequently, the first five have been selected as the basic parameters in this summary attempt to delineate the nature of management.[2]

Planning

In the simplest terms, to plan is to decide on a course of action. A plan is futuristic in nature even though it might involve planning for the near future or in the long run. Planning will usually involve forecasting in some form or another. As a current example, in planning a high school sport program today, one would certainly be advised to consider the forecast related to financial restraints in public education during the next 10 years. Unless one is embarking on a new endeavor, the forecast will probably be initiated by first determining where the present course will lead. Modifications in the forecast will be based on anticipated changes. The forecast is the basis for the second step in the planning process, the establishment of objectives.

The objectives are the desired end results for the program. Sometimes one finds distinctions made among such terms as goals, objectives, and desired outcomes. However, such distinctions are not needed here. The important thing for managers is to determine what they would like to see accomplished, whatever that may be called. It might be said that objectives represent the very heart of the plan-

[2]The basic information that is included in the analysis of these five functions is derived from R. Alec Mackenzie, "The Management Process in 3-D," *Harvard Business Review*, Vol. 47, No. 6, November-December 1969, pp. 80–87.

ning processes. Without them, there is no clear sense of direction. With unobtainable or ill-conceived objectives, there is virtual certainty that the remainder of the planning process will not take shape. It is most important that the objectives be sufficiently realistic and concrete to facilitate the development of the ensuing strategies. This might be demonstrated through a hypothetical example in college sport. An athletic department might decide that an objective or goal was to move from NCAA IAA to Division 1 competition in football. The college has a stadium that seats 20,000 people. The financial forecast indicates that raising sufficient funds to enlarge the present facility or build a new one is unlikely. The geographical area is also not known for the attraction of football fans. In such a case, the proposed goal would be an unrealistic objective that would likely prohibit any further steps in meaningful planning.

With the establishment of realistic and concrete objectives, there is a basis for the development of appropriate strategies for reaching those objectives. "How?" and "When?" are the key questions to be addressed in the strategical plans. Strategies represent the blueprint of the planning process. Another way of looking at the strategical component is to recognize that strategies pave the way for the remainder of the planning process.

Once the strategies are determined, management is ready to move to the considerations that represent the bulk of the planning phase. The actual planning will be particularly manifested in the design for program, budget, and procedures. Program planning includes the establishment of priorities, sequence, and timing. It is obvious that there has to be a very close link between the program planning and the strategies that were earlier determined. Program planning really represents a detailed guide for reaching objectives and carrying out the strategies.

Budgeting is the most concrete aspect of the total planning process. The budget should be a direct reflection of everything else that goes into the total planning component of management. Thus, one should be able to examine the budget and have a fairly clear idea of what is planned for the total program. If there were a need to take a shortcut in determining the plans of a particular organization, budget examination would be the item for attention. This, of course, is based on the assumption that the budget is consistent with the other aspects of the planning process. In particular, there should be a strong correlation between the program priorities and those priorities that are indicated by the dollar figures in the budget. Should that not be the case, something is askew in the planning process.

Thus far, we have considered those aspects of planning that are largely preliminary to the execution of the other managerial functions. However, it is most important to note that planning is a continuous process; it does not stop when we begin to organize, and it continues to be important throughout the entire managerial cycle. Two forms of continued planning are particularly evident. They are the standardization of methods and policy development. Even though each of these might begin in the initial planning phase, they cannot fully materialize until the program has been in effect for a certain period of time. The initial strategies provide a base for the standardization of methods. Nevertheless, there will be a need to make certain modifications before the procedures are set.

Policy development might be viewed as the capstone of the entire planning process. Essentially, it involves making standing decisions on important recurring matters. Brink (1978) presents a fine description of how policy fits into the total management process. He cites three basic components of management—objectives, policy, and implementation. He sees policy as being the essential link between the other two components. Even though the establishment of policy is integral in complete planning, it obviously also takes time to establish policy. That's why policy development is a continuous process.

To date, policy development for school and college sport programs seems to show a number of deficiencies. In particular, policies are needed with respect to program structure, financing, athletes, and coaches.

To summarize, the planning processes begin with forecasting and end with policy development. However, even though planning is the beginning of management in action, it does not cease when one moves to the other functions of management. Planning is an ongoing function. To a large extent this is also true of the other managerial functions. Although there tends to be a chronological flow involving planning, organizing, staffing, directing, and controlling, one function does not cease as another is assumed.

Organizing

It should also be noted at this point that there is no hard line between the various functions of management. Although the dividing lines are evident, one function leads into the other. The link between planning and organizing is particularly apparent. It might even be argued that organizing is a form of planning. Nevertheless, the major difference involves implementation or action. The action begins with the process of organizing. But planning will also be evident while the organizing is being done. The overlap is most apparent at the outset with the establishment of an organizational structure.

The organizational structure provides the base for the remainder of the process of organizing. It is manifested through the presentation of an organizational chart, which offers a pictorial focus for understanding how the organization is to be managed from a personnel perspective. In addition to setting forth the basic positions within the organization, the chart can also assist in delineating relationships. This serves, too, to define the liaison lines, which, in turn, facilitates coordination. Once again, a point of overlap is evident among the managerial functions because coordination is also an important component in the function of directing.

The need for a sound organizational structure cannot be overemphasized. One of the greatest potential pitfalls within any organization, particularly a large one, is that "the left hand doesn't know what the right hand is doing." The organizational chart, delineating the relationships, will help to avoid that pitfall. Beyond that, the next step in organizing is to create position descriptions.

At least four things may be accomplished through the creation of valid position descriptions. First, they will define the scope of the various positions. This is needed primarily in order to avoid undesirable overlap among the positions. Second, positional relationships can and should be identified in the description. Who reports to whom, and who works with whom? As noted earlier, to some extent these questions are answered through the organizational chart, but the descriptions provide the necessary details. Third, the descriptions are used to define responsibilities. This may well be their most important use. The responsibilities are a logical extension of the scope of the position and represent a further breakdown of the scope. Finally, the descriptions should also indicate the authority that goes with each position. It is well known that there must be appropriate authority to accompany the responsibility. The descriptions can assist in reaching that objective.

The organizing function culminates with the establishment of position qualifications. It involves defining the qualifications for persons in each position within the organization. In general, the position descriptions will more or less dictate the qualifications that are established. However, there may be desired personal or general qualifications that extend beyond the needs in the position per se. These are qualifications that extend beyond a specific kind of position. Often they are qualifications that are sought for a certain grouping of positions within the organization (e.g., middle management).

Whether the position qualifications are quite specific or more general, this step of establishing the qualifications also tends to be one of the key components in managerial effectiveness. It is usually most desirable that the qualifications be specified as clearly as possible. But, as noted earlier, there may be those qualifications that cut across positional lines. The importance of establishing appropriate position qualifications is particularly demonstrated when we move to the next managerial function, that of staffing. Many of the potential problems in staffing can be avoided through careful attention to this last aspect of organizing. Once again, we see the close link between the various managerial functions.

Staffing

The key to fulfillment of the staffing function is to be found in effective recruitment and selection of personnel. In addition to the selection process, staffing also includes the orientation, training, and development of staff. However, these aspects of staffing will be facilitated if the manager chooses competent people for positions in the organization. Nowhere is this better exemplified than in the areas of college and professional sport, where the successful coach knows that recruitment and selection are the name of the game. The coach's ability to orient, train, and develop the athletes is directly dependent on what happens up front in terms of selection. In fact, head coaching is a good place to look if one wishes to observe concrete evidence of any aspect of management in action.

When one approaches recruitment, the immediate consideration is the culminating point of organizing, which involves the position qualifications. In essence, recruitment is an effort to obtain the best-qualified person for a given position. If the manager does not launch recruitment from the position perspective, the ensuing efforts in staffing are likely to be misguided. Once again, professional sport can be noted as dramatic evidence of this point. Those who conduct the drafts of college talent fully understand the need to establish the fit between position qualifications and the subsequent recruitment and selection.

Selection is really a further refinement of everything that goes into recruitment from the perspective of establishing that fit. Recruitment will provide the pool of talent that generally meets the qualifications for the position. The actual process of selection is the cruncher in the effort to meet the needs in the position. Here we observe one of the more widespread pitfalls in ineffective management. The recruitment may be handled quite well. The position qualifications are carefully established, and the position is thoroughly advertised. However, things break down in the selection process. At that point the manager may turn to personal or political considerations that tend to work at cross-purposes in the principal effort to establish the fit between the qualifications for the position and the qualifications of the selected personnel. There is, of course, a human factor here that will always exist outside any ideal format of management.

The remaining aspects of staffing are a bit different in that there may be a tendency to overlook or minimize them within certain organizations. This is certainly not true of coaches, who know that they have to orient, train, and develop after they select. But there are other situations wherein the needs for orientation, training, and development are more subtle. That certainly does not negate the idea that effective staffing includes more than appropriate selection of personnel. Selection is the keystone to the ensuing steps in the total staffing function.

Orientation has the purpose of familiarizing new people with the nature of the organization of which they are now members. It can assume any one of several forms, both formal and informal. Much of the informal orientation is of a spontaneous nature, but the manager must plan for the informal as well as the formal means. Other staff members can be particularly useful in facilitating the orientation process. Orientation should include information regarding the objectives of the organization, the strategies that are used in pursuing those objectives, and the policies that have been established to guide the work within the organization. Within many organizations there is often a need to include additional information about other groups or individuals who are external to the organization but with whom there are close working relationships. As an example, a school or college athletic director would include information about the institution's conference or league as part of the orientation for a new coach. Some of the orientation can be accomplished through written material. Other aspects of orientation, particularly the more informal, will be oral.

Training is related to orientation, but it is different in one important respect. Orientation relates to the total environment of the organization, with the recognized need to become familiar with the broader situation. By contrast, training focuses on in-depth instruction and practice in the work that is required of the person who is assuming the position. Another way of looking at the contrast is to note that orientation is largely organization-centered whereas training is job-centered. As with orientation, training may also be either formal or informal. However, training is more frequently of a formal nature. Much of that will depend on the particular makeup of the position that is involved. It is to be expected that a head coach will utilize quite formal means to train the athletes for various positions on the team. On the other hand, the training of an academic professor of sport management may be fairly informal.

The last component in complete staffing is the one that is most likely to be overlooked in many situations. Development is actually an extension of training. It is the improvement of knowledge, attitudes, and skills. Development offers the potential to advance beyond the immediate situation. The reason that it may be overlooked is that it is not absolutely necessary for fulfilling the minimal demands of the current position. However, without development, there is also little opportunity for growth. For this reason, the effective manager will provide opportunities for development. If this doesn't happen, the mangager will likely encounter future problems as he or she carries out the managerial functions of directing and controling. Lack of opportunity for development is a principal morale problem within many organizations.

Directing

Management in action is probably most clearly identified in the directing function. It is not necessarily the most important function, but much of the direction may take care of itself if management has been effective in planning, organizing, and staffing. But directing is the point at which it all happens.

Within most organizations, directing begins with the process of delegation. Naturally, the larger the organization, the greater the need for delegation. To delegate is to assign responsibility and exact accountability for results. Lack of clear delegation of responsibility is another one of the more noticeable pitfalls in management. With the delegation of responsibility, there must also be the accompanying and appropriate delegation of authority. Nevertheless, aside from considerations of authority, the *way* in which responsibilities are delegated can pose a problem. Frequently, things are left unsaid in the process of delegation, and this contributes to a fuzziness that may limit the entire directing function.

The need for coordination points to another dimension of directing that is a real challenge for anyone who is involved with management. Directing also includes the management of differences among the members of the organization. The coordination will not materialize unless the differences are taken into account. This is a dual process of encouraging independent thought on the one hand and resolving conflict on the other. It is often most difficult to strike a balance between those two considerations; nevertheless, the efforts in this regard are central in the directing function of the management process.

The management of differences also points to another demand in terms of providing competent direction, namely, the management of change. There is always a need for some change based on both internal and external variables. The effective manager is able to chart a steady course in leading the organization toward the pursuit of its objectives while at the same time stimulating creativity and innovation in achieving those objectives. Again, this is not an easy task, but the process of directing is limited without it. One frequently hears reference to the idea that an organization lacks direction. That may mean the objectives have not been clearly defined. It may also mean that management has been unable to cope with the need for creativity or change in the pursuit of the objectives.

There is one other aspect of directing that actually affects the entire function—motivation. Without motivation, there is a good probability that relatively little will be accomplished in terms of other efforts at providing direction. The importance of motivation has perhaps been overemphasized, yet one can scarcely consider delegation, coordination, management of differences, and the management of change without factoring in the need for motivating. Some authorities believe that motivation is *the* most significant concept in the entire process of management. Without it, any manager will be severely limited in performing the various managerial functions, from planning to controlling. And yet it is particularly in the directing function that we observe the efforts to motivate.

Controlling

Control is basically aimed at ensuring progress toward reaching objectives according to whatever plan has been set forth for the organization. As with the other functions, there are several elements involved in controlling the managerial situation. With respect to controlling, these elements are largely chronological although the cycle or continuous nature of the functions is also evident here.

The first step in controlling is to establish a reporting system. A key factor in the system is a determination of what critical data are needed. This is particularly true in a large organization; management must decide what kind of data will be essential in the control process. An excess of data will likely deter any further steps in the effort toward controlling. In addition to determining the kind of data, the reporting system should also provide accountability for how the data are to be reported and when they are to be received.

The reporting system provides one of two essentials for launching the controlling function. The other essential is the development of performance standards. It is not sufficient to have the critical data; there must also be a means of determining how the data will be utilized. Performance standards set the conditions that will exist when the key duties are well done. The data can then be compared with the standards to provide the basis for evaluation.

As noted earlier in this chapter, evaluating is sometimes viewed as one of the principal functions of management. However, many feel that it makes more sense to consider evaluating as an aspect of controlling. This attitude is based on the idea that evaluation leads to control because when we evaluate, we attempt to determine the extent to which the actual performance varies or deviates from the standards which have been established. In turn, this will provide some measure of the extent to which the objectives or goals of the organization are being reached. Again, we see evidence of the cycle or continuous flow of the management process. Somethimes evaluation will result in replanning or in an adjustment of the plans that were made earlier in the management process.

A key factor in determining any need for the adjustment of plans is the evaluation of the extent to which the group has deviated from the standards and objectives that were originaly established for that group. If there is considerable deviation, adjustment of plans may be warranted. By contrast, individual deviation is more likely to be handled through other forms of corrective action such as counsel or additional training.

Ultimately, the controlling process will result in some form of reward system. Depending on the nature of the organization and the individuals in that organization, reward can be manifested in any one or more of several forms. Within many organizations, remuneration is the most concrete and meaningful form of reward. However, praise and discipline are other common results of the evaluation process. The way in which reward is handled is critical for carrying out all the other functions of management. Obviously, what is done in terms of remuneration, discipline, and praise will have a strong bearing on effectiveness in staffing and directing. Somewhat more indirectly, the reward system will also reflect on the utility of the earlier planning and organizing.

PUTTING IT TOGETHER: SPORT AND MANAGEMENT

Thus far we have independently examined the nature of two extensive human activities—sport and management. As indicated at the outset, this book is based on the premise that these activities share a common denominator, namely, the management of the sport enterprise. Furthermore, there is reason to believe that the sport enterprise can be managed more effectively in many instances and that this, in turn, will enhance the viability of the various sport programs. However, as with many propositions, the case cannot merely be stated: it also has to be won. This chapter began with some observations about the nature of sport through an analysis of the ideas of Weiss, Novak, and Cady. An examination of the nature of management, using the model set forth by Mackenzie, followed. Now we are faced with this question: How can the ideas of effective management be utilized within the management of a sport program? This question might be answered by noting the management concerns that are either implied or stated in the works of Weiss, Novak, and Cady.

As already stated, *Sport: A Philosophic Inquiry* offers a solid rationale for anyone who is involved with the management of an elite sport program. At the same time, Weiss's work points to certain management needs in sport. One of these stems from the author's strong emphasis on standardization. Within the management process, this is a factor basic to both the planning and controlling functions. In particular, standardization is important in developing performance standards for athletes and coaches.

"The Game" actually reflects the importance of the entire management process in that setting. How the game is handled is a direct indicator of the effectiveness of management. Weiss's model for the game cannot be achieved without careful attention to planning, organizing, staffing, directing, and controlling. Game management requires essentially the same functions as other forms of management. Those who manage school and college sport programs might well begin by assessing what is being done with respect to contest management. Effective procedures or deficiences relating to any one of the five functions (e.g., planning) could point to similar strengths or weaknesses in the management of the total sport program.

At least two other principal managerial concerns can also be directly elicited from the focus provided by Weiss's work. First, the athlete is at the center of the stage. If things are right with the athlete, there is a good probability that things will be right with the progam as a whole. Thus, the athletic director must plan, organize, staff, direct, and control with the needs of the athlete at the forefront. Some recent occurrences in the collegiate sport realm serve only to reinforce the point that management is not always effective in this regard.

Second, Weiss's "ideal coach" offers a model for staffing considerations. We have to admit that the actual staffing will invariably fall short of the ideal; there are bound to be coaches who are only like supervisors in their operation. Yet there is a continuing need to seek coaches who can contribute to the total development of the athlete. This brings us back to the point that the athlete should be the principal concern to management.

In summary, Weiss's message for the management of a sport program is more implicit than direct. Yet he lays bare the parameters of priority considerations in planning, organizing, staffing, directing and controlling a school or college sport program that is aimed at the pursuit of excellence.

By contrast, Michael Novak's message for management is considerably more direct. Moreover, the strong focus on the sport fan makes the message particularly meaningful for those who manage programs at the level of NCAA Division I competition. At the same time, implications are there for the management of any school or college sport program.

Novak's discussion of women and sport particularly points to planning consid-erations. Questions related to priorities, revenue-producing potential, and the possi-ble development of new sports all point to the need for careful planning, extending all the way from forecasting to the development of strategies and policies. In fact, a women's sport program probably epitomizes the acute need for fulfillment of the planning function in the managerial process. The need for careful planning is always heightened in a dual context of little involvement and marked change.

The tie-in between management and Novak's analysis of the relationship of sport to politics and morality has been noted earlier in this chapter. Quite obviously, the staffing function looms as the principal managerial concern here. Even though the jury may still be out with respect to transfer effects in this general area, it is apparent that coaches must be selected with some thought regarding their ability to provide a solid ethical base for the athlete's development. This is especially true in selecting coaches for junior high and high school programs.

Novak's discussion of regionalism also has implications for the management of sport programs. Regional differences can be a significant factor in decision making. Here are some examples of regional emphases on certain sports that may serve to illustrate this point: wrestling in Oklahoma and Iowa, soccer in the St. Louis area, basketball in Indiana and North Carolina, football in Texas and Pennsylvania, la-crosse on Long Island and in the Baltimore area, field hockey in the Northeast, women's basketball in Iowa, and ice hockey in Massachusetts and Minnesota. Of course, this is not to imply that these sports do not receive considerable attention in other locations. We always have to begin with the recognition that at least baseball, football, and basketball are truly national sports. However, the relative emphasis on one or more sports is an important consideration in planning, organizing, staffing, directing, and controlling a program.

It would be a challenge to find a theoretical reference on sport that has stronger implications for mangement than *The Big Game: College Sports and American Life*. This is partly due to the very design of the work. In the first part, Cady presents the theoretical framework for college sport in the United States. Based on that frame-work, the second half speaks directly to management.

As noted earlier, the management function of controlling is the key theme throughout the book. Cady cites numerous areas of control for college sport. How-ever, it is also clear that his entire exposition reaffirms the close connection within the continuous cycle of the mangerial process. One cannot obtain the kind of control that Cady is seeking without careful planning, organizing, staffing, and directing. This is particularly evident when we reexamine his discussion of coaches, student athletes, recruiting, and financial aid. To achieve what he considers desirable for intercollegiate athletics requries a fulfillment of all the effective managerial compo-nents. The following statements by Cady more or less exemplify the close integra-tion of the various functions in the total management of an intercollegiate athletic program.

The best resource available to a president who must control his intecollegiate athletics will always be considered resoluteness in support of his own positive people. Coaches, directors, faculty representatives, deans of students, registrars who carry the president's word for sound control can win it for him, most of the time against the gates of hell . . . He cannot do it alone because he cannot and must not afford the energy taken from more central, imperative duties. But he can win with his own team. I don't think there is any other way.

To do that requires the same attention to assembling your people and making support evident as the accomplishment of any other mission. The great difference is that success in controlling athletics is indeed a journey, not a destination (p. 190).

Summary

In this chapter we discussed a theoretical framework for the more practical considerations that will be addressed thoughout this book. The sport enterprise has its own distinguishing characteristics that mark it as a particular kind of human activity with broad social implications. The works of Weiss, Novak, and Cady are examples of efforts to understand the nature of sport better. Likewise the nature of management can be identified through an examination of the principal functions that are performed by anyone who has managerial responsibility. Sport programs in the schools and colleges provide dramatic evidence of the need for effective management, all the way from the coach to the high school principal or the college president. This book is designed as a guide for all those who are involved with the management of school and college sport programs. Much of the discussion in the ensuing chapters will focus on collegiate sport. The main reason for this is the fact that collegiate sport has provided the pattern for interscholastic sport. Naturally, we expect to find differences in terms of such considerations as departmental size, revenue, and general complexity of the program. However, the parameters of sport and effective management are essentially the same at both levels.

REFERENCES

Brink, Victor. *Understanding Management Policy—and Making It work.* New York: AMACON, 1978.

Cady, Edwin H. *The Big Game.* Knoxville, Tenn. The University of Tennessee Press, 1978.

Mackenzie, R. Alec. "The Management Process in 3-D." *Harvard Business Review,* Vol. 47, No. 6, November-December, 1969, pp. 80–87.

Novak, Michael. *The Joy of Sports: End Zones, Bases, Baskets, Balls, and Consecration of the American Spirit.* New York. Basic Books, Inc., Publishers, 1976.

Weiss, Paul. *Sport: A Philosophic Inquiry.* Carbondale and Edwardsville, Ill. Southern Illinois University Press, 1969.

2

Planning A School Or College Sport Program

CONCEPTS AND PROBLEMS

Distinction Between Individual Objectives and Institutional Objectives

The Program Should Reflect the Objectives

Variables in Arriving at Program Priorities

Relative Importance of Suitable Scheduling

The Budget Should Reflect the Total Planning Process

Utilization of MBO in Budget Planning

Distinction Between Procedures and Policy

Five General Areas for Procedural Concern

The Evolution of Policies

The Principal Policy Domain in School and College Sport

As indicated in Chapter 1, planning will usually begin with some form of forecasting. The nature and extent of the forecast will largely depend on the circumstances that surround the particular organization. For example it can easily be seen that forecasting is a major component of planning for anyone who is involved in the management of an investment business. It is not so easy to identify the specific need for forecasting when planning a school or college sport program. Nevertheless, the need for some kind of forecasting is evident. Projected financial restraints, shifting populations, decline in enrollment, and changes in sport popularity all represent potential bases for forecasting when one is initiating the planning for a sport program. To what extent any of these will be a major factor depends on the specific time and circumstances, but all these conditions tend to be significant factors in the current planning for school and college programs.

OBJECTIVES

Regardless of the influence of any forecast, the next step in the planning process is always a requirement if any type of meaningful plan is to materialize. The objectives for the program must be established. Those who are responsible for the management of school and college programs face a special challenge in an attempt to set objectives. It is a challenge that is shared by all those who are involved with the management of any service organization. There must always be a dual consideration of individual or personal objectives and those that are advanced for the organization or institution as a whole. These two categories should not be and are not necessarily mutually exclusive, yet the principal reference points tend to be quite divergent. This should become more evident as we analyze the following possibilities for setting objectives for school and college sport programs. Administrators will have to make some hard decisions in setting any of the objectives. Frequently, these decisions will have to begin with a basic choice involving the balance between individual and institutional needs.

Individual Objectives

When all is said and done, individual objectives are largely those things that the individual hopes to obtain from an involvement with the program. They are personal to the extent that they may or not be shared by others with the same or a different kind of involvement. If individual objectives are to be used as a focus for planning, management will probably have to begin by determining the kind and degree of consensus.

Identifying individual objectives for school and college sport programs is a complex matter because various constituencies of individuals must be considered. Furthermore, these constituencies are frequently at cross-purposes in terms of basic needs. The logical place to begin is with a consideration of the sport participant. Yet that category can be complicated in itself without considering other forms of sport involvement. Sport participants cover a large range stemming from the variety of sports and the level of participation. However, beyond that, other individuals are also very much involved with school and college sport programs. Parents have to be considered. This is particularly true at the high school level. However, this constituency cannot be overlooked at the college level in view of the fact that parents are frequently financing the cost of the education. What does the parent hope that the son or daughter will obtain from participation in the sport program? That may or may not be the same as the student's objective.

Then there is at least one other external constituency that is likely to yield differences in meeting individual objectives. The spectators yeild their own individual perspectives. These spectators may be parents; they may be alumni; they may be townspeople or friends of the school or college. On the other hand, they might just be sport fans or those who enjoy watching the sport contest. In any event, each individual in the spectator category also has a certain expectation regarding what is to be expected in the sport program.

With these diverse possibilities in mind, management must plan a program than will be based to some degree on a consideration of individual objectives. Without such consideration, the chances of adequate financial support for the school or college sport program are minimal. The only real question that remains is the extent to which individual objectives should be balanced against the broader institutional considerations. What might an individual hope to obtain through involvement with a sport program?

Fun. Many educators and parents might consider fun a strange and even inappropriate consideration to use in beginning to identify individual objectives for a school or college sport program. After all, an educational institution is supposed to be first and foremost a place where people go to learn and learning is associated with rigorous discipline and hard work. Somehow or other, it is difficult to expect the objective to include fun within that context.

Regardless of the arguments for and against associating fun with education, the fact remains that Americans have chosen to link sport programs with schools and colleges. This fact has to be coupled with the recognition that fun in some form or other is close to the heart of the sport enterprise. Words other than *fun* might be used to express basically the same idea. For example, play, enjoyment, and pleasure are similar in their conception. But regardless of the particular word chosen, the relationship to sport should be clear. Guttmann (1978) describes sports as being "playful physical contests." He also vividly points to the bond among sport, play, and fun: "In his many guises, the 'spoilsport' stands ready to dispel the illusion and to allow the rainbow world of play to fade into the light of common day" (p. 14).

Guttmann goes on to point out that in many respects modern sport has moved a long way from the play spirit. This probably accounts for the fact that the following objectives also are legitimate possibilities in identifying individual objectives for a sport program. Nevertheless, a logical conclusion is that the very origin of sports makes it impossible to overlook the possibility of having fun through a playful physical contest (sport) as an individual objective for involvement with a sport program.

Now how one proceeds to plan for the opportunity to have fun is entirely another matter. In many respects, the idea of planning seems to be contrary to the notion of having fun. A possible solution to this apparent dilemma is to begin by noting the reactions of those people who do have fun through their sport participation. People know when they have had fun while participating in a sport. The conditions surrounding such participation can be used as a basis for planning.

Before leaving this discussion of an individual's objective revolving around the idea of having fun, one other point should be mentioned. Sport may be fun for the spectator as well as for the participant. The irony of the situation is to be found in the strong possibility that the athlete may not be playing for fun though he or she is providing fun for the spectator. Consequently, when a sport program is planned from the standpoint of the "fun" objective, it is not a simple matter of deciding that the program should offer fun for those involved. Decisions regarding the balance between participant and spectator satisfaction weigh heavily when one is considering the impact of this objective on school and college sport programs.

Skill Acquisition. Any consideration of this objective for a sport program immediately prompts the recognition that even the individual objectives are not mutually exclusive. Those who have had the experience of having fun through sport are likely to agree readily that a certain level of skill is necessary in order to attain fun from playing the sport. On the other side of the coin, the actual learning of the skill is not much fun. It usually involves concentration, practice sessions, and frustrations that are contrary to the play spirit. Overall, there is a challenge to be met in acquiring the necessary skills to participate in a sport. The immediate objective could be one of merely attempting to meet that challenge. Yet there is also the strong possibility that the objective to acquire skill is also a facilitating agent in reaching toward other objectives in the sport programs. In addition to enhancing the fun potential, the acquisition of skills is also inextricably linked to the pursuit of excellence and positive social experiences.

Consequently, from a management perspective it is not a simple matter of deciding that the acquisition of skills should be one of the individual objectives for the sport program. Within the context of school and college sport programs, there is good reason to believe that the acquisition of skills will somehow or another be identified as one of the objectives. From there, critical planning decisions have to be made as to how this objective relates to other program objectives and what should be done to facilitate the acquisition of skills in sports.

Pursuit of Excellence. In the first chapter we noted that Paul Weiss advances the idea that the pursuit of excellence is the principal reason for the attraction of sport. Assuming there is merit in his argument, we would have to conclude further that the pursuit of excellence might also be considered a prime objective for a school or college sport program. However, with this other consideration in mind, we now definitely can see that management has to make some choices.

From a very superficial standpoint it would seem that the pursuit of excellence ought to be accepted readily as an objective for many sport programs. This might be particularly true in the school or college setting owing to the general tendency to associate educational endeavors with the pursuit of excellence. However, in the subsequent planning for the achievement of this objective, it doesn't take long to realize that it may work at cross-purposes to the achievement of other individual objectives.

The most obvious restriction is that the objective will relate to only a very limited number of participants. That restriction is inherent in the very idea of what is involved in pursuing excellence; such pursuit is not for the masses. By contrast, the two preceding objectives tend to be very much mass-oriented. When it comes to program and budget planning, the administrator will recognize that something has to give. Facilitating the pursuit of excellence requires a commitment to program and resources that makes it most difficult to plan for the achievement of other objectives.

On the other hand, it is also not difficult to see that the pursuit of excellence is likely to emerge as the top priority objective if the spectator is used as the principal reference point. The spectator's identification with the sport program is largely with that pursuit of excellence, be it of team or individual or both. By contrast, the other individual objectives are very much participant-oriented.

The pursuit of excellence also provides the closest link between the individual and institutional objectives. At least it is the closest in terms of what is most readily apparent. Public relations' support for school and college sport programs is obviously related to the spectator's identification with the pursuit of excellence. More about that will be said later when institutional objectives are analyzed.

Social Development. It is difficult to select the most appropriate wording for the potential objective of social development for a school or college sport program. Perhaps what makes this so difficult is the variety of associations and connotations that come to mind when we consider the social process and sport. As an example, within recent years there has been much discussion centering around the idea of character development through sport. Although that topic tends to be primarily a psychological consideration, the social implications are there as well. For the most part, the recent tendency has been to view the claims of character building with considerable skepticism owing to the value-loaded nature of the concept. Many people have somewhat jokingly suggested that sport produces characters rather than character. In a somewhat different vein, socialization is a widely discussed concept among sociologists. Socialization is certainly a legitimate objective for a sport program. However, that too tends to be a bit suspect because it seems to center on a basic conformity to the social order.

In spite of all the complications centering around what happens to people socially in sport and through sport, it seems fairly apparent that sport can serve as a prime medium for social development. To put it simply, sport can offer ample opportunity for social contacts under a variety of circumstances. With that recognition, it seems safe to say that some type of social development is likely to occur. Therefore, from a managerial perspective it might be best to stick with the simple idea of social development in lieu of more lofty or sophisticated sociological propositions.

In any case, it is quite obvious that social development is not as definitive an objective as the acquisition of skills, or the pursuit of excellence. If we are involved with management by objectives, it becomes difficult to measure the degree of social development. Of course, the same could be said regarding any attempt to evaluate the amount of fun that participants derive from a program.

At the same time it can easily be seen why social development might be set forth as a key objective for a sport program. This would probably be particularly true at the high school level, where developing social contacts are so significant. Another interesting feature of the social development objective is that it does not seem to be in inherent conflict with the other individual objectives for a sport program. In particular, there would appear to be a strong positive correlation between the idea of having fun and social development. In the final analysis, social development should be advanced as a by-product of other program objectives. Yet program content can be at least partially determined by a decision involving the social development objective. For example, the high school athletic director may choose to emphasize team sports as a principal facilitator of social development. This might mean a focus on football, soccer, basketball, and baseball for boys as well as field hockey, basketball, volleyball, and softball for girls.

Contribution to Physical Fitness. The wording for the individual objective is also a critical consideration. People do not become physically fit as a result of participation in a sport program. Physical fitness is a complex concept involving a host of variables and conditional elements, yet a sport program can and should contribute to the physical fitness of the participants.

Selection of physical fitness as a principal objective for a sport program is almost certain to have a great influence on the other components of planning. To begin with, if the objective is to have any real meaning, program content should be selected with great care. Among sports, we find considerable variation in physical demands and effects. There is evidence of virtually no plannning if physical fitness is set forth as a prime objective, followed by a program that reveals a variety of sports, selected at random or only according to student interest. As a prime example, the more physically demanding sports often may not be the most fun for many of the participants.

More than anything else, an emphasis on the physical fitness objective clearly points to a program that is participant-oriented rather than spectator-oriented. This tends to set it apart from three of the other four objectives that were identified earlier. Skill acquisition is the only other individual objective that is clearly based in the participant's frame of reference. However, before physical fitness is highlighted as an objective for a school or college sport program, one other consideration is worthy of attention: a sport program can contribute to the physical fitness of the participants. Yet sport may not be the most effective exercise mode to make such a contribution. Those who seek to contribute to physical fitness might well choose exercise per se. In many respects it is more a case of physical fitness for sport rather than of sport for physical fitness. This complexity has to be considered by management before meaningful planning can take place.

Institutional Objectives

The preceding objectives were advanced from the perspective that they are individually oriented. That is they are possibilities regarding what an individual consumer might seek through involvement with a sport program. The consumer could be a participant or a spectator, but it is obvious that each objective is not equally applicable to each type of sport consumer. These objectives are important because management naturally wishes to offer a program that meets the needs and interests of the consumer, which, in turn, are reflected in the individual objectives. However, that is not the whole story when it comes to setting the objectives for a sport program within the context of an educational institution. Certain institutional considerations exist apart from individual objectives. Those who are responsible for the management of programs within the institution must recognize that support for any program is a complex variable. Furthermore, any program will only prosper to the extent that it is supported. If the individual objectives are to be reached, the institution must also work toward other, broader objectives that tend to be of a facilitating nature. As I see it, the following objectives fall within that category.

1. *Enhancing the Image of the School or College.* The first thing that should be considered is enhancing the image of the school or college because the other objectives are largely dependent on the degree to which the school or college is able to achieve and maintain a positive image.

Image is a strange and tricky concept. It seems to be something that defies precise definition and yet always lurks in the background as a prime consideration. Reputation is a concept closely related to that of image. We all know that schools and colleges acquire certain reputations, apparently for a variety of reasons. Ideally, one might like to think that the reputation of an educational institution is based solely on academic standards. However, to do so would be to ignore the complexities surrounding image development generally, especially those associated with American schools and colleges. Many of these institutions are better known for their sport programs than for any academic achievement. On a more positive note, sport has often been used as a principal means of gaining good public relations and financial support, which, in turn, have enabled the institution to upgrade the quality of its academic offerings. In other words, it has not been a simple matter of choosing between academics and sport. Some colleges with exceptionally fine academic reputations are also well known for the achievements of their sport teams.

It is quite obvious that this institutional objective tends to have a strong positive correlation with the individual objective of pursuing excellence through sport. The association of the school or college with relatively excellent sport teams or athletes becomes a major factor in enhancing the image of the institution. By contrast, it would be difficult to draw any type of correlation between image enhancement and any of the other individual objectives that were discussed earlier. Of course, those objectives can contribute to the welfare of the institution, but only the pursuit of excellence offers the medium for public relations support. As a classic example, can one even begin to guess what basketball has meant to De Paul University? It is no small wonder that many of those people who are responsible for the management of school and college sport programs have decided to pursue the individual objective of pursuing excellence and the institutional objective of enhancing the image of the school or college.

Before we leave this discussion, one other point should be noted. Support for the school or college could possibly be listed as a separate institutional objective. However, there is good reason to believe that such support is directly related to the image of the institution. For this reason, potential support for the school or college is tied up with the objective of enhancing the image.

2. *Developing School Spirit.* Any attempt to analyze the significance of school spirit as an institutional objective is not entirely unlike the preceding attempt to get a handle on image enhancement. The parameters of school spirit are also not easily described. Furthermore, there are plenty of skeptics today who would argue that if there was ever something called school spirit, it is no longer present. I would have to admit that in terms of the traditional "rah rah" approach, things have changed considerably in most of the schools and colleges. But that is not to say that all pride for, or identification with, the school has disappeared. Many students still receive satisfaction in the accomplishments of the school, and sport continues to rank high among the more visible areas of accomplishment. The frequently heard chant of "we're number one" is dramatic evidence of the fact that something that could be called "school spirit" is still present.

The concept of identification is key to any attempt to understand the basis for school spirit. When it is present, students and teachers tend to identify with the success (and even failure) of those groups or individuals (or both) who represent the school. The spectator side of sport often provides one of the more visible means for such identification.

From a management standpoint, one can easily see why there might be definite attempts to develop school spirit. Esprit de corps has long been recognized as an important factor in organizational success. Enthusiasm for the honor of the group usually implies that the members of the group are willing to work toward the achievement and maintenance of that honor. When school administrators cite the development of school spirit as an objective for the sport program, there is an expectation —or at least a hope—that the identification with the sport team will transfer or extend to a broader identification with the school at large. Whether or not this is true is debatable. It does appear that sport can frequently be used as a rallying force for other institutional pursuits.

The development of school spirit also tends to relate most positively with the previously cited objective of image enhancement. This is a bit like the "chicken and the egg" controversy, but in general one would suspect that the image serves more as a facilitator of the spirit than the reverse. However, in either case, both of these institutional objectives are inextricably related to the pursuit of excellence as an individual objective. Once again, it can be seen that program content will be headed in a certain direction if the development of school spirit is set forth as an institutional objective.

3. *Positive Association with the School.* It is also difficult to word the objective of positive association with the school, but the difficulty does not negate its potential significance as an institutional objective. There is some overlap with the previous objective in that school spirit could also serve to facilitate a student's positive association with the school. The major difference is that the various means of generating school spirit are more limited in their approach. Aside from the pursuit of excellence, other individual objectives might also serve to provide a positive association with the school. In other words, the student might positively respond to the school situation as a result of the fun of sport participation, acquisition of skills in sport, social development, or the contribution toward physical fitness. These are not necessarily equal possibilities, but they all exist as some kind of possibility.

Basically, the objective in question proceeds from the assumption that some students (perhaps many students) need something other than the rigors of academic pursuit to motivate them to adjust to, and benefit from, the total school setting. As such, this objective is not unique to sport. Music, drama, and industrial arts, among others, could be cited as program areas that might set forth this institutional objective. Once again there are those who would argue that the rationale behind this objective is unsound from an idealistic point of view. If there is to be a positive association with the school, it should come from the pure challenge and satisfaction gained from academic achievement in the traditional sense. Be that as it may, the fact remains that some students are in school only because they are required to be there. This, of course, is particularly true at the high school level. In recognition of that fact, management might well choose to set an objective for the sport program that serves to facilitate a positive association with the school.

The word *college* has purposely been omitted from the statement of this objective and the preceding one. This is not to imply that there is no need to develop college spirit or that a college sport program should not be designed to enhance a positive association with the college. Instead, the intent is to stress that these two objectives appear to be more distinct possibilities at the high school level. Age differentiation and a different set of motivational circumstances seem to point to the more acute need for sport to serve those other purposes for the high school.

4. *Contributing to the Total Educational Program.* From an institutional perspective, one other distinct possibility exists in setting forth an objective for a sport program—the contribution to the total educational program. The objective rests on the assumption that sport participation can be educational in itself; sport need not, and possibly should not, be used as a facilitator in support of other school or college programs. Reference to this objective tends to be a favorite in statements issued by the NCAA and other school and college sport organizations who choose to draw attention away from the more materialistic side of sport.

The objective may be most legitimate in its intent and even in its implementation. However, the word *consistency* should serve as a caution for any school or college sport administrator who chooses to "hang his hat" on this objective. To begin with, most of the possible individual objectives do not correlate particularly well with the idea that sport participation is first and foremost educational in nature. The basic idea behind providing for the fun of participants in a recreational sport program is that it will serve as a diversion from educational endeavors. Beyond a doubt, the pursuit of excellence in anything is educational, but management will soon have to face up to the "numbers game" if it chooses to explain the educational component of its program from that perspective. Is it reasonable to postulate a program that is directed only toward the education of a relatively few participants? It could indeed be argued that social development is educational, but with that line of thinking the school or college begins to lose whatever special leverage it has as the educational arm of society.

The last two individual objectives would appear to offer the best possibility for supporting any institutional objective of sport contributing to the total educational program. However, even the implementation of these objectives has to be carefully planned if there is to be any sort of legitimate basis for advancing the educational claim for the sport program. Skill acquisition per se could be called educational, but the instructional sport program occupies a tenuous spot in the academic framework if there is no theoretical structure for the teaching of sport skills. Much the same can be said about the physical fitness objective. Thus, any sort of meaningful educational objective could only be reached when knowledge about exercise is related to the sport participation. Once again, we see the need for strong consistency between stated objectives and program content.

PROGRAM

As noted earlier, the program should be a direct outgrowth of the objectives. If that is not the case, a red flag, signaling the inconsistency, should hover over the managerial environment. The program represents the essence of what the organization is able and willing to offer. With respect to a sport management program, this is manifested first and foremost in the sport or sports that are offered by the organization. A program is a fairly straightforward matter with a professional sport team because it centers on a single sport. Much the same is true of many private sport organizations, such as a gymnastic, tennis, or swimming club, where one sport tends to represent the focus of the program. However, planning a sport program in the schools and colleges is a much more complicated matter. Basic decisions have to be made regarding the sports to be offered. Beyond that, program content will also be very much determined by decisions related to the instructional, intramural, and interscholastic or intercollegiate components of the total program. When these decisions are made, the structure for the program is eventually revealed in three ways: scope, priorities, and scheduling.

Scope

Essentially, decisions here revolve around one basic question: what should be offered? Even though the question is basic and simple, the answers are not easily reached owing to the variables that surround the decision. Following are some of the factors that must be taken into consideration before the question regarding scope can be answered. These factors are not necessarily listed in the order of either chronology or priority. When the program is planned, most of these factors have to be considered somewhat simultaneously.

1. *Needs and Interests of the Students.* One part of program planning that relates directly back to the objectives concerns the students' interests and needs. The program content should reflect them as they are established through the individual objectives. For example, if social development is cited as a principal objective, it would be difficult to explain a program that places relatively little emphasis on team sports. Similarly, one might wonder how a junior high school could set forth any objective revolving around the idea of fun if no intramural sport program is offered.

Any tendency to overlook this factor in program planning might be explained by the difficulty in arriving at the information. The most obvious way to determine people's interests is to ask them. However, in the planning of a program for a large student body, this is more easily said than done. Needs are even more complicated in terms of determination. To a limited extent, surveys can be used to obtain the desired information. More about that will be said later under planning procedures. Beyond surveys, management will have to rely rather heavily on informal feedback and continued observation. National, regional, and local sport popularity will certainly be significant as a basis for student interest. Thus, if racquetball is an "in sport," one would expect this to be manifested in any expression of student interest.

In school programs, particularly at the elementary and junior high levels, parents should be consulted in the effort to determine the needs and interests of students. There is reason to believe that many school sport programs have been woefully deficient in this aspect of planning. Of course, parental input is not the final answer in any attempt to arrive at a determination; nevertheless, the additional insight may be significant. Furthermore, the parental involvement may assist in reaching some of the institutional objectives that have been established for the program.

2. *Available Facilities.* Earlier it was stated that the factors to be considered in planning for the scope of the sport program are not necessarily listed chronologically or according to priority. That remains basically true, but if there is reason for any sort of priority consideration, facilities would have to rank at the top or near the top of the list. This is because facility availability is the most direct factor in determining what can be offered. Of course, there is always the possibility that additional facilities could also be planned, taking into consideration the other factors that enter into the planning decision. That possibility brings us to the recognition that facility planning is only realistic when financial resources are likely to be sufficient. This, in turn, gets us involved in forecasting and budgetary planning procedures. By now, it can easily be seen that planning is not a simple chronological progression.

When all things are considered, facilities will serve as a twofold factor in planning for the scope of the program. The immediate availability of facilities will be a limiting factor in determining what can be offered. Choices based on other variables will be made within that limitation. In turn, long-range planning for facilities will be based both on the availability of financial resources and on the other factors that contribute to decisions regarding the scope of the sport program.

3. *Qualifications of the Staff.* In some respects, a consideration of staff qualifications is not unlike our discussion of facilities. The similarity is found in the dual need to consider always both the current situations and future possibilities. Qualifications of the staff will also be a limiting factor in determining what can be offered. What should be offered will point to the need for additional staff or the extension in qualifications of the existing staff or both.

The difference between these two factors is that the matter of staff qualifications offers greater flexibility than is found in the facility situation. Financial resources for additional facilities often are just not available. The personnel budget may also be tight, but there is always some turnover even when it is not possible to increase the staff. Furthermore, the current staff might extend their qualifications to one or more other areas of the sport program. More about this will be said in Chapter 4 on staffing. However, the important point here is that the existing qualifications must be considered in planning for the scope of the program. This represents a potential pitfall that is far too often overlooked. Staff flexibility should not be interpreted to mean that anything can be offered regardless of the qualifications.

4. *Regional and Climatic Considerations.* There is at least one other factor that should be taken into consideration in planning for the scope of the sport program, namely, regional and climatic considerations. This factor involves any special circumstances stemming from the region and climate where the school or college is located. To some extent, climate is a built-in factor and doesn't require much thought or discussion when it comes to planning the offerings. However, this is probably more true of timing or scheduling than it is of the scope as such. Climate is a factor influencing the scope to the extent that certain sports are likely to be more or less popular as a result of climatic conditions. Regionalism is a broader consideration and a very definite factor in appropriate program planning. For various and partially unknown reasons, one finds quite a divergence of interests and emphasis in sports on the national spectrum. Even within a given state, differences can be noted within the regions of that state. Although regionalism may not rank with the other factors as being critical in determining the scope of the program, it is nevertheless a significant point for consideration.

Priorities

In many respects, the determination of priorities is the essence of program planning. For one thing, this tends to force the hard decisions that have to be made by management. Generally speaking, it is much easier to arrive at the scope and timing than it is to decide where the emphasis should be placed. As a matter of fact, the priorities can also influence decisions involving the scope and the scheduling. Perhaps most importantly, priorities point to those conditions that represent the variables in the total sport program. It is not just a matter of determining priority among sports. The establishment of priorities begins with more general considerations involving the intercollegiate (or interscholastic), intramural, and instructional components. At this point one notes particularly the strong need to assess the individual and institutional objectives. Here the interests and needs of the students may be even more critical than was indicated in planning for the scope of the program. Somehow or other, priorities must reflect such interests and needs, yet other variables enter into the picture that complicate the entire planning for program priorities. Following are some of the variables that are likely to be important factors in establishing the priorities.

Nature of the Educational Institution. The nature of the educational institution is a variable that is particularly evident with respect to colleges and universities. A college is not a college, and a university is not a university. By that we mean that it is very difficult to make generalizations regarding the makeup of American colleges and universities. This is perhaps the most distinguishing feature of American higher education.

The spectrum of differences among colleges and universities is also reflected in the nature of the various sport programs. It is readily apparent that certain large universities have primarily used sport (notably football or basketball or both) to enhance the image of the university and thus to gain the support of alumni and the public. That will be a critical factor when the time arrives to determine priorities in program planning. Other institutions are very much identified with success in a given sport (e.g., De Paul, basketball, Johns Hopkins, lacrosse). Then there are institutions that are steeped in a long academic tradition that permits a more independent decision regarding sport priorities. At one time such institutions relied more heavily on the prominence of the football team, but today (even though football may still have top priority in some cases) the sport program need not be the principal concern in image enhancement. The Ivy League institutions and the University of Chicago are examples of this category.

Some colleges are established within a general orientation that more or less limits the development of the intercollegiate program. The overall perspective of the college points to priorities in the intramural, club, or instructional components. An example here would be Hampshire College in Amherst, Massachusetts.

Note that there are a great many institutions that are in a gray area regarding sport priorities. Some of these have recently attempted to move out of the gray zone by establishing a top priority sport. In most cases, the decision has gone to basketball owing to economic considerations. However, as the competition gets keener with so many seeking the top, this may result in a reassessment of the priorities.

Within the gray area, there are many institutions that face even more difficult decisions in planning for program priorities. With limited resources, they seem to be more or less equally committed to the intercollegiate, intramural, and instructional components. In some cases, it is also difficult to determine the priorities among sports. In other situations, such priorities appear to be manifested in selected sports that are the scholarship sports. Yet the scholarship sports may not be yielding the results that are generally sought for the institutional objectives. Management decisions for planning program priorities will continue to be most difficult for those institutions that fall within this general category.

National, Regional, State, and Local Considerations. The variable of national, regional, state, and local considerations was discussed to some extent when the regional and climatic considerations for planning in the scope of the sport program were analyzed. With respect to priorities, this general category represents an even more critical factor in program planning. There are many aspects of this variable, any one of which could be most significant in establishing the sport program priorities for a given institution.

One might begin by considering the national situation. Here the "trinity" of American sports might offer the principal frame of reference. To date, it would appear that the majority of schools and colleges have been heavily influenced by at least two thirds of that trinity in their program development (baseball being the exception in terms of school and college spectator sports). In terms of variability, the question largely centers on the extent to which schools and colleges will continue to be guided by the trinity in setting forth future priorities. There are those who point to the growth of soccer in the United States and who contend that soccer will someday replace football in popularity. It is true that several schools and colleges have dropped the football program in recent years. Yet it appears this is done primarily for financial reasons rather than on the basis of popularity per se. At this point in time, the trinity still remains as a significant national frame of reference for sport orientation.

Regional and state considerations serve only to enhance further the possibilities that the priorities will reflect the sport traditions in the area. There is long-standing evidence of the relative popularity of school and college football in the Midwest and Southwest. The emphasis on schoolboy football is particularly evident in states such as Ohio, Pennsylvania, and Texas. Basketball holds a special place in Indiana and the region of the Atlantic Coast Conference.

The local dimension further complicates the total priority picture. Soccer is a key sport in the St. Louis area as lacrosse is in the Baltimore and Long Island areas. The fact that basketball has been recognized as "the city game" is another angle in assessing priorities that arise from local considerations.

Those examples that have been cited may not be the most outstanding or the most appropriate for getting a hold on the variables surrounding sport priorities stemming from national, regional, state, and local considerations. However, they should suffice to convey the idea that effective program planning ought also to take into account this kind of variable.

The Educational Level. In terms of total sport program planning for all schools and colleges, at least one other variable deserves special attention, namely, the educational level. As noted earlier, program priorities are reflected in more than just emphasis on certain sports. An even more basic consideration is that related to the priorities among the instructional, intramural, and interscholastic or intercollegiate components of the complete sport program.

With respect to the theory behind the total sport program, there seems to be a general tendency to suggest that all three components should have more or less equal status from the junior high school through college level. Few would dispute the idea that the instructional component should have top priority at the elementary school level. Yet as one examines the situation in the broad spectrum of junior and senior high school and collegiate institutions, there is reason to doubt that the actual programs always reflect the stated priorities.

Intramural sport represents a principal area for questioning. The logic behind the objectives for a junior high school program might indicate that intramural sport should have top priority. Yet the record shows that there are relatively few strong intramural programs in either the junior high schools or the senior high schools. By contrast, the strongest program support for intramurals can be found at the collegiate level. That, too, may be consistent with the objectives for a given collegiate program. However, overall, one wonders whether sufficient attention has been given to the educational level in determining priorities for the total sport program.

Scheduling

Scheduling as a broad area of planning represents such an important factor in the school and college environments that it could even be advanced as the name of the game within that managerial setting. For example, if the schedule is suitable, the situation is generally fine; and if there is something wrong with the schedule, everything is wrong. Effective scheduling is a critical aspect of planning in all three of the major components of the complete sport proggram. However, the difficulties in arriving at appropriate scheduling are dramatized in the interscholastic or intercollegiate arrangements. Therefore, we can begin by noting some of the managerial concerns that apply to that component.

Interscholastic or Intercollegiate Scheduling. To arrive at a suitable interscholastic or intercollegiate schedule, we must take into consideration several factors. These are not necessarily factors that apply equally to all schools and colleges. Nevertheless, the following can be said to represent the general territory for planning an appropriate interscholastic or intercollegiate schedule.

1. *Objectives of the Program.* Once again we see how pivotal the objectives are in the total planning process. Within other limitations, the schedule should reflect the objectives of the program. Numerous examples could be cited to reinforce this idea, but the following few will convey the basic tie-in between objectives and scheduling. The pursuit of excellence was identified as one of the possible individual objectives. There is evidence that an individual athlete may demonstrate a relatively high degree of excellence aside from the schedule or particular level of competition. The same could be said for a given team although this is probably less

likely to be the case. Nevertheless, all other factors being equal, the pursuit of excellence in a sport is likely to be a direct reflection of the level of competition. It is not accidental that the more highly qualified athletes generally prefer to play for a team that typically has a schedule of top flight opponents.

From the institutional vantage point, two other examples serve to illustrate the close connection between the objectives and the sport schedule. It is difficult to enhance the image of the school or college through sport without a schedule that facilitates the necessary visibility. Many of the traditional collegiate powers in sport have met this objective either through a conference arrangement that provides a first-rate schedule or through the scheduling of independents that tend to be perennially strong.

The other institutional example may be more apparent at the scholastic level. The schedule can also be a factor in developing school spirit. The most obvious connection here relates to the scheduling of traditional rivals. However, the scheduling of a new opponent could be equally significant in facilitating the development of school spirit. This is most likely to occur when the new opponent offers something by way of a special geographical or cultural link with the school or college.

2. *Travel.* With budgetary restrictions being what they are today, the travel factor has to rank near the top of the list when it comes time to plan any athletic schedule. This is especially true for high schools and small colleges although all institutions cannot afford to overlook this factor. There is not much more to be said about this most important consideration other than to note that travel generally represents a relatively large proportion of the typical athletic budget. The real difficulty in planning resides in the realization that a schedule that reduces travel costs often works at cross-purposes to the other factors that influence the desired schedule.

3. *General Institutional Relationships.* The factor of general institutional relationships is a bit more difficult to pinpoint. Nevertheless, it represents a potentially significant consideration for many schools and colleges. In the establishment of an athletic schedule there is often an attempt to provide a schedule that will reflect the broader relationships among the schools and colleges. Sometimes this relationship is manifested in a tradition of academic and social compatability. The so-called Ivy League is a classic example of a conference and scheduling arrangement that takes heavy account of this factor. However, it is not just the "Ivies" who focus their schedule within the context of general institutional relationships. Several of the collegiate conferences are arranged from a similar premise. The "Big Ten" and conferences comprising the Southern universities are other notable examples showing that the general orientation of the institution is a significant factor in scheduling arrangements. This type of consideration also influences the scholastic realm, wherein we find parochial leagues and other conferences that are structured according to common elements in socioeconomic conditions.

4. *The Competitive Level.* If the various factors to be considered in planning the athletic schedule were to be listed in order of priority, probably the competitive

level would have to head the list. A strong argument can be made for the idea that an appropriate schedule is one that first and foremost provides for general equality in the ability level among the opponents. However, any priority decision in this regard is not as simple as it first appears. The record shows that some institutions must be giving greater weight to the factors involving program objectives, travel, and general institutional relationships. If that were not the case, we would not find as many examples of schools and colleges that are perennially near the bottom of their conferences in most sports. This could be dismissed as merely representing poor planning. Yet perhaps a more reasonable answer is to be found in the complexities that surround the entire planning of the schedule. Thus, it becomes difficult to set forth a definitive priority that applies to all situations. At the same time, the competitive level has to be a prime consideration. This is probably particularly true with respect to scholastic sport programs. One wonders how any of the program objectives can be approached when there is generally a great disparity in the level of ability among the opposing teams.

5. *Basic Spectator Appeal.* Before we leave this topic of the factors to be considered in athletic scheduling, one other consideration—basic spectator appeal—should be noted. This is complex in itself in that it is not a parallel consideration to the four previously mentioned. For one thing, it tends to cut across or overlap all the other factors. For a given institution, the program objectives may not be aimed at spectator appeal. In another case, the program objectives may be such that spectator appeal becomes *the* factor in scheduling. Further evidence of overlap is found in the realization that institutional relationships and equality in competitive level might also bear heavily on spectator appeal. Then, of course, there is the additional complication that spectator appeal is really only a significant consideration with respect to two of the school and college sports. Nevertheless, in spite of the limitations and complications, it seems apparent that the idea of basic spectator appeal has to be recognized as an additional factor in planning for an athletic schedule.

Intramural Scheduling. The key to effective scheduling of intramural sport activities is found in a consideration of two variables: student interest and student availability. Those who plan intramural sport schedules must approach this managerial function from a posture of basic flexibility. Thus, it is more difficult to identify a set number of factors that tend to guide the scheduling in a certain direction. Student interest, of course, will be facilitated by schedules that provide for competitive opportunities at approximately the same level. Beyond that, the conditions that influence the scheduling of intramural sport activities are really quite different from those noted with respect to interscholastic or intercollegiate sport.

The availability of facilities is another important consideration in intramural sport scheduling. In many cases, it seems as though the intramural schedule must be built around the instructional schedule and the practice schedule for athletic teams. Depending on total program objectives, that kind of priority can also be debated. Nevertheless, the entire consideration of facilities points to the need for more coordination in planning intramural and instructional schedules.

Scheduling of Instruction. One point of view holds that some of the more ineffective planning in school and college sport programs can be found in the scheduling arrangements for the instructional area. Structural limitations tend to be particularly acute at the public school level although the basic limitation extends to some college programs as well. The essence of the difficulty is related to the scheduling of gym classes and the subsequent barrier associated with a program of physical education. This, in turn, has led to an artificial, organizational division between an intramural sport program and a physical education program. It further contributes to a general splintering effect in the management of school and college sport programs. Those who manage these programs also seem to be entrenched in their thinking that instruction is something that must take place during the normal school day whereas intramural sport is an after-school activity.

The following steps might be followed in planning a schedule for sport instruction.

1. Management begins by making a basic decision regarding the particular sports for which instruction can be offered in a given semester. For the most part, this decision will be based on a twofold consideration of available facilates and available *qualified* instructors. However, earlier planning, involving program priorities, might also bear on this decision. Eventually, this first step will result in a tentative schedule for instruction in selected sports (swimming, gymnastics, golf, tennis, etc.). Generally speaking, this step is now followed in planning for instruction in most college sport programs. However, it should be noted that the step represents a radical departure from scheduling a gym class in the public schools.

2. In scheduling the time for classes, there is no sacred dimension accorded to the "school day." The only real restriction here might be bus limitations (particularly in consolidated school districts) or instructors' conflicts with coaching responsibilities. Any restriction involving bus schedules may not be as severe as thought in many cases because it is not uncommon for parents to bring children to various forms of sport instruction outside the school setting. Any possible conflicts involving coaching, instruction, and intramural sport responsibilities can be handled through effective management by sport coordinators. More about that will be said later in the discussion of the organizing and staffing functions in sport management. It is enough to note here that the instructional planning proceeds within the entire framework of time that is available for the total sport program. Most of the classes may still be scheduled during the normal school day, but that is not a built-in restriction.

3. For any given span of time (usually a season, quarter, or semester) a schedule of sports and class times is then distributed. Thus, a sample instructional sport schedule for a junior high school might show the following schedule for the fall term.

Swimming	M W F	10 A.M.
Basketball	Tu Th	2 P.M.
Golf	Sat.	10 A.M.
Football	M W F	11 A.M.
Field Hockey	Tu Th	9 A.M.
Gymnastics	Friday	8–10 P.M.

The number of offerings in any term would, of course, depend on the size of the school and the results of following the first two steps in planning. The preceding example is not designed to indicate that these would necessarily be the selected sports or the most desired times for instruction. The precise schedule would depend on the needs and resources within the particular sport program.

4. Students then indicate their preferences for sport instruction within that term. In most cases, it might be advisable to give each student the opportunity to indicate a first, second, and third choice. That decision will largely depend on the size of the total program. I recommend that the selection at the elementary and junior high levels should be made through joint, student-parent decisions. Prior to each term (or other scheduled span of time), the student would take home a copy of the schedule. Preferences would be selected and returned to the school.

5. The preference sheets are then utilized by the school to plan a final sport instructional schedule for the term. At this point, it will probably be necessary to make some last-minute adjustments in most cases, again within the limits of available facilities and available *qualified* instructors.

As one looks over the steps, it is apparent that this is basically the kind of scheduling arrangement that is now followed in most college sport programs. Thus, I would again stress that the need for more effective planning in the instructional area is particularly evident in the public schools. However, planning at the college level could also be improved considerably through better coordination between the instructional and intramural units. In a total sport management program, as conceived in this text, these would be administered as an integrated unit along with the intercollegiate component. Basically, for the majority of the student body, most of the sport participation would be through the medium of intramural activities. It is assumed that the bulk of sport instruction would have been received during the earlier years of education. Therefore, under this framework, sport instruction at the college level is offered as a supplement to the regular intramural sport program on the basis of needs and interests. What this also implies is that there would no longer be any physical education classes, as such.

BUDGET

If one is searching for the most concrete example of effective planning (or the lack of it), the budget is a good place to begin the search. The budget should be a direct reflection of everything else that is involved in the total planning process. Should this not be the case, there is evidence that management has a need to reexamine the entire structure that provides the basis for planning decisions.

Essentially, budget planning includes three major steps: (1) analysis of resources, (2) establishing the procedures for budgetary control, and (3) presentation of the budget. These steps can probably be most effectively approached through *management by objectives* (MBO) or at least some modified form of that total system of management. Within the business community, MBO has become a widely publicized concept in recent years. Yet it appears that there has been a relatively small attempt to apply MBO to the management of school and college sport programs. For this reason, the basic format will be presented as the frame of reference for budget planning in the hope that at least some of the ideas may contribute to more effective planning of the budgets for school and college sport.

Basic Premise of MBO

Deegan and Fritz (1975) present a most usable analysis of MBO in their book entitled *MBO Goes to College*. Although they focus on the applicability of MBO for general management in higher education, the ideas obviously have equal applicability for the management of school and college sport programs. Consequently, their thoughts provide the basis for the following suggestions as to how MBO might be utilized in planning school and college sport budgets.

MBO is designed around a very definite philosophy of management. In simple terms, it could be called ''participative management.'' This means that all the members of an organization have a personal responsibility to work within a framework in which outputs (results) are the only claim upon the resources (inputs) of the organization. The results provide the justification for approving, modifying, or abandoning programs of action. The assessment of results is accomplished through a comparison of the level of performance with the objectives that have been mutually agreed upon between the employee and the immediate administrative superior. More will be said about MBO in that context in the latter part of this book when we discuss the controlling function in management. Here it is important to note that the budget is planned within the framework of the desired level of performance.

Goals or objectives (these two words are used synonymously) describe what the organization plans to accomplish. Thus, they are also the basis for budget planning. Furthermore, an objective should not be confused with an activity. Therefore, we do not budget for an activity. We budget for an objective. An activity merely facilitates efforts to reach the objective.

There are three major elements in any complete system of management: resources, activities, and results. MBO is always carried out within the context of those three elements. It is also important to recognize that MBO is a total system of management. As such, it exists in support of the five basic functions of management that have been used as the general parameters for this text. MBO is not an alternative to the functional approach in management; to the contrary it should assist in carrying out the functions of planning, organizing, staffing, directing, and controlling.

Kinds of Objectives

At this point it is important to note that objectives as used in the MBO context are not the same as those that were discussed earlier in this chapter. There we distinguished between individual objectives and institutional objectives. However, both of these categories represent a higher level of objectives that are part of the overall purpose or mission of the organization. These might be called fundamental objectives or goals. Collectively, they present the basic reason for the existence of the program.

By contrast, the MBO objectives are the measurable results we hope to produce while aiming at the higher level objectives. It is for this precise reason that MBO objectives are directly related to budget planning. They represent concrete steps on the way toward fulfilling the broader purpose of the program. In terms of budget planning, dollar values can be assigned to the expenditures involved in reaching these concrete steps.

Another way to understand the difference between the two levels of objectives is to recognize that each is one of five steps in sequential program development. The five steps are as follows:

1. The establishment of purpose or mission. Here is where the school or college would set forth its individual objectives or institutional objectives (or both) from the possibilities outlined earlier in this chapter. These tend to be continuous in nature even though they may be altered over a period of time.
2. Setting forth a statement of values to which the institution is committed. This statement should be in support of the mission or the higher level objectives noted earlier.
3. Arriving at immediate goals or objectives under the MBO framework. In most cases, these would be established on a yearly basis, and they provide the basis for budget planning.
4. Policymaking. Policies are guidelines for subsequent decisions. This aspect of planning will be discussed later in this chapter.
5. Program or action steps. This last step would be manifested in the actual conduct of the sport program.

Thus, it can be seen that budget planning under thre MBO context is the third step in total program development. The specifics of such planning, as outlined in the following discussion, should be noted within the broader frame of reference.

Categories of MBO Objectives

The entire picture surrounding the objectives for any program is further complicated through the recognition that MBO in itself involves a consideration of three different categories of objectives. These are routine, problem-solving, and innovative objectives.

1. *Routine Objectives.* Routine objectives relate to regular commitments within the program. The intent here is to show improvement from the present level to a desired level of performance. In terms of sport scheduling, an example might be to reduce the percentage of away contests from the present level of 55 to 40. This change would be reflected in an accompanying budget reduction for the cost of transportation.

2. *Problem-solving Objectives.* Problem-solving objectives are identified because of some form of basic dissatisfaction. The current results are definitely below par, and the objective is aimed at finding a solution. Here it is important to note that problem solving should not be confused with fighting brushfires. Every organization has brushfires. However, an organization also encounters some problems from time to time. They key to noting a legitimate problem is found in the difference between the present level and a reasonable desired level of performance. For example, a high school athletic director might note that he or she is currently dissatisfied with the present level of qualified women coaches and that at present there are two women on staff with the expected coaching qualifications. The reasonable desired level is to have five qualified women coaches, and the objective is to reach the desired level. Again, the implication for budget planning is obvious.

3. *Innovative Objectives.* It is obvious from the heading that innovative objectives deal with something new. *Change* is the key word in understanding an innovative objective. The development of an innovative objective begins with an idea for change. It proceeds with a recognition of the results —the concrete improvement or benefits that would be expected from the change. However, to achieve any benefits always involves costs. These may not always be dollar costs. They may be costs involving time, energy, people, or opportunity. As far as the budget is concerned, the proposed change may actually result in a reduction of dollar costs, but the cost will be evident in some way or another. Examples of innovative objectives in school or college sport might be providing a

new security system for spectator contests or developing a new transportation plan for team travel. Budget planning would reflect such change in one way or another.

Key Result Areas

With respect to all three categories of objectives, one common denominator should be noted. All the objectives are derived from the identification of key result areas. What is a key result area? It is an answer to the following questions: "What is it I am trying to measure? What are the things I am accountable for? What are the major component parts of my job?" (Deegan and Fritz, p. 136).

It is important to keep in mind that key result areas are not objectives. Rather, they are the areas of concern that will lead to the development of specific, quantifiable objectives. Ultimately, the budget will reflect these areas of concern and the accompanying objectives. Deegan and Fritz repeatedly emphasize that one must not fall into the "activity trap" when identifying key result areas. To avoid that pitfall, they suggest that the development of key result areas should begin with the use of nouns rather than verbs in listing the responsibilities of the job and the areas of managerial concern. They also suggest four possible sources for identifying the responsibilities of the job: (1) organization chart; (2) job description; (3) special programs, projects, and committee assignments; and (4) particular items of attention during the last few weeks or months on the job. Following these general guidelines, a high school or college athletic director might identify these key result areas for budget planning purposes:

Sports (would include a listing of each sport offered).

Coaches (would include a listing of each coach—probably used as an alternative for sports).

Athletic training.

Transportation.

Officials.

Promotion.

Equipment (might be a separate category under each sport).

Facility maintenance.

Recruitment (might also be a separate category under each sport).

Sports information.

Game management.

Staff recruitment.

Staff development.

The preceding, of course, are just examples of key result areas that an athletic director might use for budget planning. There is no magic list or particular list that can be recommended for every athletic director. Each athletic director would select the key result areas that appear to be most appropriate for his or her situation. The cited examples are quite general areas of concern for the management of interscholastic or intercollegiate sport. It is also possible that an athletic director might choose to select any one of the more general areas and break it down to identify other key result areas. For example, the key result areas under the general context of game management might be noted as follows:

tickets

concessions

parking lot

security

officials

radio and television

maintenance

ushers

Before we move on to a further development of the MBO concept, a few words are in order concerning the preceding examples of key result areas. They were selected on the basis of implication for budget planning. It is important to recognize that MBO extends well beyond any direct budgetary concerns. As noted earlier, MBO is a total system of management. For instance, these key result areas would at least be more remote as far as having an immediate import in planning the budget is concerned.

athletic eligibility

coaching evaluation

academic counseling

athlete's safety

coaching techniques

instructional procedures

However, in the final analysis, it is also safe to say that any key result area is likely to relate to the budget in one way or another. After all, the budget is essentially a dollar-and-cents reflection of the entire planning process. When the budget is being planned, it is logical to assume that the athletic director will select those key result areas that are criticial in his or her budgetary situation.

Routine Objectives in Planning a School or College Sport Budget

A definite format for the presentation of the various objectives is set forth by Deegan and Fritz. Their format will also be used here to show how the various MBO objectives can be employed as a basis for budgetary planning. Once again, it is important to keep in mind that these objectives are only examples. They are not presented as the ones that should represent the framework for all school and college sport budgets. It is hoped that they will assist in demonstrating how budget planning can be carried out through the MBO context.

In setting forth routine objectives, four principal steps are involved: (1) selecting the key result areas that are of a routine nature, (2) determining the indicators of success, (3) determining the present level of performance, and (4) deciding on the desired results for the next period. With respect to this aspect of planning, it is important to note that we are much more interested in substantive ideas than in any rhetoric that surrounds the ideas. Therefore, it is suggested that the objectives should initially be listed in tabular form. The following examples will illustrate this.

As stated earlier, the key result areas represent the most critical aspect in the total MBO process. However, the indicators of success are also most instrumental in the fulfillment of the process. Deegan and Fritz cite four broad types of indicators of success: quantity, quality, time, and cost. These are not listed as the indicators for success under the routine objective format. Instead, they provide the guidelines for determining what is to be measured. In other words, as an athletic director you would be setting forth indicators of success that have a quantitative, qualitative, time, or cost dimension. How many students are served? (quantity) How many games are won? (quality) How long is the preseason practice? (time) What is the cost of the football program per player? (cost) Quite obviously, the cost dimension is the one that relates most directly to budget planning. However, it doesn't take long to realize that the budget will also be determined by objectives that result from other indicators of success. Following this line of thinking, the following are some possible routine objectives for the management of school or college sport programs:

Sample Routine Objectives For School or College Sport Programs

1	*2*	*3*	*4* Desired Level		
Key Result Area	*Indicator*	*Present Level*	*Minimum Acceptable*	*Expected Average*	*Maximum Probable*
Sports					
Football	Ticket sales	$1,368,000	$1,300,000	$1,500,000	$1,800,000
	Number of full-time coaches	6	7	6	5
Golf	Total expenditures	$25,615	$26,000	$24,000	$21,000

BUDGET

1	2	3	4 Desired Level		
Key Result Area	Indicator	Present Level	Minimum Acceptable	Expected Average	Maximum Probable
Game management	Number of security personnel	6	6	7	8
	Program and concessions revenue	$102,000	$90,000	$105,000	$120,000
Transportation	Percent of away games	52%	50%	50%	40%
	Average cost per athlete	$30 per year	$30 per year	$28 per year	$25 per year
Intramural sports	Percent of budget allocation	10%	15%	20%	30%
Facilities	Amount spent on plant improvement	$50,000 per year	$50,000 per year	$100,000 per year	$200,000 per year
Athletic training	Cost of supplies	$125,000	$140,000	$120,000	$100,000
Promotion	Number of radio stations covering sport programs	2	2	4	6

Although key result areas and indicators of success have been discussed earlier, further explanation may be necessary in interpreting this table of objectives. The present level, of course, represents the situation at the time of initial planning. Generally speaking, the data would be assessed on a yearly basis because this represents the time frame for most budgets. Determining the desired level is a bit more confusing.

Column 4 (desired level) represents the crux of the planning under the idea of "participative management." The figures under the three subcolumns would be determined through negotiations between the immediate supervisor and employee (e.g., athletic director and coach). In all cases they should reflect realistic appraisals of *results* to be achieved. It is important to note that the maximum probable figure is not always the highest figure; it is the desired optimum figure from a realistic perspective. For example, sometimes it may be necessary to reduce costs; in that case, the maximum probable figure would be the lowest of the three figures. The expected average is merely an estimate of what can reasonably be anticipated in terms of results. The minimum is just that: success in the key result area is in jeopardy when the result falls below that minimum.

As noted earlier, the examples already given were selected purely at random. They do not necessarily represent priority routine objectives. In some cases, the budgetary implications are most direct; in other cases (e.g. number of radio stations), the influence on budget planning is more subtle. It is hoped that the examples cited are sufficient to show how the routine objectives under the MBO framework can assist with budget planning.

Problem-Solving Objectives in Planning a School or College Sport Budget

The form of planning involving problem-solving objectives begins by identifying a key result area that currently falls well below the accepted norm. Deegan and Fritz suggest that this part of the planning process is initiated when the administrator completes the following sentence: "I am dissatisfied with the current level of   " (p. 199). They also list nine steps in determining whether it is really a problem and in making plans for solution of the problem (pp. 197–198).

1. Identify the problem (by completing the above sentence).
2. Determine the present unsatisfactory level.
3. Define a reasonable desired performance level.
4. Isolate the difference between the present and desired levels.
5. Brainstorm possible causes of the problem.
6. Decide which causes are the most crucial.
7. Identify alternative solutions.
8. Evaluate proposed solutions.
9. Make commitment to time and action plan.

Following that model, a college athletic director might outline this problem-solving objective as part of his or her budget planning.

1. Statement of problem: I am dissatisfied with the current level of number of athletes who do not receive their degrees.
2. Present level: 60 percent of all varsity athletes complete their degree work.
3. Reasonable desired level: 80 percent of all varsity athletes complete their degree work.
4. Reason for desired level: to have the percentage more in line with that for all the students in the college and with athletes at other colleges with comparable academic standards.
5. Possible causes:
   Competitive recruitment (obtaining athletes with deficient academic ability).

Lack of athlete's motivation for academic pursuits.

Poor teaching.

Insufficient academic advising.

Attitude of coaches.

Time demands in athletics.

Housing situation on campus.

Social life on campus.

External influence on athletes (professional sport and other job opportunities).

Limited curricula (choice of majors).

Faculty attitude toward athletes.

6. Most Likely Causes:

Competitive recruitment.

Inadequate provision for academic advising and tutoring.

7/8. Alternatives and Evaluation:

Contribution = assessment of the degree to which the proposed solution is likely to solve the problem.

Cost = in addition to dollar costs, this would include an assessment of all resources necessary to solve the problem —includes time costs, energy costs, people costs, opportunity costs.

Feasibility = is the proposed solution likely to be one that can be implemented?

Note: Each proposed solution is assessed on a scale of 1 to 10, with 10 indicating the optimum for that category of assessment.

Options	Contribution	Cost	Feasibility
1. Faculty involved in recruiting	9	3	1 (14)
2. Alumni involved in recruiting	3	5	7 (15)
3. Expanding the recruitment area to be covered by the coaches	7	1	10 (18)
4. Lowering the athletic standards for recruitment	8	1	1 (10)
5. Providing additional funds for advisement and tutoring services	9	1	9 (19)
6. Volunteer faculty assistance for advisement and tutoring	7	9	1 (17)
7. Eliminate all recruitment	8	1	1 (10)

9. Action plan: An analysis of the preceding options would indicate that three of them emerge as the best possibilities. They are expanding the recruitment areas to be covered by the coaches, providing additional funds for advisement and tutoring, and volunteer faculty assistance for advising and tutoring. However, the last-mentioned ranks extremely low on the feasibility scale. For this reason, it appears that the problem can best be met by expanding the recruitment area to be covered by the coaches and providing additional funds for advising and tutorial service.

Specific action would be to increase the budgetary allocation for the next fiscal year as follows.

Recruitment—$75,000

Advisement and tutorial service—$20,000

Once again, it is important to keep in mind that the preceding is only a hypothetical example of how the development of a problem-solving objective could be used to guide the budget planning. It could well be that the possible causes of the problem, most likely causes, and solutions would appear quite different in an actual college situation. Nevertheless, it is hoped that the basic idea behind this form of planning has been conveyed.

Innovative Objectives

Of the three types of job-related objectives (MBO objectives), the innovative objective is perhaps most readily understood because there is a natural tendency to associate objectives with innovation. The real key here, particularly from a budget-planning standpoint, is to understand the actual commitment that lies behind the goal statement.

Innovation begins with an idea for change or initiation; it is creative in nature. As such, an innovative objective is sharply contrasted with a routine objective. When using an innovative objective as a partial basis for budget planning, there must be an indication that the proposed innovation will result in some form of payoff or benefit. The idea is the seed of exploration of the possible results; the idea is not an objective as such. The actual objective will be manifested in a statement of the proposed results that stem from the idea. Once again, it is important to note that the word *results* is a key factor in the MBO concept.

Improvement is not made without associated costs of some type. In explaining the format for their innovative goal worksheet, Deegan and Fritz succinctly describe the cost consideration: "By costs we mean more than dollars, obviously. We mean all resources which might be spent. Thus we are thinking of dollar costs, time costs, energy costs, people costs, opportunity costs, frustration costs, any and all costs expended to achieve the intended results." (p. 223).

As with the routine and problem-solving objectives, Deegan and Fritz's format is also used here to show how an innovative objective can be factored into the budget planning for school or college sport.

Sample Innovative Objective Work Sheet for School or College Sport Program

Innovative idea: to provide summer sport camps for this community and the surrounding area
Desired results: 1. Increased revenue of $25,000 per year
                  2. Additional salary for staff ($20,000 total)

3. Improved community relations
4. Fuller utilization of facilities during the off-season

Method	Timetable
1. Meet with staff to discuss interest in the proposal	1. By July 1
2. Visit sport camps at other schools and colleges—$300	2. By Sept. 1
3. Check effect on liability and insurance	3. By Sept. 15
4. Obtain commitments from instructors and other staff	4. By Oct. 15
5. Prepare schedule for camps	5. By Dec. 15
6. Distribute flyers and other announcements for advance publicity—$500	6. By Feb. 1
7. Receive applications for enrollment (including deposit)	7. By April 1
8. Plan final schedule	8. By May 1
9. Distribute information on changes—$200	9. By June 1
10. Begin camps	10. By July 1
11. Monitor results	11. July 1–Sept. 1
12. Evaluation	12. Oct. 1

As with other examples, this one may not be appropriate or on target for many situations. Yet it should demonstrate adequately that the development of an innovative objective can also be a significant component in budget planning. If nothing else, it should show that there must be an accompanying budgetary consideration whenever there is a proposal for innovation or change.

PROCEDURES

A fourth aspect of planning involves the establishment of procedures for the general conduct of the program. For at least three reasons, this is a fairly difficult area to pinpoint. (1) There is a natural tendency to confuse procedures with policy. (2) Many procedures arise out of the dynamics of the particular situation. Therefore, it is difficult to discuss them in a more global manner. (3) Planning procedures tend to overlap with the actual procedures in organizing, staffing, directing, and controlling a program. Nevertheless in spite of these inherent limitations, there are at least five areas that generally call for the establishment of planning procedures for the total management of school and college sport programs. This list may be far from inclusive, and much of its applicability will depend on the particular structure and demands of the school or college. It is hoped that any confusion between policy and procedures will at least be somewhat clarified at the end of this chapter.

Personnel

Obviously, personnel procedures form an area of planning that most clearly overlaps the other functions of management, particularly staffing and evaluating, as an aspect of controlling. However, there are certain basic decisions involving personnel that fall into the early planning category; and procedures are needed to implement those decisions. How will the personnel be obtained? What should be the work load for teachers and coaches? How should personnel be evaluated? What should be the procedures for the selection, retention, advancement, and dismissal of personnel? Who should participate in the personnel decisions? These are all questions that call for early decisions about procedures.

Selection of Personnel The term *personnel* is used here in its broadest sense to include all the staff and students who are involved with the school or college sport program. In many organizations, it is natural to restrict personnel considerations to those decisions involving the management of the staff. However, in a school or college setting, student personnel decisions are equally as important. Procedures are needed to respond to the following questions regarding the selection of staff and students.

Staff.
   1. Who should participate in the selection process? Should there be a personnel committee that has staff selection as one of its functions? To what extent is this primarily an administrative decision?
   2. How will the various positions be advertised? How will the applicants be screened? Today there are standard affirmative action guidelines for these procedures. However, each department will have to establish additional procedures for the specific implementation of these guidelines.
   3. Should there be general guidelines for appointment? If so, what is the nature of these guidelines? Specific criteria for appointment will be covered by the position description. However, it is possible that a department might choose to establish some general procedures to guide the appointments.

Students. It is assumed that for the most part the selection of students is a lesser concern in public schools owing to the very nature of those institutions. However, all schools and colleges will need certain procedures to govern the selection of students for instructional classes. It is also assumed that each coach will also establish his or her own procedures for selection of team members. Beyond that, each college and private school will need procedures in response to the following questions revolving around recruitment of athletes.

   1. To what extent will recruitment be employed?
   2. What will be the general guidelines for recruitment?
   3. Will alumni be used in recruitment? How?
       (Note: For the most part these three questions bring us into the area of policy. However, as will be pointed out later, policy development occurs over a period of time. Therefore, some preliminary planning procedures must be provided.)
   4. At the college level, how will the NCAA regulations be enforced at the institution?

Staff Workload
1. What is a full teaching load?
2. In terms of split responsibilities, how is the work load determined for the various responsibilities? For example, what would be the relative distribution of the work load among the following responsibilities?
   Coaching
   Teaching
   Intramural sport
   Sports information

Evaluation of Personnel

Staff
1. Who should participate?
2. What are the criteria for evaluation?
3. When does the evaluation take place?
4. How is the evaluation conducted?

Students
1. What is the basis for evaluation in classes?
2. Are grades assigned? If so, what type of grading system is employed?
3. What are the athletic awards? How are the recipients of these awards determined?
4. What are the intramural sport awards? How are the recipients of these awards determined?

Retention and Dismissal of Personnel

Staff
1. What are the criteria for reappointments?
2. What are the conditions for reappointment?
3. Is there a tenure system for coaches? If so, how is eligibility for tenure determined?
4. What is the procedure for dismissal of a staff member?

Students (questions related to eligibility of athletes)
1. How are national, state, or conference eligibility requirements (or a combination) enforced?
2. What are the institutional eligibility requirements?

Staff Advancement
1. Is there a system for promotion? If so, what are the procedures that guide the consideration for promotion in rank or other positional status?
2. How are salary raises determined?

As one looks over this list of questions related to personnel procedures, it is obvious that blanket answers cannot be provided (or even suggested) that will apply to all schools and colleges. So much depends on the specific nature of the managerial environment. Yet these are procedural questions that at some point in time must be addressed as part of the total planning function in the management of school or college sport programs. Much the same can be said about the questions to be considered under the other procedural areas.

Procedures for Facilities

This is another critical area for procedural planning. Although there is no attempt here to set forth a hierarchy for the planning of procedures, it is safe to say that such planning is off to a good start if sound decisions are made with respect to personnel and facilities. Generally speaking, the procedures related to facilities fall into any one of four categories: long-range planning, maintenance, priorities for usage, and scheduling.

Long Range Planning: The success of most school and college sport programs may ultimately depend on the degree to which sound judgment has been employed in the long-range planning for facilities. Any deficiencies in this regard may be largely attributed to the host of variables that influence such planning. From an external perspective, these variables relate to the cultural, social, legal, political, technological, and economic factors that influence facility development. Internally, one has to consider program philosophy, financing, personnel, and current utilization. It seems that one might be prepared at least to approach these variables if the following procedural questions are considered:

1. Who will participate in facility planning?
2. What will be the strategy for presenting a facility plan?
3. What criteria will be employed in determining the need for facilities?
4. How will the financing of new facilities be pursued?

Maintenance. Although the procedures for maintenance are also an integral part of the total planning picture, this is not a topic that readily lends itself to textbook discussion. It is clearly a case where the hands-on, directing function is the name of the game. Nevertheless, there is little doubt that certain basic questions must be addressed as part of the total picture involving facility procedures:

1. Who is directly responsible for the maintenance of facilities?
2. What type of maintenance schedule will be employed?
3. What provision will be made for adherence to safety standards?

In terms of the actual maintenance of sport facilities, answers to the preceding questions will only scratch the surface. Yet there is good reason to believe that many of the typical maintenance problems can be avoided if these basic questions are addressed as part of the preliminary planning process.

Priorities In any multiple-use environment, determination of priorities for the use of facilities is always a complicated matter. Sport programs in the schools and colleges exemplify this complexity owing to the extremely diversified nature of a total sport program. With respect to multiple use of sport facilities, priorities must be determined among sports; among male, female, and coeducational sports; and among instructional classes, intramural activities, and interscholastic or intercollegiate teams. Once again, it is most difficult to be specific about a set of priorities that will be appropriate for any given institution. There are too many variables stemming primarily from the program objectives and the nature and scope of the existing facilities. However, later decisions involving the direction and control of facility usage will be facilitated if the following questions are considered in the early planning for procedures.

1. Who is ultimately responsible for determining priorities?
2. What will be the basis for determining priorities?
3. What provision will there be for reconsideration of priorities?

Scheduling of Facilities: Whenever there is a problem associated with facility usage (which appears to be the more typical situation), some type of master schedule is really a necessity. Therefore, the procedural planning should be directed toward an effort at obtaining that master schedule while allowing sufficient flexibility for extenuating circumstances. This can be facilitated if these procedural questions are addressed:

1. Who will prepare the actual schedule?
2. What scheduling period will be employed (weekly, monthly, seasonal, semester)?
3. When should schedule requests be submitted?
4. What are the mechanics for making schedule changes?

Scheduling Games, Tournaments, and Classes

Beyond facility scheduling per se, there is a much broader aspect of sport scheduling that begs for procedures resulting from preliminary planning. This includes a wide range of considerations related to the instructional, intramural, and interscholastic or intercollegiate components of the total sport program. These are the more basic scheduling decisions, which, of course, will ultimately have a bearing on the decisions related to facility scheduling.

Instructional Scheduling: Sport Coordinators. Earlier in this chapter, some fairly detailed suggestions were presented about scheduling, under the context of program planning. Thus, to some extent the planning procedures for scheduling have already been discussed. However, there are additional procedures that are also part of the total planning picture.

It seems that the real key to effective procedures for instructional scheduling revolves around the effective use of sport coordinators.

1. How many sport coordinators should be appointed? This is a procedural question that can be determined only on the basis of needs and resources within the

particular institution. In general, the size of the institution and the size of the sport program will be the most important determining factors. Chances are that there will also be a positive correlation between those two factors. Therefore, it is logical to assume that in an extremely large university, there is likely to be a separate coordinator for each sport; for example, a basketball coordinator, a wrestling coordinator, a golf coordinator, and so on. In smaller colleges and most high schools, it might be necessary to appoint a smaller number of coordinators who have responsibilities for more than one sport. The possible combinations of sports are too numerous to mention. The point here is that a coordinator would not be appointed for a sport in which he or she did not have a relatively high level of expertise. For this reason, the determination of the number of sport coordinators in an important procedural matter.

2. How will the classes be scheduled? This questions calls for basic procedures related to time, place, and level of instruction. It is assumed that each sport coordinator would submit a separate schedule to be considered for determination of a master schedule.

3. How will the teaching assignments be determined for the various classes? This is an extension of the question related to work load. After the basic work load for each instructor is determined, there must be procedures for converting that work load to actual teaching assignments.

4. How will the classes be evaluated? By and large, the evaluation process is part of the controlling function that will be discussed later in this book. However, basic procedures related to evaluation should also be set forth in the earlier stage of planning.

Intramural Scheduling: Sport Coordinators. As noted earlier, much of the success in planning an integrated school or college sport program will depend on the degree to which the planning can mutually provide for the needs of the instructional, intramural, and interscholastic or intercollegiate components. The establishment of appropriate procedures, revolving around sport coordinators, is again a key factor in facilitating that intent. Interscholastic or intercollegiate scheduling poses its own special problems owing to external considerations, but there is no reason why the scheduling for instructional or intramural activities should not be centralized through sport coordinators. In fact, it would seem that this is the only logical way to avoid many of the conflicts involving time, place, and personnel. Thus, we suggest that each sport coordinator should submit a combined schedule for classes and intramural activities. In doing the planning for the intramural components, sport coordinators will also have to consider various procedural questions:

1. What will be the basic units of competition? Answers to this question will once again largely depend on the specific structure and group dynamics of the particular institution. However, these are among the prime possibilities. The nature of the particular sport will also be a determining factor in selecting among the possibilities:

Colleges	Schools
Class units	Geographical units
Fraternity or sorority units	Independent groups
Dormitory units	Sport club groups
Independent groups	Groups representing other
Geographical units	school activities—
Department groups	band, theater, debate,
Graduate student groups	and so on
Faculty groups	Homeroom units
Sport club groups	
Social groups	

2. What types of meets, leagues, and tournaments will be utilized? Again, the nature of the particular sport is often a critical factor in establishing the procedure. This is another reason why such planning should revolve around sport coordinators. Planning for meets is quite specific to certain sports such as track and field, swimming, and gymnastics. Other sports lend themselves to procedural planning for tournaments or leagues, or both. Procedures will be based on a selection of possibilities such as these: round robin (including variations), single elimination, double elimination, semidouble elimination, consolation, challenge, ladder, pyramid, funnel, spider web, or bump board tournaments. In addition, various sports employ even more specific types, such as the "best ball" tournament in golf.

3. How should the intramural schedule be integrated with the instructional schedule? There is no standard answer to this question, but the procedure has to be established. It is assumed that in most cases the sport coordinator would begin by providing the instructional schedule for the sport or sports for which he or she is responsible. However, again this should not be the gym class type of arrangement wherein instruction takes place only during the course of the normal school day. Conceivably, any period of time from 8 A.M. to 8 P.M. Sunday through Saturday might be utilized. Once the instructional schedule is established, the sport coordinator can proceed to plan a competitive intramural schedule built around the variables of time, place, and available supervisory personnel. The important element throughout the planning is that sport instruction and competitive intramural activities are not viewed as separate programs that are in basic conflict. These two elements of the total program should be designed to complement each other. This is why the sport coordinator is the key to effective procedural planning.

Interscholastic or Intercollegiate Scheduling. It could be argued that an appropriate schedule is the real key to success in an interscholastic or intercollegiate program. This, of course, is a generalization that is subject to criticism from various directions when we consider that many factors contribute to such success. One always has to be begin with the athlete. Beyond that, the quality of coaching and the quality of the facilities loom as significant variables. Nevertheless, these quality control factors are not likely to achieve potential if the athletic department is not able to provide a suitable schedule. For this reason, interscholastic or intercollegiate scheduling procedures are also an integral component of the total planning picture.

1. Who should do the scheduling? This is a crucial question in school and college sport programs because there frequently is inherent conflict between the perspective of the coach and that of the administration regarding what is considered to be a desirable schedule. Ultimately, the answer should depend on the objectives of the program and the capabilities of the personnel within the department. Final decisions, of course, are the responsibility of the athletic director. In general, the procedure should be one that provides for input from coaches and key members of the administrative staff.

2. When should a schedule be prepared? This is another one of those procedural questions that does not readily lend itself to textbook answers. In many cases, the answer will in large part be provided by conference arrangements and standing agreements with traditional opponents. Within recent years, the tendency has been to prepare schedules well in advance. However, it would appear that there is also a need for some flexibility in the scheduling procedure to facilitate an adjustment to the current situation.

3. What are the factors to be considered in arriving at a suitable schedule? Answers here should also largely depend on the objectives of the program. It seems that the following will usually be among the prime considerations:

Sufficient number of home contests.

Anticipated gate receipts (guarantees for away games).

Travel costs.

Traditional opponents.

Possible new opponents to advance the level of the program.

Possible new opponents with similar program objectives.

Inherent institutional relationships.

Financial Procedural Planning

Needless to say, all other aspects of planning will remain at the planning stage if there is insufficient attention to the procedures to be followed in financing the program. Consequently, at the outset management must consider some of the more basic questions that relate to the financing of any program. In some cases, these questions are particularly acute in school and college sport programs owing to the variety in financial arrangements.

What are the Financial Limits? One of the more characteristic features of financing in educational institutions is that a number of individual units are all competing for existing funds. This in itself calls for a recognition of a certain kind of limitation and the development of a procedure to cope with that limitation. What case can be made for the sport program to receive an equal share of funds among other programs? Is the administration inclined to cut back the sport program in favor of other priorities? What is the nature of the competition? These are questions that call for a procedure to be followed in pursuit of the competitive dollar. Basically, what is needed is a strategy to gain financial support for the sport program.

Aside from competition among competing units in the institution, there is also a more general institutional limitation that affects the planning for school and college sport programs. In addition, each institution faces a financial limit in competing for existing funds. This kind of limitation has been most evident in many parts of the United States in recent years. Classic cases in point can be found in the restrictions placed on schools as a result of Proposition 13 in California and Proposition 2½ in Massachusetts. Proposition 13 directed a 57 percent cut in property taxes as of July 1, 1978. The effects of Proposition 2½ are more gradual. It states that, beginning in 1981, all personal property (excise) and real estate taxes must be reduced to an evaluation of $25 per $1000. A community is required to make 15 percent reduction in its taxes each year until the 2½ percent evaluation is reached. In both states, the effects of the legislation on the sport programs is very evident. Administrators have been faced with dramatic evidence of coping with financial limits. Financial procedural planning assumes a new dimension.

As an alternative to institutional funding, many school and college sport programs are increasingly exploring possibilities for other sources of funding, some of which tend to make the program more of an independent enterprise. However, this has another kind of limitation and points to another question that is always integral in planning the procedures for financing the program.

What Are the Possible Sources of Revenue? Athletic programs are somewhat unique in that they typically have available a couple of funding sources that are not available to all units in the educational institution. These sources are gate receipts and student fees. In addition, of course, many universities have particularly benefited from television contracts as a principal source of revenue. Beyond that, revenue is also obtained through booster clubs, fund-raising drives, endowments, donations, concessions, and parking fees.

Within recent years it has become increasingly apparent that athletic departments must do additional planning for generating revenue in spite of the usual sources of revenue that have often been available to them. For this reason, fund raising has emerged as a principal procedure for many school and college sport programs. Bronzan (1977) offers an excellent account of procedures that can be employed in fund raising. The March 1981 issue of *Athletic Purchasing and Facilities* also includes a series of practical articles related to fund-raising procedures. Both of these works point to the need and potential for this kind of planning for sport programs. The reader may wish to consult these works for additional ideas regarding sources of revenue. Regardless of the choices, the following questions are integral to the total financial planning.

1. Revenue for what? What is the basis for the need for revenue or additional revenue?
2. What percentage of the total revenue can be anticipated from the various sources?
3. Who will make the contacts in fund raising?
4. How will the funds be initially allocated?

Planning Procedures for Marketing

The subject of fund raising points to one other area of planning that also calls for some early decisions regarding the procedures to be followed. This is the broad field of marketing. Every program has to be marketed in some form or another. Here marketing is considered in a sense that extends beyond the direct selling and buying of a commodity. In the case of an extensive spectator sport program at the college level, it is easy to see that the program has to be marketed in order to generate sufficient gate revenue or television revenue or both. However, beyond that most concrete example, every school and college sport program must establish procedures for assessing the relationship between the services that can be provided and the needs of the consumer, be that a spectator or a participant or both. In short, there is a need for a market analysis as a preliminary component in planning. What might be involved in a marketing analysis for a school or college sport program? The following questions and answers address the problem.

1. How should the objectives of the program be presented? Earlier in the chapter we looked at possible program objectives from the standpoint of both the individual consumer and the institution. A strategy has to be developed that will present these objectives in a manner that is understandable and basically appealing to the consumer. The marketing strategy might be to focus attention on a particular objective. This does not necessarily imply a program priority. However, it can be useful in gaining entry to a greater acceptance of the program. For example, management might choose to focus on the football team as the medium for identity with the institution while recognizing that the consumer will ultimately lend support as well to objectives associated with the intramural sport program.

2. What special services can be provided? Every program has its strengths and weaknesses. In terms of strengths, what can be advanced as the principal benefits

from an involvement with that school or college sport program? With regard to spectator sport, there may be a possibility of stressing the accomplishments of a certain team or a star player on that team. In the case of participant sport, the special service may be manifested in the form of new facilities, expert instruction, or unique opportunities in developing sports. In other words, what does the program have to offer that might not be found through other sources?

3. What is the nature of the market? Who are the consumers? How have they changed in recent years? Based on current projections, how might they change in the near future? These are general questions in marketing that should be considered in planning a school or college sport program. For example, spectators might be showing a shift in interest from one sport to another. Another possibility is that a particular sport is beginning to attract a different kind of spectator. Participants may be seeking new modes of participation or gravitating toward sports with general popularity (e.g., current interest in racquetball).

4. What are the community or alumni attitudes (or both) that might have a bearing on success in reaching program objectives? Programs in all schools and colleges will to some extent (often to a considerable extent) be shaped by the social environment in which they exist. Community attitudes tend to steer school programs, and alumni attitudes are a significant factor in the development of college programs. Part of the market analysis should include an attempt to assess those attitudes. Subsequently, a marketing strategy should be developed in an effort to provide a means of program implementation that will not conflict with these attitudes. For example, possibly the community attitude is such that the people only think about interscholastic competition to the exclusion of other components of the total sport program. If the earlier planning calls for the development of other aspects of the program, a marketing strategy will have to be aimed at a shift in the attitudes toward the program.

5. What is the nature of the competition for the service that is provided? This question is not directed toward the competition between schools or the competition for funds within an institution. From the standpoint of a market analysis, this question of competition focuses on the competition for the service that is offered to the consumer. Thus, with respect to college spectator sport, management must analyze the competition for the entertainment dollar. The market for participant sport in the schools and colleges must be analyzed in relationship to other agencies, be they public or private, that also offer a service in the form of participant sport opportunities.

6. What is the extent of the projected market? A market analysis will ultimately result in some projection figures relative to the potential consumers. Within the context of school and college sport programs, this would likely include projections on the number of athletic participants, the number of intramural sport participants, instructional enrollment, and spectator attendance. Therefore, it is quite obvious that a market analysis is an integral procedure in the planning function of

management. Without it, there will be difficulty in organizing and staffing the organization.

POLICY DEVELOPMENT

One major component of planning remains to be considered—the broad area of policy development. It is being considered at this point because it occupies a different place in the total process of planning. Setting objectives, planning the program, budget planning, and the planning procedures are all matters that call for initial attention. By contrast, even though policies will ultimately represent some of the factors of planning, they evolve over a period of time. Therefore, it seems appropriate to think of policies in the form of policy development. Before examining the potential policy domain in school and college sport programs, it might be useful to consider the nature of policy from a general perspective. This might help to clarify any possible confusion between procedures and policies.

The Nature of Policy   Grumm (1975) makes a distinction between two forms of policy that appears to be a meaningful point of departure for anyone who is attempting to understand the idea of policy.

> Policy might still be conceived in a narrow, restricted sense or in a broad, encompassing sense. In the narrow sense it can be thought of as an authoritative declaration or prescription consisting of a statute, an appropriation, a set of rules, an executive order, or a judicial decision. In this sense, it is a decision reached by the political process to take some action or compel some action. Or more broadly it might be conceived as a general pattern of decisions and actions by government authorities that are tied together by a common and general goal to which all of the decisions and actions are directed. The latter definition would probably conform more with conventional usage (p. 441).

This latter conception of policy would be very useful in gaining a clearer understanding of sport management policy. Particular attention should be given to the "general pattern of decisions and actions." This reinforces the idea that policy is a planning component that evolves over an extended period of time.

It is obvious that Grumm's distinction is presented within the framework of governmental policy. However, his basic conception of policy would be applicable to policy in any context, be it educational policy, management policy or sport management policy. The only different is that we would be thinking of a general pattern of decisions and actions by management in lieu of government authorities.

In discussing management policy per se, Brink (1978) presents a conception of policy that at first seems to complicate the picture. However, in the final analysis, his ideas fit in quite well with Grumm's usage of policy in the broader sense.

> It is not enough to know where we want to go. We must also determine how we are going to get there. This means that we must have policies and related plans. These policies and related plans are needed at each organizational level. At the highest

organizational level, the policies are known as strategies and are supportive of the highest-ranking goals of the enterprise. At each lower organizational level, there are also policies that should be supportive of the policies formulated at the next-higher organizational level and be supported by the policies formulated at the next-lower organizational level. There is thus an interrelated chain of policies moving from the lower to the highest organizational level. . . . Although policies tell us how we are going to achieve our objectives, supporting actions are still needed to implement those policies. These supporting actions include lower-level operational plans and definitive actions to carry out the previously developed policies. Both types of action constitute the third requisite, which we call implementation. Obviously, well-established goals and well-designed policies will not be realized if they are not effectively implemented (pp. 6–7).

The initial complication is found in Brink's idea that there are three basic components of management: objectives, policies, and implementation. One is more or less given the impression that these components of management proceed in chronological order. In other words, management moves from the establishment of goals or objectives to the development of policies and then to the implementation of the program. This seems contrary to the conception that policy is a general pattern of decisions and actions. After all, the actions are the implementation. The sequence of objectives, policies, and implementation also seems to contradict the earlier point that policies evolve over a period of time.

The apparent difficulty in arriving at a consistent conception of policy can be overcome by recognizing that policy is sometimes referred to in a more generic sense to include procedures. Brink refers to the fact that policies and related plans are needed at each organizational level. It would seem that, at the lower levels, such policies are more of a procedural nature. These procedures are also the concrete elements in the implementation of the program. But ultimately the organization moves to policy development, which, in Grumm's terms, is a general pattern of decisions and actions. Over a period of time such policy will provide the essential link between objectives and implementations in accordance with Brink's conception of the three basic components of management. Thus, we have initial planning procedures to determine how we will get there. Eventually, we have policy to provide a steady light in our efforts to reach the objectives of the organization.

The Policy Domain in School and College Sport

Based on what has been said about policy in general, it should be evident that it is virtually impossible to set forth policies that are generally applicable to school and college sport programs. Policies not only evolve over a period of time; they are also developed from the general pattern of decisions and actions within the particular sport program. Therefore, when one thinks about the planning for policy, the best he or she can do is to point out the potential territory or domain for policy development in school and college sport. The following should be among the prime considerations in the planning of policy for school or college sport or both.

Athletes. Any policies related to athletes are likely to be aimed at an attempt to control the relationship between the needs of the athlete and the objectives of the program. How does the athlete fit into the total structure of the school or college? Are athletes to be treated like any other student? If not, what are the areas of exception? What are the bases for such exceptions? The answers to such questions could lead to policies involving admissions, athletic eligibility, retention or dismissal, advising, and tutoring. At the college level, the answers would also be applicable to decisions involving housing and meal arrangements. In some cases, particularly at the school level, the answers might also lead to a policy related to a separate code of conduct for athletes.

In addition to the role of the athlete in the school or college, the role of the athlete in the sport program prompts certain policy considerations. How should disciplinary cases be handled? How will the administration proceed in attempts to resolve conflicts between a coach and members of the athletic team? Will athletes be restricted in their involvement with other aspects of the sport program? What means will be used to reward or recognize athletic achievement?

All these questions point toward a policy domain that is largely within the institution. Particularly at the college level, there may also be a need for policy involving the athletes' interface with the public. Are there to be restrictions involving the athletes' contact with the media? If so, what would be the form of such restriction? In what ways will athletes be permitted or encouraged (or both) to serve as representatives of the institution or the sport program or both? Within certain college sport programs there will be "blue-chip" athletes who are highly pursued by professional scouts. Invariably, this type of situation will have to lead to the development of some kind of policy.

Coaches. Although policies involving athletes are ultimately the bottom line considerations in athletic programs, those involving the coach rank close behind owing to the unique role of the coach. Not unlike the athlete, the coach may well be a subject for policy determination on three fronts: role within the institution, role within the sport program, and interface with the public.

1. *The Insitution.* Will coaches be considered for tenure? If so, on what basis will tenure be awarded? If not, what will be the terms of employment? Are coaches to be evaluated on the same basis as another teacher or faculty member? At the college level, will coaches be eligible for academic rank? What will be the basis for determining the coaches' potential involvement with an academic program?

2. *The Sport Program.* What will the basis for determining when coaching should be a full-time position? When a coach has split responsibilities between coaching and the intramural or instructional components (or both), how will the total performance be evaluated?

3. *The Public.* What limits, if any, are to be placed on the coach with respect to communication with prospective athletes, the media, and parents

and regarding general public appearances? To what extent is the coach a spokesperson for the institution? What type of reporting system is to be used in controlling the public relations aspect of the total program?

Other Policies. We could continue to raise questions about other aspects of the sport program that apparently also call for the development of some kind of policies. However, for at least two reasons, it seems more appropriate to rest the case here. First of all, there is good reason to believe that athletes and coaches represent the principal territorial need for policy development. This is based on the assumption that athletes and coaches represent the two most significant variables in sport programs. In general, when things are right with them, everything is right; and when things are wrong with them, everything is wrong. That generalization could be challenged by suggesting that finance is really the bottom line consideration and that the really significant policy area is finances. Although such an argument has considerable merit, there is a second reason why it is difficult to set forth the remaining territory in the policy domain.

Most of the other policies will ultimately be developed from the procedural considerations. Finances comprise a classic case in point. The reader will recall that we noted several questions that call for financial procedures. Within the context of each institution, some of those procedures will ultimately be stabilized in the form of policies. The same will be true of other selected procedural considerations. You will recall that a policy is a general pattern of decisions and actions that are tied together by a common goal. Therefore, it becomes difficult to spell out the complete territory for developing policies. But it is also difficult to imagine the absence of a need for policies involving atheletes, coaches, and finances.

Summary

In this chapter we have attempted to analyze the entire planning function as it relates to the management of school and college sport programs. It should be evident that this is a most extensive function, ranging from forecasting to policy development. Setting objectives is probably at the heart of the entire process. Yet each aspect of planning has its own kind of importance.

When one thinks of planning, the initial idea is that planning is the function that takes place before any implementation or action. To some extent this is true; many of the planning components are up front considerations. However, it is also important to keep in mind that planning is a continuous process. This is particularly evident in the area of policy development.

The relative importance of planning cannot be overemphasized. As trite as this may seem, the person who fails to plan is planning to fail. Sport programs in the schools and colleges only dramatize this need for careful planning. For the most part, these programs arose spontaneously amid a relative abundance of available funds. However, the situation today dictates a different managerial approach. Thus, the entire planning function is a priority consideration for immediate attention.

REFERENCES

Athletic Purchasing and Facilities. Vol. 5, No. 3, March 1981.

Brink, Victor. *Understanding Management Policy—and Making It Work.* New York. AMACON, 1978.

Bronzan, Robert T. "Preparing Leaders for Non-School Youth Sports." *Athletic Purchasing and Facilities.* Vol. 6, No. 3, March 1982, pp. 12–16.

———— . *Public Relations, Promotions and Fund Raising for Athletic and Physical Education Programs.* New York. John Wiley & Sons, Inc., 1977.

Deegan, Arthur X., Roger J. and Fritz. *MBO Goes to College.* Clearwater, Fla. Art Deegan & Associates, 1975.

Grumm, John. "The Analysis of Policy Impact." In *Policies and Policymaking,* Fred I. Greenstein and Nelson W. Polsby (eds.). Reading, Mass. Addison-Wesley, 1975.

Guttmann, Allen. *From Ritual to Record: The Nature of Modern Sports.* New York. Columbia University Press, 1978.

3

Organizing a School or College Sport Program

CONCEPTS AND PROBLEMS

Key Considerations—Work Unit Size and Span of Control

Distinction Between Line and Staff Personnel

The Situationally Defined Nature of an Organizational Chart

Four Elements in a Complete Position Description

Common Staff Positions in Collegiate Sport

Communication Skills—The Common Denominator in Managerial Qualifications

"Intramural" and "Extramural" Qualifications for a Coach

Specific Qualifications for Certain Staff Positions

As noted in Chapter 1, to some extent the line between planning and organizing is a fine one. There is a natural flow from planning a program to organizing it. The major difference is that organizing signals the action point. When we organize, we set the wheels in motion for the remainder of the total process of management. Nevertheless, the planning does not stop because it is an ongoing process throughout the managerial cycle.

Organizational considerations are largely related to the structure for the program. How many managerial positions should be identified? What are the lines of authority and responsibility? Who reports to whom? What are the relationships among the various positions? To what extent will efforts be made to integrate the work in the various components of the total program? These are basic organizational questions that should lead to decisions about the structure for the program. Before turning to the specific organizational considerations in a school or college sport program, we might find it helpful to look at some general factors whenever and wherever a unit is organized.

GENERAL FACTORS IN ORGANIZING

Why do we organize? The most basic need for the organizing function is to provide the machinery or network for carrying out the planning function. The organizational structure should offer a means for determining how each group member can contribute to the achievement of the goals or objectives of the organization. Thus, from a simple standpoint, the division of work is a principal consideration when we organize. However, there is much more involved. In addition to deciding who does what, we also organize to provide the means for interaction, communication, and cooperation among group members. Although there may be considerable variance from organization to organization regarding the extent of independent work, all members of any organization are to some extent dependent on the work of their fellow group members. To state it somewhat differently, one never completely works in isolation within an organizational structure.

The organizational structure also provides a means for indicating responsibility. Such notation of responsibility is a natural corollary of the division of work. In the structural framework this is usually indicated through the designation of leaders for the various subunits within the organization. Within the relatively larger organizations, the assignment of responsibility is often particularly critical at the middle management level. It is generally not too difficult to pinpoint responsibility at the top level of management. As we move through the organizational matrix, it becomes increasingly clear that the responsibility must be indicated as precisely as possible.

However, the subject of responsibility also prompts consideration of the fact that there are essentially two main types of organizations—the formal and the informal. Generally speaking, a formal organization has status, authority, and power even though these elements will be found in varying degrees within the formal organization. Thus, we find that provisions for responsibility and accountability are built into the structure of a formal organization. By contrast, an informal organization tends to be more ad hoc in its structure. It frequently coexists with or within a formal organization. The goals of an informal organization are generally less prescribed and of a short-term nature. Also, the focus tends to be more on individuals than on positions. A committee might be thought of as a vivid example of an informal organization. For the most part in this chapter, the discussion will center around the organizing function within a formal organization. However, it is important to keep in mind that the informal organization is also an important component in the total spectrum of management.

Steps in Organizing

Brinckloe and Coughlin (1977) list six basic steps in organizing that generally apply to formal organizations:

1. Work must be broken down into specific tasks, so that it can be fitted to the specialized skills of the people in the organization.
2. Activities must be grouped into units of workable size: no unit should be so large that it is unmanageable or so small that it is inefficient.

3. Resources must be provided, and responsibility delegated commensurate with the stated objectives of each unit. It is a sign of managerial inexperience to expect results from a person or group when the necessary tools for such results have not been supplied.

4. Duties of every unit and every employee category must be defined; employees may not live up to management expectations otherwise.

5. Personnel must be assigned to the units to flesh out the organization, which until then is simply a paper structure.

6. Tasks and relationships must be specified in detail. This can be the most difficult of all because in any organization there are overlapping areas where two or more groups seek jurisdiction. (If Personnel is to handle all disciplinary actions, this delegation must be made very specific because line supervisors may feel discipline is traditionally their responsibility and tend to exercise it in the absence of clear and unmistakable instruction to the contrary.) (p. 70.)

With respect to these steps, two concepts emerge as being particularly significant whenever one is organizing. The first is the work unit size, and the second is the span of control. For either there is no magic formula for arriving at the desired organizational structure. Brinckloe and Coughlin set forth the general parameters about size in their second step. However, within the context of any given organization, management will have to make decisions about the size of the units in terms of their being manageable and efficient. Span of control is the key concept in the sixth step. What is the scope of the jurisdiction for decision making? Here a couple of guidelines may be useful in arriving at the structure. The span of control should probably be shorter when the work tends to be relatively complex. Also, when the tasks are closely related, a need for a greater span of control is indicated.

If we depart for a moment from the general factors in organizing, I think we can see that the six steps are applicable to the organization of school and college sport programs. However, the athletic director begins with a certain built-in advantage in making some of the decisions related to the steps in organizing. The sport team quickly emerges as an identifiable unit, and the coach is the apparent choice for a line position as the leader of that unit. The organizational lines become a bit more fuzzy when we move to the instructional and intramural components of the total sport program. For that reason, earlier in the text, I suggested that the appointment of sport coordinators would facilitate the organizing function. Particularly at the college level, the task of organizing will become more complex when decisions have to be made relative to the staff positions for the work in financial management, fund raising, public relations, promotion, sport information, scheduling, and facilities management. At that point, the athletic director will have to pay particular attention to the sixth step, as outlined by Brinckloe and Coughlin. The coach's span of control is quite obvious. However, it is easy to see that the line supervisors within an athletic department might extend their boundaries if the tasks and relationships are not specified in detail.

Line Versus Staff Personnel

Reference has been made to line positions and staff positions. That distinction should also be clarified before moving on to other general factors in organizing. Line personnel are so named because they are within the line of authority. Thus, of course, they are also within the line of responsibility. Essentially, they are responsible for achieving the objectives of their respective units and contributing to the achievement of the overall objectives of the organization. Staff personnel basically function in a service capacity. They advise, direct, and control, but their work is in support of the line operation. Therefore, it might be said that they provide a service to the line personnel.

Staff personnel further tend to consist of two basic types: general staff and specialized staff. Quite frequently, a general staff position is filled by someone who has qualifications that are similar to those of the administrator of the unit. Thus, within the collegiate sport structure it is not unusual to find an associate athletic director or an assistant athletic director who has basically the same qualifications as the athletic director. Any difference in the basic qualifications is most likely to be in the years of experience in managing an athletic program. As might be expected, specialized staff usually have a specialized background that qualifies them for a particular role in the staff side of management. Within collegiate sport departments, the athletic business manager and the sports information director are vivid examples of specialized staff. Although the professional preparation may not be as specialized, the ticket manager and the director of sport promotion would be other examples of specialized staff positions. In general, all of the specialized staff personnel have an expertise that focuses on a restricted portion of the organization's activities.

From the overall management perspective, an effort to avoid potential conflicts between line and staff personnel is often a key consideration. With the increased technology and subsequent specialization of today, the need to solidify line-staff relationships is particularly acute. In organization, it is important to convey the basic distinctions between the functions of the line personnel and the staff personnel. The key is to indicate that staff personnel advise, suggest, and recommend to the line personnel in the latter's decision making. Stated somewhat differently, staff personnel are in support of the managerial line. At the same time, considerable conflict can be avoided if the staff personnel realize that they have the freedom to work in their area of expertise without domination by the line personnel. Also, when they make a recommendation, there must be provision for it to be made from a legitimate base without their being cast in the role of "yes people."

Within some organizations it is possible to establish a structure that does not provide for line-staff distinctions. This is particularly true in the more informal and less complex organizations. However, it would appear that the work in collegiate sport departments lends itself to line-staff organization. This is most evident in the large university setting. By contrast, the relatively small high school sport program would probably be organized on a purely line basis.

Organization Charts

Simply stated, an organizational chart is a pictorial description of how an organization is structured. Obviously, the only real significance of the chart is to be found in what it represents. On the other hand, it may be most useful, especially in complex, formal organizations. Internally, a chart helps to point out the lines of authority, responsibility, and accountability, as well as the general flow of communication within the organization. Externally, a chart can be useful in explaining how the mission of the organization is pursued.

A few principal variables tend to characterize the makeup of organizational charts. One of these is the degree of flexibility that is indicated by the structure. Edginton and Williams (1978) set forth a continuum of organization structures, extending from the "organic organization" to the "mechanistic organization" (p. 124). The former tend to be the more informal organizations although organic features can also be found within formal organizations. Thus, we find that the continuum of flexibility is an applicable frame of reference. The degree of flexibility will be determined by the amount of specialization, standardization, centralization, and traditionalism within the organization.

Generally speaking, an organic structure is more individually oriented than task-oriented. The focus tends to be more on the overall goal of the organization. According to Edginton and Williams, "Control, authority, and communication move through a wide network rather than a single hierarchial structure " (p. 125). In terms of organizational charts, a couple of implications are immediately evident with respect to organic structures. The first is that there is less likely to be a need for a chart as such. That is, a chart and flexibility do not necessarily go hand in hand. Secondly, if there is an organizational chart for an organic unit, it is much more likely to be of a horizontal or "flat" nature. The chart would reflect diffusion of authority in lieu of hierarchical command structure. It would seem that many high school sport programs and some college sport programs might reflect the seemingly organic structure.

The mechanistic structure might be called the "classic" structure for an organizational framework. Systematicness is a key concept in the mechanistic structure. The adaptability of a mechanistic framework is dependent on the work of the organization's being relatively fixed and routine. Thus, the work is task-oriented, and there is generally a high degree of standardization in carrying out the work. Most formal, well-established organizations are likely to fall somewhere on the mechanistic side of the continuum. A military organization is a vivid example of a mechanistic framework. Moreover, the mechanistic structure can also be found within the context of certain school and college sport programs, particularly in the large university setting. Therefore, some organizational charts will be included later in this chapter.

Position Descriptions

Perhaps it is more common to hear reference to a job description than to a position description. However, for purposes here, the words *position* and *job* are being used interchangeably. From a technical standpoint, I suggest that a job usually connotes a more mechanical or manuallike task assignment, tied in with labor. A position might imply a professional role. However, either a job or a position draws its organizational significance from the manner in which it fits into the total structure. Therefore, it does not seem important to hold to a firm distinction in this context.

The heart of a position description is to be found in an identification of the duties to be performed by the person who holds that position. However, a complete position description contains much more. Famularo (1979) identifies four general areas that are typically included in a position description: "function, responsibility and authority, relationships and accountability" (p. 144). The function component of a position description provides an overview of the job. Basically, it is the raison d'étre for the position. If the general purpose of the position cannot be described, there is reason to believe that the legitimacy of the position might be questioned. A concrete example from the realm of school and college sport might help to illustrate what is intended in the function segment of a position description. The example is the position of coach. In this case, the function is easily determined. It is only necessary to determine this: coach of what? Should the appointment be as head basketball coach, we already have arrived at the function dimension in the description. Even though it is easy to relate coaching to function, we will find that the function aspect of other positions in school and college sport is not always as easily determined.

It is obvious that responsibility and authority should go hand in hand if the position description is to be a workable organizational tool. Without authority there can be no meaningful responsiblity, and without responsibility authority loses its focus. The key to setting forth both in a position description is to be as specific as possible. The description should list the major specific responsibilities that are assigned to the position. It should also identify the line of authority in carrying out those responsibilities.

The relationships section is actually an extension of the authority component. In addition to spelling out the relationships within the line of authority, the description should also delineate other relationships between the incumbent and those who work closely with him or her in the organization. For example, in a college sport program it would seem desirable to set forth the relationship between the director of sport promotion and the sports information director.

It might also be said that the accountability section is an extension of the responsibility component. In so far as possible, there should also be reference to the specific standards that will be utilized in assessing performance. For example, it might be spelled out that an athletic business manager is accountable for presenting an accurate and meaningful description of budgetary receipts and expenditures. The accountability factor is further reinforcement that the position description generally is a written agreement between the employer and the employee.

This also suggests that position or job descriptions serve several purposes. Fundamentally, of course, they help to fill out the structure of the organization. Beyond that, they all contribute to the execution of other managerial functions. Up front, they are a principal tool in recruitment and advertising positions. On the other end of the managerial spectrum, they can be used as a basis for evaluating employee performance. In between, position descriptions can also serve as guides for personal development and motivational instruments. They also have potential public relations use in describing the function of the organization. Hendersen (1976) goes beyond these purposes in placing the job description in total management perspective. He states that job descriptions can be used in "(1) personel administration, (2) compensation administration, (3) legal compliance, and (4) collective bargaining" (p. 2). The potential significance of job descriptions is heightened when they are considered in the light of the major functions within personnel administration: "manpower planning, recruiting and screening, hiring and placement, orientation, training and development, and career ladders" (Henderson, pp. 3–4). In summary, it might be said that position descriptions are a blueprint for action.

Pitfalls in Organizing

In the first part of this chapter, an attempt was made to set the stage for the organizational considerations in school and college sport by identifying some key areas of concern in any organizational effort. Before proceeding, we might well also note some pitfalls that should be avoided if the process of organizing is to be an effective managerial function.

1. It would appear that organization often breeds further organization. Why is that a potential pitfall? I suggest that there are at least two inherent problems with the proliferation of organizational efforts. The first is that this can easily lead to a situation in which there is more attention to the organization than there is to the action that is to flow from the organization. In an extreme case, this becomes organization for organization's sake. The second problem is that too much organization also tends to create excessive specialization. When that results, the following cliché often applies: "We can't see the forest for the trees." Consequently, even though organizing is one of the principal managerial functions, ev-

ery manager must be conscious of the need to monitor the balance on organizational efforts in relationship to the total managerial process.

2. At the other extreme, we also find a potential pitfall. This revolves around the problems associated with a static organization. Just as there can be too much focus on the organizational structure, there can also be a tendency to become complacent about the structure once it is established. From time to time, internal or external changes or both call for a new look at the structure. The key here is to know when to make the organizational changes and how to adapt to the internal and external factors that signal the need for reorganization. As with planning, organizing is also an ongoing process.

3. Within any given organizational structure there is also a need for some degree of flexibility. Earlier in this chapter we noted that there is a continuum of flexibility among organizations, extending from the organic organization to the mechanistic organization. However, even the mechanistic structure must offer some provision for flexibility. Personnel cannot perform effectively if they have some feeling that they are completely bound by the structure. That is another pitfall to be avoided.

4. Finally, there must be an effort to avoid any major descrepancy between the ''paper'' organization and the ''real'' organization. In other words, the organizational prospective must be meaningful in its potential for implementation, and the actual organization should be reflective of the design. Otherwise, the expression ''it looks good on paper'' is a true, but unfortunate, description of the situation.

VARIABLES IN ORGANIZING SCHOOL AND COLLEGE SPORT PROGRAMS

When embarking on any organizational effort, one should begin by considering the various possibilities for the structure. Within some organizations, the possibilities are somewhat limited owing to the very nature of the organization's environment and mission. Such a limitation does not generally apply to school and college sport programs. The variance among educational institutions and within the realm of sport point to several up-front considerations before any decisions can be made regarding the specifics of the unit structure.

School, College, or University

The most apparent variable is that found when we compare school programs to college programs. Beyond that, variability between college and university programs also has to be taken into account. In introducing this text, we mentioned that the word *college* would be used to include both college and university sport programs. However, with respect to organization, differences have to be considered. As a matter of fact, in some cases the organization of a small college sport program will more closely parallel that of a school than of a university sport program.

In the schools and some small colleges, a fairly typical pattern is to organize sport under the rubric of physical education. The inherent limitations in such an organizational arrangement were referred to in Chapter 2 under the topic of instructional scheduling. Nevertheless, in spite of any opinion that might be held about this being a limitation, physical education does exist as an umbrellalike organization. Where a sport program is organized in the context of physical education, any change would be manifested in the form of reorganization. For instance, the structure advocated in this text would in most instances call for a reorganization to remove sport from the physical education umbrella.

Even when sport is within the physical education domain, we find great variety in the structuring of the organizational framework. In some cases, the physical education director is also the athletic director; in other situations, we find separate directors of physical education and athletics. The circumstances surrounding the intramural sport component are even more complex. In many of the smaller schools, it may be difficult even to identify the intramural director within the organizational matrix. Sometimes intramurals are a responsibility of the athletic director. Likewise, we can find that the physical education director takes direct responsibility for intramurals or that the intramural director is on a management level with the athletic director and the physical education director.

Both the intramural component and the intercollegiate component point to one of the major differences we often find between the sport organization in large universities and schools and small colleges. There is a general tendency to separate both the intercollegiate program and the intramural program within the large university environment. In the case of the intercollegiate program, this organizationally manifests itself in the appointment of an athletic director who reports directly to the president, chancellor, or some similar higher administrative officer. With intramural sport, it may mean that it is a semi-automonous unit under the Dean of Student Services or similar office.

Based on things said earlier in this book, it is obvious that an integrated sport program is being advocated that involves the intercollegiate, intramural, and instructional components. That would have a major influence on the proposed structure. Yet most of us are seldom in a position where we can organize a program from scratch. We usually have to begin with the organization as it currently exists. In other words, organization is more likely to take the form of reorganization. It's also likely that in most cases we will be only partially successful in achieving our ideals. For these reasons, it is important that we begin by recognizing the current variables involving the differences in structure among school, college, and university programs.

Nature of the Institution

Obviously, there is some overlap between this variable and the one that was just discussed. Part of the nature of a given educational institution stems from its primary identity as being either a school, a college, or a university. The size factor is also significant in determining the nature of an institution. This, too, is generally related to the institution's status as a school, college, or university, with the school typically being the smallest of the three organizations and the university being the largest. However, beyond those two factors, other variables in the nature of an institution should also be considered when organizing a sport program.

One of these variables involves the differences between private and public institutions. All other factors being equal, the private institution typically offers greater opportunity for organizational flexibility because it is not as bound by state legislation and other restrictions related to the public service. On the other hand, the degree of flexibility can be offset by the traditional pattern within the private institution. This is likely to be particularly evident in select prep schools and private colleges with long-standing traditions.

At the university level, we find a variety of organizational arrangements involving colleges, schools, divisions, departments, and programs within the university. For example, one university may establish colleges and departments as the principal administrative units. In another, school status may more or less replace college status, or there may be a combination thereof. Still others may be organized into divisions. Various possibilities exist. The important point here is that the sport unit must be structured within the context of the particular mode of organization within the institution. For example, if a college of sport management seems like a viable organizational proposal, that should be considered as a possibility. In other situations, it might be much more realistic to seek school, division, department, or program status.

Overall, the variable related to the nature of the institution involves an assessment of the lay of the land or the general modus operandi before proceeding with a specific organizational format. If this is not done, there is a much greater probability that the organization will remain at the "paper" stage of development.

Men and Women

All units within an educatinal institution tend to have their share of organizational uncertainty. It might be said that there is no such thing as a "perfect" organizational structure. Nevertheless, sport programs face one organizational challenge that is not typically found in other educational programs—how to put the men and women together or keep them separate. The basic reason for this unique challenge probably goes back to the very nature of sport. The physical dimension of sport points to the physical differences involving the participation of men and women in sport. This probably explains, at least in part, why the historical pattern

was to have separate departments of physical education for men and physical education for women. However, things are changing and have been changing for some
time. As women explored their sport horizons through new opportunities and more
in-depth participation, the consideration of the most appropriate organizational
structure become even more significant. Today by and large we find relatively few
remaining separate departments of physical education for men and physical education for women. However, the increased participation of girls in interscholastic
sport and women in intercollegiate sport has brought about a shift in the
organizational challenge to determine the most appropriate structure for these programs. The range of variability extends from complete merger to various kinds of
partial merger to completely separate units.

Nelson (1980) surveyed the impact on women's athletic programs when athletic departments merge. Her findings show that the tendency is to place the wom-
en's program under the existing male athletic structure, including the retention of
the male athletic director, when the merger is made. She concluded:

> The merger itself has no positive effect on the women's program. The enactment of Title
> IX has vastly improved women's programs, regardless of the administrative structure.
> But the merger has profoundly reduced the status and power of female administrators
> and has made them more vulnerable regarding employment security.
> If women's athletics are to protect the gains made in recent years—and allow for future
> growth—it will be imperative for women to control women's athletics, independent of a
> male Athletic Director acting as superior. As discussed earlier, a male Athletic Director
> will be primarily concerned with the welfare of men's—not women's—athletics. He
> will probably pressure his female Associate Director to send her teams to championships
> sponsored by men's national organizations (p. 29).

The preceding conclusion represents opinion based on a limited sample of 40
institutions in a national survey. However, it does point to the significance of the
men and women variable as one of the major organizational considerations in school
and college sport programs. Obviously, further study is needed to determine how
many programs have been merged and how the merger is evaluated by both women
and men. In the meantime, this variable continues as a focal consideration in
organizing a sport program in the educational institution.

Objectives of the Program

In the preceding chapter, it was mentioned that the program objectives were the key
to effective planning. The objectives also represent another major variable in
organizing the program. At least that is true if the organization is to be meaningful.
Meaningful organizational structure will reflect both the objectives and the subsequent action.

How do the objectives influence organizational structure? A couple of examples may help to answer that question and show why this variable also has to be

considered in the earlier phase of organizing. The objectives may be such that they call for a strong balance among the intercollegiate, intramural, and instructional components. In other words, the emphasis might be placed on the skill, fun, social, and educational objectives that we discussed earlier in the text. From the organizational standpoint this would suggest that the sport coordinators and coaches might be on an equal level in the line relationships.

On the other hand, the objectives could also be in the institutional direction of using the sport program to enhance the image of the college and to gain more support for the college. This clearly points to a priority regarding the intercollegiate component and to a further priority among sports. This would suggest that the football and basketball programs (and hockey in some institutions) might have a separate organizational position that reflects such a priority. In other words, they would be organizationally distinct from the other components of the total program.

Unfortunately, it seems all too common to find an organizational structure that is really a sham in terms of what takes place within the operation. It might appear that the wrestling coach is on a par with the head football coach. There is nothing wrong with either way as long as the organizational chart does not represent a hypocritical situation. It might even be said that a careful consideration of objectives in organizing the program is a mark of institutional integrity.

Personnel

Of the variables to be considered in organizing, one other is an important variable in any organization, not just school and college sport programs. Depending on the circumstances, this could well be the most significant of the variables. When all is said and done, the personnel appear as a major consideration in deciding the specific form of organization. In most cases, it is much more effective to fit the structure to the personnel than it is to attempt an adaptation of the personnel to the structure. Sometimes the latter can be accomplished but often only in part. This is one of the major reasons why organizing is an ongoing function. It is never a simple matter of establishing the structure and leaving it in the original form. It also prompts attention to the fact that a textbook discussion of the organizing function will only carry us so far. There is value in considering various guidelines and models, but beyond that the accommodation to personnel has to be made.

Some examples in the contemporary collegiate sport realm might serve to illustrate the relative significance of the personnel variable in the organizational structure. Paul "Bear" Bryant occupied a unique role in the Athletic Department at Alabama. It was not the usual structural position for a head football coach owing to the relative success and special qualifications of Bryant. The tradition was so well established that Ray Perkins was also given the additional role of athletic director shortly after his appointment as head football coach at Alabama. In a different context, it would be difficult to identify the role of De Paul's Ray Meyer in your standard collegiate athletic department's organizational chart. After 40 years at De

Paul and with much success, Meyer occupies a position that extends beyond that of a head basketball coach in the usual collegiate context. There is no doubt about it; the personnel variable permeates the organizing function almost as much as the staffing function.

SCHOOL AND COLLEGE SPORT STRUCTURES

Any meaningful organization chart will have to be developed within the context of particular needs and circumstances of the institution. The situationally defined nature of organization charts is evident after one notes the difference among three actual charts for college sport programs (Tables 3.1–3.3) and three typical charts for high school sport programs (Tables 3.4–3.6). Owing to the situational differences, it seems more appropriate here to focus on models for an integrated sport program with the understanding that such models would have to be adapted to the local variables. Before the proposed models are presented, it also seems desirable to define some of the titles that will be used in the organization charts and position descriptions.

Director of the Sport Program. The person who is ultimately responsible for the total sport program with its intercollegiate (or interscholastic), intramural, and instructional components.

Director of Sport Instruction. The person who is delegated the responsibility for the instructional as well as the intramural components of the program. This position would be found only in the larger programs. The various sport coordinators report to the individual who holds this position.

Athletic Director. The person who is directly responsible for the intercollegiate or interscholastic sport program. In the smaller program, the director of the sport program will also be the athletic director.

Sport Coordinator (basketball coordinator, field hockey coordinator, etc.). The person who is directly responsible for the intramural and instructional components for a given sport. In the smaller programs, this person will also be the head coach of that sport.

Structures for School Sport Programs

As might be expected, the organization of a school sport program will tend to be much more simplistic than the college organization. This is due to the relative size of the institution and the generally more restricted focus in program objectives. The major difference revolves around the addition or omission of what can be called "staff" positions. Such positions would include trainers, the business manager, the sports information director, the director for sport promotion, the ticket manager, and the manager of facilities. It is rather unlikely that most high schools will have sufficient resources to fund any or even a few of these positions. Trainers, of course, are the best and most needed possibility. However, even in that case, the position of

Table 3.1 Staff Activities and Sport Activities

STAFF ACTIVITIES

SPORT ACTIVITIES

Chancellor

Athletic board

Director of athletics

Secretary

Asst. A. D. Williams fund

Sec.

Asst. A. D. spec. projects

Sports A. D. business

Sports info. director

Men & womens basketball

Asst. coaches secretaries part time coaches

Asst.

Asst.

Men

Part time

Sec.

Women

Asst.

Sec.

Head football coach

Sec. | Sec.

Asst.

Asst.

Asst.

Asst.

Asst.

Asst.

Asst.

Asst.

Part time

Sports network director

Video-tape

Asst. A. D. non-revenue sports

Men & womens track

Men & womens swimming

Men & womens tennis

Men & womens gymnastics

84

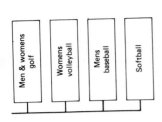

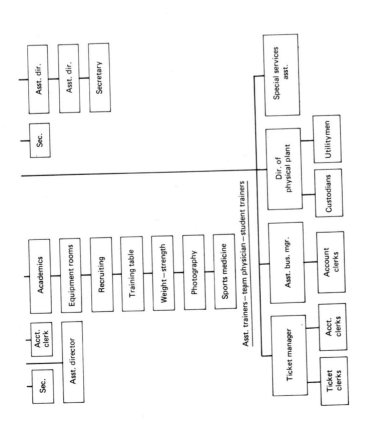

Table 3.2 Organization Chart for University of Louisville's Department of Intercollegiate Athletics

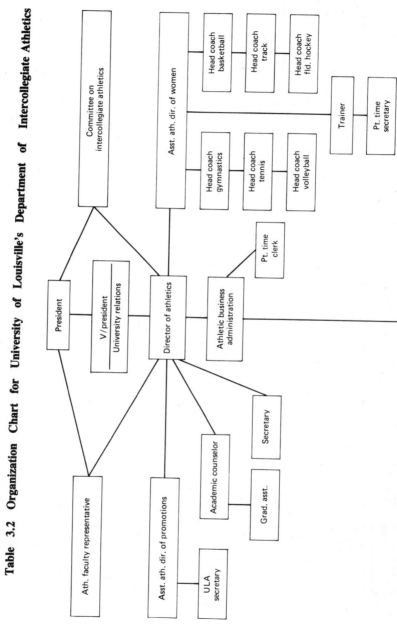

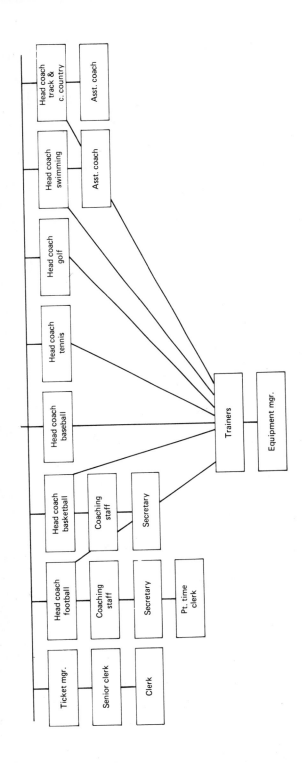

Table 3.3 Organization Chart of University of Delaware

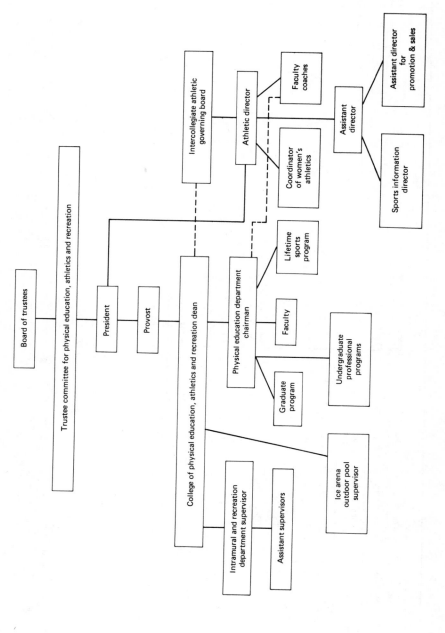

Table 3.4 Stage I. Small High School Athletic Program Formal Organizational Structure

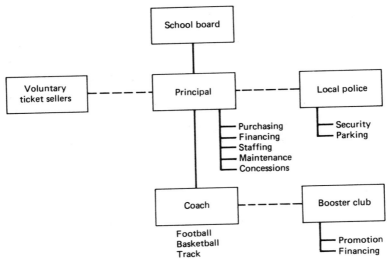

trainer is much more likely to be a part-time one that is filled by a coach or another teacher in the school system. For that reason, the position of trainer or of any of the other staff positions is not included in the proposed organization charts. Nevertheless, it is important to remember that this does not negate the importance of the position of trainer. If the school has sufficient resources, the position of a full-time trainer should be the first staff position to be included.

When we consider the possible structure for a school sport program, there is really only one central question: how should the interscholastic, intramural, and instructional components be related? A simple approach would be to suggest that we already have the essence of the structure by merely noting that there should be a director for each of the three components with all three reporting to the director of the total sport program. However, earlier in the text it was suggested that, for a variety of reasons, it seems desirable to integrate the intramural and instructional components through the medium of sport coordinator. For that reason, the organizational structure would take on a different form.

In terms of the basic structure for school sport, that leaves us only with a decision relative to the relationships among the coaches and the sport coordinators. Within the larger schools, there may also be a consideration as to whether there should be a separate position of athletic director who reports to the director of the complete sport program. However, with or without a separate position for the athletic director, the key question is whether a coach should report to a sport coordinator. Thus, three basic types of organizational structures are suggested as possibilities:

Table 3.5   Stage II. Medium Size High School Athletic Program Formal Organizational Structure

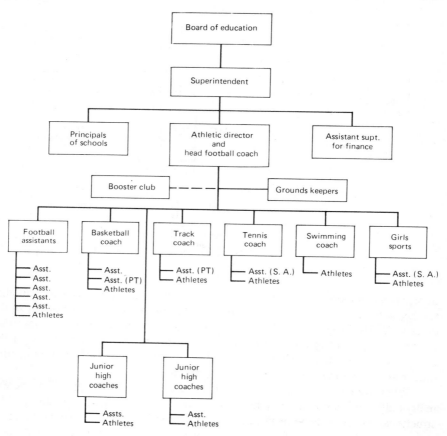

The role of instructor (mentioned in chart under Structure A, page 92) includes responsibility for intramural supervision in sports that are taught by that instructor. Some of the instructors may also be coaches, and some of the coaches may also be instructors. This would be particularly true in the smaller schools. In the very small schools there would be a further collapsing effect in terms of the organizational matrix. Thus, one individual might serve as the sport coordinator, coach, and instructor for a given sport.

Of course a fourth basic possibility would be to have an athletic director who reports directly to the school principal. This is not outlined as a prime choice be-

Table 3.6   Stage III. Large Size High School Athletic Program Formal Organizational Structure

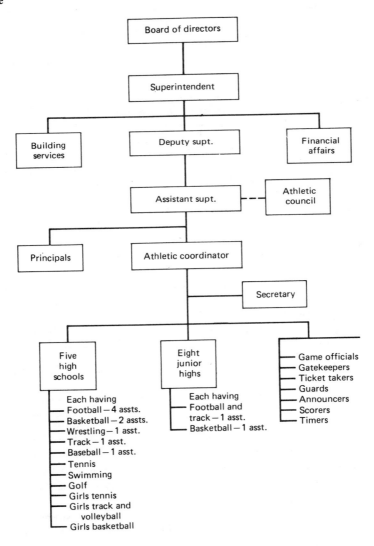

91

Structure A

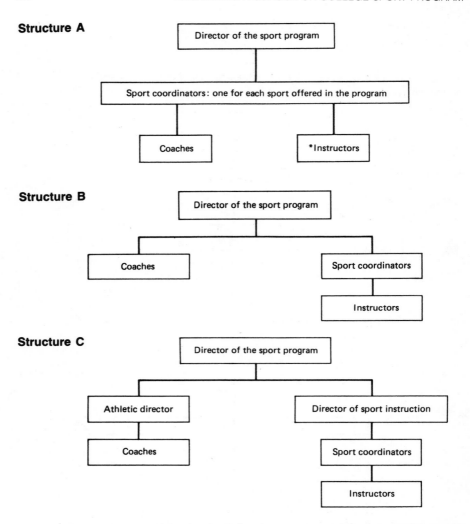

cause it is contrary to the idea of an integrated sport program that is being advocated in this book. In essence, when such a choice is made, it connotes a program that first and foremost is designed for institutional purposes at the expense of student and parent interest and needs. This seems to be a fairly indefensible position, particularly at the high school level.

As we examine the three types of proposed structures, strengths and weaknesses of each can be noted. Structure A could be called a "clean" structure to the extent that it represents unified vertical development within a given sport. Everything about the sport is centralized in the hands of the sport coordinator for that sport. Thus, the golf coordinator is in complete charge of the golf program, extending from golf instruction to intramural golf matches to the interscholastic golf team. A possible weakness of the arrangement is that it might only serve to accentuate what already exists in terms of esoteric emphasis within a given sport. Perhaps a more obvious limitation might be that the coach is one step removed from the director of the total sport program. Depending on the program objectives, this could be a problem.

This possible limitation of Structure A also points to the strength of Structure B. Here we have both the coaches and the sport coordinators reporting directly to the program director. This provides for more administrative control at the top level. However, any advantage in this regard may be offset by the splintering effect within the total sport program wherein a coach and a sport coordinator are vying for resources in the same sport.

Structure C adds another dimension with a similar advantage and disadvantage as that noted for B. The only real difference is that we have added another layer of administrative control. Therefore, Structure C is more likely to be suitable for a larger school system. From the standpoint of program objectives, the more basic choice is likely to be between A and B or C.

Perhaps only one other thing needs to be noted in terms of a structure for a school sport program. Earlier it was suggested that a trainer is the best and most needed possibility for a full-time staff position at the school level. When a school is fortunate enough to have the resources for such a position, it would seem to make the most sense to have the trainer report to the director of the total sport program. This is based on the assumption that the trainer should be available to be involved in the prevention and care of athletic injuries wherever needed in the program. The staff (not line) relationship between the director and trainer would connote the total responsibility of the trainer.

Structures for College Sport Programs

When we move from the school to the college structure, it is primarily a matter of proceeding from the simple to the complex. The one exception might be a very small college program that more or less resembles the school structure. However, as noted earlier, the provision for various staff positions tends to be one of the more characteristic features of a college sport structure. The other major feature revolves around the line of administrative accountability for the athletic director. In terms of actual practice, we find a whole host of arrangements wherein the athletic director may report to a college president, chancellor, provost, vice-president for student affairs, or a dean of physical education. Here again none of these possibilities are being suggested in keeping with the theme of the text, namely, the management of an integrated sport program. It is, of course, assumed that, in the smaller colleges, the director of the sport program and the intercollegiate athletic director will be one and the same person. That still leaves the decision as to whether that person should report to the president, the chancellor, the vice-president for student affairs, or the dean of some college. Thus, this book proposes that the athletic director should report either to the director of the total sport program or (in the case of a combined position) to a higher administrative officer in the college or university. In terms of organization charts, there is no advantage in attempting to set forth the higher administrative positions for such reporting. Whether the sport program ultimately comes directly under the president, chancellor, vice-president for student affairs, a dean, or some other higher administrative official will depend on the structure of the particular college or university. In line with the school structures, three basic types of organizational structures are also proposed for the college sport program:

Structure A

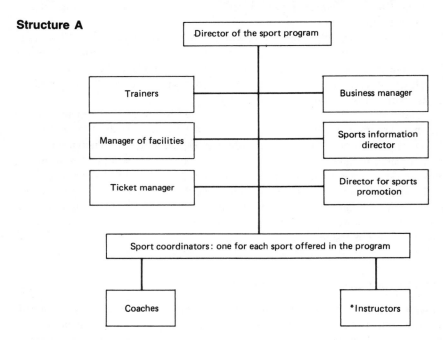

As with the school situation, the role of each instructor also includes the responsibility for intramural supervision.

Structures A and B are fairly straightforward. Basically, they indicate a differentiation between line and staff positions with the sport coordinators, coaches, and instructors holding the line positions and the remainder being staff positions. The only thing to be added is that the number of staff positions will vary from one upward, depending on the size of the institution. This is based on the assumption that there should at least be one full-time trainer at the collegiate level. Within the very small college, the director of the sport program may have to assume one or more of the other staff responsibilities: On the other hand, within the very large university, there may also be more than the six types of staff positions that have been included

Structure B

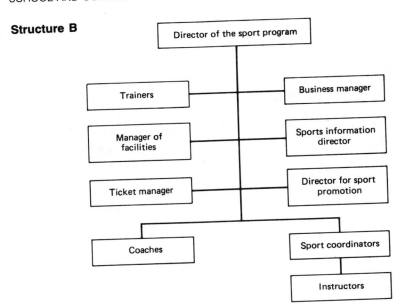

Structure C

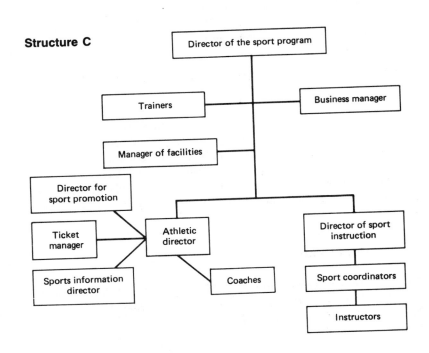

in the proposed structures. Only those that are fairly commonly identified are included.

Structure C poses certain complications because some basic decisions have to be made relative to the staff relationships with the director of the sport program and the athletic director. The proposed structure suggests that the business manager, trainer, and manager of facilities should have direct staff relationships with the total sport program. This is based on the recognition that these positions relate to all aspects of the program. At the same time, it seems to make sense to have the director for sport promotion, the ticket manager, and the sports information director report directly to the athletic director. These positions are involved with the intercollegiate athletic component. Nevertheless, possibilities for other arrangements also exist.

Aside from the three basic structures that have been outlined, certain modifications could be made. For instance, the director for sport promotion could be designated as a principal staff position, with the ticket manager and sports information director reporting as staff associates to the person who holds that position. This kind of arrangement would be based on the assumption that there is a certain common denominator among promotion, tickets, and sports information and that promotion is the ultimate focus.

Before we leave the topic of organizational structures one point should again be stressed that is particularly true of the type C structure. Within the relatively smaller institutions there is bound to be some collapsing effect within the organizational matrix. In other words, there will be fewer positions, based on need and more limited resources. Thus, as an example, a given institution might have one person who is responsible for promotions, tickets, and sports information.

POSITION DESCRIPTIONS FOR SCHOOL AND COLLEGE SPORT PROGRAMS

Earlier in this chapter we noted that position descriptions typically include four elements: function, responsibility and authority, relationships, and accountability. In light of these elements it is impossible to set forth position descriptions that are generally applicable to any school or college sport program. They will have to be developed out of the dynamics of the given institution. However, the following are suggested as examples and reasonable possibilities for the structures, which might include these positions.

Director of the Sport Program

1. *Function.* To manage the entire sport program for the college, including the intercollegiate, intramural, and instructional components.
2. *Responsibility and authority.* Major areas of responsibility and authority include the following.

- Budget preparation and presentation.
- Personnel selection, evaluation, and development.
- Facilities planning, development, and maintenance.
- Establishing sound institutional relationships.
- Providing effective public relations with other college sport programs and the public at large.
- Providing the necessary leadership to meet the objectives of the program.

3. *Relationships.*

- Works with the other principal administrative officers within the college to meet the general goals of the college and to establishe the role of the sport program within the total educational setting.
- Delegates authority and responsibility to line and staff personnel, as appropriate.

4. *Accountability.* Reports to the vice-president for academic affairs.

Basketball Coordinator

1. *Function.* To manage the entire basketball program for the college, including the intercollegiate, intramural, and instructional components.[1]
2. *Responsibility and authority.* Major areas of responsibility and authority include the following.

- Preparation and presentation of a proposed basketball budget.
- Maintaining control of the basketball budget.
- Making recommendations for selection of basketball coaches and instructors.
- Submitting requests for purchase of basketball equipment and supplies.
- Evaluation of basketball coaches and instructors.
- Submitting an intercollegiate, intramural, and instructional schedule for basketball.
- Coordinating use of facilities for the entire basketball program.

3. *Relationships.*

- Works with the other sport coordinators to meet the objectives of the total sport program.

[1]This position would be based on Structure A, wherein both the coaches and the instructors report to a sport coordinator and the director of the sport program is also the athletic director. A similar position would exist for all other sports in the program. In the smaller institutions, the basketball coordinator would also be the head basketball coach (collapsing effect in the organizational matrix).

• Delegates authority and responsibility to coaches and instructors.

4. *Accountability.* Reports to the director of the sport program.

Head Basketball Coach

1. *Function.* To coach the intercollegiate basketball team.

2. *Responsibility and authority.* Major areas of responsibilty and authority include the following.

• Recruitment, selection, and preparation of team.
• Supervision of team managers.
• Preparation and presentation of an intercollegiate basketball budget.
• Supervision of players' academic progress.
• Public relations for the basketball program.
• Representing the basketball program at conference, regional, and national meetings.

3. *Relationships.*

• Works with the other coaches to meet the objectives of the total intercollegiate program.
• Delegates authority and responsibility to assistant coaches, managers, and captains.

4. *Accountability.* Reports to the basketball coordinator.

Head Basketball Instructor

1. *Function.* To manage the instructional intramural components of the basketball program.[2]

2. *Responsibility and authority.* Major areas of responsibility and authority include the following.

• Preparation of an instructional schedule.
• Preparation of an intramural schedule.
• Selection and supervision of intramural officials.

---

[2]Once again this type of position is postulated for a very large university having the need and sufficient resources for an individual to be solely in this position. More commonly and more realistically, one can expect to find various forms of combined positions. For example, the basketball coordinator might be the head basketball instructor. There might also be various combinations of sports. Thus, an institution might have a racquet sports coordinator or a head instructor for racquet sports. With such an example, it is assumed that such an individual would also be the coach for racquet sports. Naturally, all position descriptions would be modified accordingly. However, these examples are designed to explain the intent in setting forth the scope of the various line positions.

- Record keeping for intramural basketball.
- Evaluation of instructors and intramural supervisors.
- Preparation of a budget for instructional and intramural basketball.
- Teaching basketball classes.

3. *Relationships*.

- Works with the other head instructors to meet the objectives of the total instructional and intramural program.
- Delegates authority and responsibility to the instructors and intramural supervisors.

4. *Accountability*. Reports to the basketball coordinator.

Athletic Director

1. *Function*. To manage the entire intercollegiate athletic program.[3]
2. *Responsibility and authority*. Major areas of responsibility and authority include the following.

- Recruitment, selection, and evaluation of coaches.
- Preparation, presentation, and control of the intercollegiate budget.
- Preparing intercollegiate schedules.
- Public relations for the intercollegiate program.
- Representing the athletic program at conferences, regional, and national meetings.
- Maintaining the standards of student athletic eligibility (local, conference, state, and National Collegiate Athletic Association).

3. *Relationships*.

- Works with all the staff officers associated with the intercollegiate program.
- Delegates authority and responsibility to coaches.

4. *Accountability*. Reports to the director of the sport program.

Business Manager

1. *Function*. To coordinate and account for all the budgeting aspects of the program.
2. *Responsibility and authority*. Major areas of responsibility and authority include the following.

---

[3]This position is based on a Structure C organization.

- Reporting financial status to the director of the sport program.
- Putting together the annual budget submitted by other line and staff officers within the program.
- Auditing accounts.
- Negotiating and authorizing contracts.
- Making arrangements to pay officials.
- Supervise spending for travel.
- Generate financial reports.
- Handle all vouchers.
- Oversee endowment and trust funds.
- Making payment arrangements for all part time employees.

3. *Relationships*.

- Works with all the line and staff officers in the program.

4. *Accountability*. In a staff position, reports to the director of the sport program.

Director for Sport Promotion

1. *Function*. To stimulate financial and other means of support for the total sport program.

2. *Responsibility and authority*. Major areas of responsibility and authority include the following.

- Directing fund-raising drives.
- Maintaining contact with alumni.
- Developing strategies for fund raising.
- Meeting with prospective contributors for donations.
- Serving as public relations liaison with the community.
- Preparing a newsletter for the program.
- Developing other literature for fund raising and general promotion.
- Working with various support groups and booster clubs.
- Recommending policies for promotion.

3. *Relationships*.

- Works with all the line and staff officers in the program.
- Major work with the athletic director.

4. *Accountability*. In a staff position, reports to the director of the sport program.

Sports Information Director

1. *Function*. To provide the communication link between the intercollegiate program and the media as well as other public relation sources.
2. *Responsibility and authority*. Major areas of responsibility and authority include the following.

   - Preparation of press releases.
   - Compilation of statistics.
   - Promotion of outstanding players.
   - Preparation of press guides.
   - Providing arrangements for the media at home contests.
   - Coordinating the coverage for home contests.
   - Preparation of stories for the alumni magazines.
   - Providing films, slides, and photographs.
   - Coordinating the speaker's bureau.

3. *Relationships*.

   - Works primarily with the coaches.
   - Maintains some liaison with all staff and line officers.

4. *Accountability*. In a staff position, reports to the athletic director.

Manager of Facilities

1. *Function*. To manage the development, maintenance, and use of all the sport facilities.
2. *Responsibility and authority*. Major areas of responsibility and authority includes the following.

   - Maintains the liaison with the University Physical Plant Department.
   - Supervises the maintenance and repair of all facilities and equipment.
   - Assists in planning new facilities.
   - Makes arrangements for rental of facilities.
   - Makes arrangements for ushers at home contests.
   - Provides security for home contests.
   - Schedules the use of facilities.
   - Works with outside contractors.
   - Provides towel service, soap, and other supplies.
   - Supervises maintenance, equipment room, and other service personnel.

3. *Relationships*.

   - Works closely with all sport coordinators, coaches, and instructors.

- Delegates responsibility and authority to equipment room manager and head of maintenance for sport facilities.
- Maintains liaison with the University Physical Plant Department.

4. *Accountability.* In a staff position, reports to the director of the sport program.

Ticket Manager

1. *Function.* To manage the entire ticket operation from the point of advertising to the final collection of tickets.

2. *Responsibility and authority.* Major areas of responsibility and authority include the following.

- Supervision of the ticket office.
- Planning ticket sales.
- Supervision of ticket sales and distribution at the home contests.
- Recommending ticket prices.
- Designing tickets and press passes.
- Authorizing complimentary tickets.
- Stimulating season ticket sales.
- Handling ticket funds.
- Providing reports of ticket sales trends.

3. *Relationships.*

- Works closely with the director for sports promotion.
- Also maintains close liaison with the sports information director.
- Supervises work of all ticket personnel.

4. *Accountability.* In a staff position, reports to the athletic director.

Head Trainer

1. *Function.* To manage a program for the care, treatment, rehabilitation, and prevention of sport injuries.

2. *Responsibility and authority.* Major areas of responsibility and authority include the following.

- Supervising the training room.
- Supervising student trainers.
- Providing adequate coverage for all practices, home contests and away contests.
- Working with the team medical doctors.
- Submission of a budget for training supplies.
- Maintaining records on athletic injuries.

- Making arrangements for physical examination of athletes.
- Assisting with a program of off-season conditioning for athletes.
- Providng a schedule for treatment of sport injuries.

3. *Relationships.*

- Particularly close work with the team medical doctors.
- Delegates responsibility and authority to assistant trainers.
- Work with the equipment room manager in proper fitting of athletic gear.

4. *Accountability.* In a staff position, reports to the director of the sport program.[4]

Associate or Assistant Athletic Director. The position of associate or assistant athletic director was not designated in the organization charts outlined earlier in this chapter. There were two reasons for the omission. The first is that such a position would more likely be found under the Structure C organization (related to a large university setting). However, the director of the sport program and the athletic director already represent two higher management positions involved with the athletic program. Therefore, it might not be necessary to have an associate or assistant athletic director or both. The second reason is that any assistant or associate position has been purposely omitted in setting forth the basic structures. Thus, the positions such as assistant coaches and assistant trainers have been excluded as well as the position of assistant athletic director.

Nevertheless, we know that it is common to have an associate or assistant athletic director or both in many college athletic programs. Within that context, various possibilities exist in terms of responsibility and authority. Generally speaking, an assistant athletic director might have prime responsibility for student eligibility, scheduling arrangements, contest management, or team travel. Some colleges might also omit the manager of facilities position and give that responsibility to the assistant athletic director.

Any distinction between an associate or an assistant athletic director may or may not be fairly minor, depending on the particular function of the position within the program. In general, the term *associate* connotes a higher-level position than that of *assistant* within most organizations. Following that line of reasoning, one might conclude that an associate directorship would be a line position whereas an assistant directorship is a staff position. Under the line arrangement, the associate director might carry out many of the responsibilities of the athletic director. By contrast, an assistant director might have more limited scope of operation in a staff capacity.

Reference to an assistant or associate athletic director also prompts further con-

---

[4]In those structures where there is a separate athletic director, the head trainer might report to the athletic director. This could be based on the recognition that most of the work is with the intercollegiate athletics. However, if the trainer reports to the director of the sport program, this assists in establishing the idea that the services are available to all sport participants.

sideration of the organizational structure for men's and women's sports. The three basic structures have been set forth without notations of positions for men or women. The idea behind that was to set forth a completely integrated program in which the positions might be filled by either a woman or a man. In some cases, there would not be much question about the choice of a man or a woman for a particular position. Thus, one would expect to find a woman as the field hockey coordinator and a man as the wrestling coordinator. Other decisions would also be made on a "best qualified" basis, but the choice would be more difficult in many instances. For example, the tennis coordinator might be a man or a woman. This would also apply to the position as director of the sport program.

Of course, another choice would be to take any one of the three basic structures and duplicate it so that the organizational structures for men and women would be completely separated. By and large that is a local decision. However, it is also obvious that many institutions have to date opted for some form of integrated sport program with respect to men's and women's sports. Under such circumstances, the possibility increases that an associate athletic director or an assistant athletic director or both will be added to the organizational structure. Thus, we might find that the athletic director is either a man or a woman, and the situation is reversed for the associate director. Another possibility would be that there is an athletic director (either sex) with an associate athletic director for men and an associate athletic director for women.

In the final analysis, it should be evident that the entire matter surrounding an associate or assistant athletic director's position is a complicated consideration. So much will depend on the needs, resources, and dynamics of the particular institution. However, at least one factor should be made evident. In a time of tight economy, most colleges are likely to look toward a reduction rather than an expansion in the number of administrative positions.

Other Positions. The listing of positions that have been outlined in this chapter is by no means inclusive. Various other possibilities also exist. For example, a sport program might employ an administrative assistant, travel coordinator, game manager, or coordinator of admissions. More frequently, the latter three areas of responsibility will be delegated within the framework of the positions that have been outlined. In each case, the director of the sport program will have to decide which divisions of responsibility are likely to be most effective within that particular organization.

Two of the more problematic areas of organization are game management and travel arrangements. The reason for this is that both of these areas tend to cut across the usual organization lines. For instance, the coach, manager of facilities, ticket manager, sports information director, trainer, and usually others have been outlined. Consistent with the thrust of this book, the focus here w ill be on what might be sought while, at the same time, giving some thought to the general realities of the current situation in school and college sport.

POSITION QUALIFICATIONS

Director of the Sport Program. As noted in the position description for the college level, the function of the director of the sports program is to manage the entire sport program, including the intercollegiate, intramural, and instructional components. The same scope of responsibility would be involved in such a position at the high school level. A look at the "real world" indicates that by and large this position does not exist, as such, today owing to the organizational confusion surrounding physical education, sport and athletics. Therefore, this top administrative position is clearly a case of what we would be "shooting for" rather than a description of the status quo. The nearest thing we find to this at the present time is a situation in which a dean, director, or department head of physical education is responsible for the intercollegiate or interscholastic program or the intramural program or both. However, where that exists, the waters are often muddied by the diversified nature of physical education and the resulting alienation between physical education and athletics.

At the college level, the director of the sport program should have a Ph.D. in sport management or similar degree status. The doctorate is necessary in order to put the position in line with the general standards of academic appointments. Very few institutions offer a Ph.D. in sport management at the present time, but that is not to say that more degrees of this type could not and will not be offered in the future. In the interim it would probably be necessary to consider applicants with doctorates from other fields who have a strong background and interest in sport.

Communication skills have to rank near the top in a citation of the qualifications for any managerial position. The higher the level of management, the greater the need to communicate effectively. This is true of both the written and spoken word because much of the administrator's time is spent in either writing reports and letters or speaking on a formal or informal basis. The ability to speak effectively is a particularly acute need in sport management owing to the extensive public relations element in the field of sport. In fact, beyond speaking per se, the ability to present self has to be given high priority among qualifications for this position.

The scope of this position also requires an individual who is committed to the development of the total sport program. This is easier to say than achieved. Nevertheless, the success of an integrated sport program is clearly allied to an effort to reach toward this ideal. The real key to any success will result from the staffing function. More about that will be said in the next chapter. However, a few points can be noted with respect to the position qualifications as such. The director of the sport program should have some coaching experience. Clearly, the need for the coaching qualification is more evident when the individual also serves as the athletic director, as set forth under Structures A and B. The level and extent of the coaching experience may vary and will depend on the level and general nature of the sport program. Yet it is important to keep in mind that the coaches are integral line personnel in the total sport program. The cliché that "it takes one to know one" is quite applicable to the coaching situation.

On the other side of the coin, the commitment to the total sport program is also not likely to materialize if the director of the sport program has only been a coach in his or her professional career. This is less likely to be a major deficiency because most coaches have also been instructors somewhere along the line. In fact, an effective coach, in addition to possessing other talents, must be a most effective teacher. Nevertheless, that does not necessarily ensure a commitment to the instructional program. Experience indicates that it may be even more difficult to find coaches who have a true commitment to the intramural component. Yet, in terms of position qualifications, it is important to set forth the need for a balanced perspective for the director of the sport program.

One final qualification stands out with respect to this position. This, too, may be difficult to measure, but does not negate the need for seeking it from the organizational vantage point. The director must be able to work effectively with the entire college or school community. This includes extensive interface with academicians, other professional personnel, nonprofessional personnel, students, and administrators. The director is the front line person in many of these contacts, exclusive of students. When it comes to staffing, the record of previous experience will probably be the best indicator of success in meeting the qualifications.

Athletic Director. Most of the above qualifications also apply to the athletic director when athletic direction is a separate position. Perhaps the most notable exception is the degree. Although some athletic directors hold doctorates, there is no particular evidence that such a degree is required for the athletic director's position. The preferred degree would be an M.S. in sport management theory or an M.B.A. The master's degree programs in sport management are reaching a stage of development making them the degrees of the future for all athletic directors.

As mentioned earlier, coaching experience is a very important qualification for the athletic director to possess. Beyond that the athletic director should have a general sensitivity to the various needs and issues in intercollegiate or interscholastic sport.

The athletic director must also be an individual who is willing and able to work within the context of an integrated sport program. This is an important but fairly abstract qualification, which again points to the critical nature of the staffing function. It should be apparent that many athletic directors have traditionally been inclined to "do their own thing" without regard to the total sport program. That may work under certain circumstances, but it is contrary to the approach advocated here.

Coach. Perhaps volumes could be written about the position qualifications for a coach. The coach is so many different things to so many different people that it is difficult to know where to begin in setting forth the qualifications for this position.

Edwin Cady (1978) discusses these qualifications most lucidly in his chapter on the coach. He distinguishes between what he calls the "intramural" and "extramural" qualifications for the position. Most of his suggested qualifications are generally recognized in the successful coach. The intramural qualifications he discusses include knowing the game, being a gifted teacher, organizational ability, "talents of a good clinical psychologist," and integrity. The extramural qualifications include the ability to recruit, being a good colleague, and public relations ability. However, Cady puts them all together and adds the most essential ingredient with his discussion of "class" as the major qualification for a coach:

> All the foregoing qualifications require that half-definable thing, class, too. And yet a man might possess them all and remain an assistant all his professional life without a sufficient abundance and balance of certain personal gifts and qualities which no society ever has in oversupply. Any coach will tell you that the first and least dispensable is intelligence: quickness of perception and response. Second comes leadership, the power to command the loyalties and the obedience even to sacrifice which are perhaps the essentials of male bonding. With that goes an aura, the projection of what is sometimes called star quality: it makes everyone look up when one figure enters a crowded or preoccupied room. But perhaps it is more than that. If you have the eye and have seen enough of them, many people believe, you can tell a real coach just by looking at him (p. 122).

Cady's description of "class" may be a bit abstract for any listing of position qualifications as such. Yet his insight is helpful in pointing to the complexity in filling a coaching position. A listing of position qualifications will carry us only so far; the actual selection process emerges as the prime consideration.

Nevertheless, some more tangible items can be identified in determining the position qualifications for a coach. He or she should have some experience as a college athlete. That need not be the highest level or "star" type of experience. As a matter of fact, the record shows that many of the more successful coaches do not fall in that category. However, the situation is very similar to the link between coaching experience and being an athletic director. With athletes as with coaches, "it takes one to know one," The coach must be able to understand and communicate with the athletes. It is difficult to acquire that without some in-depth experience as an athlete.

In terms of degree qualifications, a bachelor's degree will suffice for many entry level positions in coaching. The degree need not be in any particular field. It is obvious that successful coaches have had various kinds of undergraduate majors. All things considered, a degree in arts and sciences is probably the most desirable in light of the strong need for communication skills and public relations ability in coaching. If the preparation is to be more directly in a professional field, the degree in sport management looks more like the degree of the future for a coach or any other position in sport management. An ideal combination is to have a coach with an undergraduate degree in arts and sciences, followed by a master's degree in sport management. The latter degree will help to prepare the coach for other management positions in school or college sport.

Sport Coordinator or Sport Instructor. With respect to qualifications, these two positions can basically be considered as one because any differences will largely relate to the level of responsibility resulting from the level of experience. The exception to that might be for a position that is being filled under Strucure A, wherein the coach for a sport reports to the sport coordinator for that sport. As with the athletic director–coach relationship, it would seem that coaching experience should be a principal qualification for a sport coordinator who is to be effective in working with a coach. Beyond that, it is assumed that any sport instructor might eventually become a sport coordinator.

The major qualification for any sport coordinator or sport instructor is in-depth knowledge and skill in the particular sport. Obviously, any coordinator must have the ability to organize effectively, direct, and control. Beyond that, not much more can be said. The record will show when someone has really been involved with aquatics, tennis, golf, or any other sport. The position qualification should focus on the in-depth involvement. Similar to requirements for the coach, the degree preparation might be in any field. The bachelor's degree would be an entry level qualification with professional advancement through a master's and (in a few cases) a doctorate in sport management.

Business Manager. In the staff position of business manager, the position qualifications should focus on specific degree requirements. Two choices are recommended. Qualifications might include either an M.B.A. (following any undergraduate degree major) or a master's degree in sport management following an undergraduate degree in business administration. In terms of something more specific, the background of candidates should show evidence of accounting experience. Other desired preparation would be in computer science, personnel administration, and legal courses.

Aside from degree work, the position qualifications should be directed toward a general knowledge of sport, particularly in relationship to the educational environment. Such knowledge might be acquired and manifested in a variety of ways. Candidates need not have previous experience as a coach or sport instructor or both.

Director for Sport Promotion. Although the specific degree requirements tend to be a bit more flexible, candidates for the position of director for sport promotion should also present evidence of certain kinds of preparation. Here the qualifications should place emphasis on knowledge in communications, marketing, merchandising, and advertising. Sales experience would be desired. In most cases, these qualifications can perhaps best be improved through undergraduate majors in business administration, advertising, sport management, or communication studies.

Beyond that, the director for sport promotion should have an extensive knowledge of intercollegiate sport. Many former coaches will work most effectively in the position if they also have the qualifications mentioned earlier plus a strong motivation for this kind of work. On the other hand, the coaching experience is not a prerequisite. The position can also be very effectively handled by those who have other kinds of experience leading to a knowledge of intercollegiate sport.

Sports Information Director. As is true of many positions, much of the work of the sports information director is learned "in the trenches." Therefore, applicants should demonstrate that they have "been there" through experience in a sports information office. If there is a preferred undergraduate major, it would have to be journalism. Short of that, the basic qualifications might be met through another undergraduate major that enables the student to take several courses in journalism. For example, an undergraduate major in sport management might have sufficient flexibility to permit the kind of preparation needed for the staff position as sports information director. Some major programs in communication studies would also be appropriate. Most importantly, the candidate should be able to demonstrate "hands on" writing experience as related to sports reporting. Prior experience with a student newspaper or a commerical newspaper or both would be most desirable.

In addition to the technical qualifications, the sports information director also needs that extensive exposure to intercollegiate sport suggested for the director of sport promotion. Again, coaching is not necessary. However, the candidate must understand coaches and be able to relate effectively with all those who work in intercollegiate athletics. It is particularly important that he or she be able to communicate effectively with all those who work in sport media in any form.

Manager of Facilities. It is somewhat difficult to pinpoint specific position qualifications for the manager of facilities. This in no way detracts from the relative importance of this position; the very nature of sport demonstrates the importance of the facilities and equipment domain. Candidates might be selected from various backgrounds. The only concrete prerequisite would be a bachelor's degree. This is needed for effective communication at this level of position within the academic environment. Some former coaches will perform well in this position, again provided they have the motivation for this kind of work. Experience shows that certain retired military officers are particularly well suited for the position. This may be attributed to the military experience in facilities management plus an ability to work with the variety of people who are involved in some form or another.

In addition, the candidate should have a knowledge of sport facilities, including design, construction, operation, and maintenance. Much of that will have to be learned on the job. When available, a course in sport facilities would be most desirable.

In the final analysis, organizational ability looms as an overriding concern in seeking candidates for the position of manager of facilities. The candidate who shows previous success in being able to organize personnel and material resources will likely meet the need provided he or she also understands the particular demands related to sport facilities.

Trainer. In contrast to the foregoing, the position of trainer represents one of the more concrete in terms of specific qualifications. The head trainer or any full-time trainer must be a certified athletic trainer with a certificate issued by the National Athletic Trainers Association. Such certification will more or less ensure the specific knowledge and skill that are required for this position. A bachelor's degree in athletic training would be most desirable. Unfortunately, relatively few institutions offer the degree as such. Falling short of the optimum, a degree in excercise science (where available) or health education would be most appropriate.

Ticket Manager. The position of ticket manager may be the most difficult one to analyze in terms of definite qualifications. From that standpoint, it, too, can be sharply contrasted with the position of trainer. Much like the sports information director, the ticket manager is most likely to qualify by "working in the trenches." Much like the manager of facilities, the position of ticket manager might be filled by a person having any type of baccalaurate background.

It may be most useful to approach the qualifications by noting certain skills that could certainly be advantageous in the positon of ticket manager. Basically he or she should have marketing skills, data-processing experience, and office skills. Beyond that, the professional development should be in the areas of ticket sales technology and the psychology of fan motivation. If the most appropriate areas of degree work had to be cited, they would probably be sport management, marketing or advertising, computer science, or psychology. Once again, a strong background of involvement with sport is assumed.

Summary

At least one thing should be clear after the reading of this chapter: to a large extent, organizing is a situationally based function. There are so many variables that influence the organizational needs. The wise manager will adapt his or her organizations to the personnel and resources of his or her unit. This, it is difficult to set forth a model for the organization of school and college sport programs. However, it is useful at least to understand the parameters in launching the organizational endeavor. We have attempted to identify those parameters.

It appears that the real key to organizing is to provide a logical flow from structure to positions to qualifications. If it is difficult to identify any qualifications, it is perhaps time to reconsider the positions. If the positions seem unclear or tenuous, there may be a need to reexamine the structure. By and large, as with planning, organizing is a facilitating function. If things work in terms of staffing, directing, and controlling, there is good reason to believe that the spadework in planning and organizing has been well done.

REFERENCES

Brinckloe, William D., and Coughlin, Mary T. *Managing Organizations.* Encino, Calif. Glencoe, 1977.

Cady, Edwin H. *The Big Game.* Knoxville, Tenn. U. of Tennessee Press, 1978.

Edginton, Christopher R., and Williams, John G. *Productive Management of Leisure Service Organizations: A Behavioral Approach.* New York. Wiley, 1978.

Famularo, Joseph J. *Organization Planning Manual.* New York. AMACON, 1979.

Henderson, Richard I. *Job Descriptions: Critical Documents, Versatile Tools.* New York. AMACON, Division of American Management Associations, 1976. 48 pp.

Nelson, Resa. "The Impact on Women's Athletic Programs When Athletic Departments Merge." Unpublished paper, 1980.

CHAPTER 4

Staffing a School or College Sport Program

CONCEPTS AND PROBLEMS

Staffing Is Integral in the Entire Managerial Process

Selection Is Only the Beginning in Effective Staffing

Relative Significance of the Interview

Complexities Surrounding the Selection Process in School and College Sport Programs

Distinction Between Orientation and Training

Orientation Should Inlcude Legal Considerations

Management Training for Coaches

Need for Both Internal and External Development

Once the position qualifications are established, the actual function of staffing can begin. It is now necessary to establish the means for obtaining the personnel to meet the position qualifications. What is the selection process? All the effective planning and organizing will be of little value if the program cannot find the people who have the desired qualifications. The coach is acutely aware of the fact that "you have to have the horses." The same idea extends to the selection of all personnel for the sport program.

Although the importance of selecting qualified personnel is well known, what is often overlooked is the need to complete the staffing function through appropriate orientation, training, and development. Therefore, in this chapter we will be considering staffing from a total perspective even though the key element is the up-front, selection process. Following are the parameters for the analysis of this complete function.

The Selection Process

1. Advertising.
2. Obtaining and processing letters of application.

  3. Obtaining and considering letters of recommendation.
  4. Interviewing.

Postselection Elements of Staffing

A. Orientation. Actions taken to familiarize the staff member with the total working environment.
  1. Policies.
  2. Standard procedures.
  3. Legal considerations.
B. Training. The focus will be on-the-job training in the form of management training for the coach. The reason for this restriction is twofold. It is assumed that training other than management training is specific to individual positions in the programs. The focus on the coach is warranted through the recognition that he or she occupies a principal line position in the department. Thus, the coach has a basic responsibility for managing a separate program.
C. Development.
  1. Internal
    a. Committe work.
    b. Working as an understudy.
    c. Working in an acting capacity.
    d. Special assignment.
  2. External
    a. Advanced degrees.
    b. Clinics, workshops, seminars.
    c. Professional organizations.
    d. Speaking engagements.
    e. Visits to other programs.

THE SELECTION PROCESS

When properly done, the selection process is long and demanding. There are many steps along the way. Of course, it's possible that one or more steps may be omitted, or there may be a general acceleration of the entire process. The exceptions to the total selection process usually occur when the time demands are such that administrators must give priority to moving quickly rather than carrying out the process of selection in its more complete, ideal form. Within the context of college sport, this type of quick decision is frequently necessary in terms of certain coaching replacements, particularly of football or basketball coaches. It may be felt that any extended search would be detrimental to the recruiting effort after the coach resigns or is released at the end of the season. Under such circumstances, we observe what might be called a "collapsing" effect in the total selection process. Nevertheless, the four basic steps in selection meet the test of what is generally considered to be desirable.

Advertising

Within recent years, the need to advertise positions has been heightened as a result of federal and state laws and regulations relating to equal employment opportunity and affirmative action. In general, these laws and regulations stipulate that in all personnel decisions there shall be equal opportunity for all persons without regard to race, color, religion, sex, age, or national origin. Consistent with this principle, affirmative action shall be taken to seek and maintain adequate representation of women and minority group members within various organizations. The effect of this legislation has been particularly evident in schools and colleges owing to their dependance on federal and state funding. The demonstration of equal opportunity and affirmative action is usually manifested in an advertising medium that offers the possibility of reaching a relatively large segment of potential applicants. Thus, as an example, it is quite common to advertise a college position in the *Chronicle of Higher Education* and the Sunday edition of *The New York Times*.

However, the need for advertising does not begin or stop with considerations involving equal employemnt opportunity and affirmative action. It should be obvious that the principal advantage of an advertisement lies in the potential to reach a large audience and a variety of candidates. In addition to newspapers, journals, and magazines, advertising of positions is also done through the medium of letters to the appropriate departments and other forms of special announcements. This is also one of the more effective forms of advertising positions in school or college sport because the notices can be sent directly to the departments that are likely to have contact with potential applicants who meet the desired qualifications. At the present time there are rapidly expanding numbers of academic program in sport management in the United States and Canada. In the years ahead these programs could offer a rich source of potential applicants. There is good reason to believe that these programs should be a focal point for advertising. This includes the advertising of coaching positions because the master's degree programs typically have many students with fine coaching qualifications.

The key to effective advertising of a professional position is to specify the nature of the position as clearly and accurately as possible. Naturally, the position description and position qualifications should be used as the basis for what is said in the advertisement. However, it is relatively expensive to advertise in newspapers, magazines, and journals. Therefore, succinctness is a top priority consideration. An advertisement that is not clearly worded is likely to attract many applicants with marginal qualifications. Among the various positions in sport management, those of coach and athletic trainer are perhaps most easily advertised owing to the relative concreteness of the position descriptions. By contrast, a position as director for sport promotion may require more thought in preparing the advertisement. Regardless of the position, it is important to specify in the advertisement a cut-off date for the receipt of applications.

Letters of Application

The next step in staffing is to obtain and process the letters of application. This is often a significant factor in staffing school or college sport programs owing to the extensive number of applications and subsequent volume of correspondence related to those applications. Current market conditions and the general appeal of the school and college sport positions are such that the applications are likely to be numerous. Therefore, this is a critical step both in terms of the criteria for evaluation and the procedure for processing the applications. The applications should be evaluated by a committee that is representative of the various groups that will be working closely with the occupant of the position.

Generally speaking, letters of application fall into one of two categories: solicited or unsolicited. Both categories are very evident in school and college sport programs. Solicited letters of application are written in response to advertisements, announcments, or other requests for applicants. In most cases, assessment will largely be based on the degree to which the applicant meets the position qualifications that have been outlined. Does there appear to be a "fit" between what the applicant has to offer and what is sought for the position? In many cases, degree qualification or previous experience result in early screening of unqualified applicants who respond to solicited applications. On the other hand, the alert applicant to a solicited application will be attempting to present a case as to how he or she meets the specific qualifications that have been delineated. By contrast, in an unsolicited letter of application the employer will often be looking for the unusual qualification that sparks the potential for enhancing the work of the organization. An example in college sport might be to receive an unsolicited letter of application from a potential fund raiser when such a position does not exist and has not been advertised.

A typical application includes two components, the letter itself and the accompanying data sheet or résumé. The principle advantage of a résumé is that it enables the applicant to highlight or provide a succint statement of qualifications mentioned in the letter of application. When applications are solicited, the submission of résumés with the letter should be required or at least encouraged. On the other hand, with unsolicited applications it is sometimes more desirable and effective to submit a résumé at a later date on the grounds that there is sufficient interest in the application to generate further consideration.

Whenever possible, the receipt of applications should be acknowledged, and this should be done as soon as possible. This is important for public relations purposes. When the search process tends to be fairly long, there should also be an appropriate number of follow-up letters to inform all applicants of the status of their applications. This step tends to be handled poorly in many organizations, partly because the bulk of paper work but also sometimes because of neglect or maneuvering in arriving at a decision about an offer for the position. At any rate, all applicants should be notified shortly after an offer has been made and accepted. Sometimes one notes a glaring omission in this regard.

Letters of Recommendation

In some respects, letters of recommendation represent the most elusive aspect of the entire selection process. They can vary all the way from being extremely helpful to virtually useless. Difficulties in assessing letters of recommendation stem from two variables that are largely outside the control of any administrator or member of a selection committee: (1) Who writes the letter? (2) Does the latter accurately reflect the qualifications of the applicant? As with letters of application, letters of recommendation also fall into the solicited and unsolicited categories. When a letter of application is solicited, it is fairly customary to request also two or more letters of recommendation in addition to the résumé. In an elaborate search process, it is often more desirable to have candidates list the names of several references who could be contacted. This has the twofold advantage of providing some selection in the source of letters and enabling one to identify particular points that should be addressed in the letters of recommendation.

The latter advantage points to a general limitation that characterizes many letters of recommendation. This is what could be called the "halo" effect that permeates letter of this type. Naturally, we are frequently inclined to write positive statements about those applicants who request recommendations. It might be said that a letter of recommendation is largely viewed as a support mechanism. That in itself may be advantageous in making decisions about appointments. However, a search or screening committee usually seeks more specific information that extends beyond the "good guy" syndrome. A search committee may be able to offset that limitation partially by asking referees to comment on particular qualifications as related to the position description. The validity of the response may still be open to question, but at least this brings the committee one step closer to effective utilization of this component in the total selection process.

One special point about letters of recommendation should be noted specifically in regard to positions in school or college sport. Many of these positions are obtained at least in part through waht could be called the "apprenticeship" route. Thus, we find young coaches who learn their work by "doing their time" under the tutelage of an experienced coach. Similar on-the-job learning experiences exist among sport instructors and sports information directors. Beyond that, the entire internship component of an academic sport managemnt program is predicated on the value of apprenticeship training. The relative importance of such arrangements should not be overlooked when one is seeking and assessing letters of recommendation. Even though the validity of a supervisor's response may be partially limited by the desire to place his or her apprentice, there is no doubt that the supervisor is in the best position to comment on what takes place in the line of action.

In short, there are letters of recommendation, and then there are "real" letters of recommendation. The validity of comments in letters or recommendation is somewhat open to question. From a management perspective there is a constant need to seek and identify meaningful letters of recommendation.

Interviewing

The interview is at the heart of the selection process. All the preliminary paper screening is necessary and important, but the interview offers a medium for face-to-face, two-way communication, which is essential to any decision involving the selection of a final candidate. The relative significance of the interview for all positions in the sport enterprise is heightened because this is first and foremost what could be called a "people-oriented" profession. That is not to suggest that any interview is a perfect indicator of future success on the job. The record often indicates the contrary. Nevertheless, the interview still has top priority in a selection process that is never perfect. Berko, Wolvin, and Curtis (1980) reinforce this opinion from the standpoint of the college graduate's initial interview.

> The initial interview is extremely important to securing the job. A study of 255 businesses that hire recent college graduates revealed that an effective initial interview ranked at the top of the list for hiring, well above a high grade point average, pertinent work experience, and good recommendations. In other words, your success in the employement process will probably depend as much, if not more, upon your skill at interviewing as it will upon your possession of task-oriented skills (p. 85).

From the management perspective, the key to a successful interview is through providing an environment and a line of communication that yield the information that is sought by both parties in the interview. In an employment interview, the environmental need can be facilitated by having the applicant interviewed by a variety of people under different environmental circumstances. This is one of the reasons a search committee is highly recommended for the selection process. If time permits, it is often advantageous to have an applicant also be interviewed by others who are not members of the search committee. Those who have carefully studied interview situations have focused considerable attention on what is known as "interrater reliability"—the extent of agreement when an applicant is interviewed by two or more people. Any differences in assessment are likely to be increased when the applicant is interviewed in a variety of environmental settings. Thus, a prospective coach might be viewed quite differently from the perspective of the dean's office, the athletic director's office, the playing field, or at lunch with other coaches. From the applicant's vantage point it is equally as important to learn as much as possible about the total environment in which he or she will be working.

The line of communication in an interview is largely determined by the degree of structure that is provided and the form of questioning that is pursued. There are two basic interview techniques: the nondirective or open-ended interview and the patterned inteview. The latter tends to focus on closed, probing, and leading questions. In a nondirective interview, the questions are more open-ended, and the applicant is asked to reflect on previous comments. Each technique has its strengths and weaknesses. When the interview is more patterned or structured, it tends to focus on specific considerations that are assessed as being important from the perspective of the interviewer. On the other hand, that can lead to the accompanying disadvantage of being too restrictive in scope. The open-ended interview has the advantage of giving the applicant the opportunity to explore those matters that he or she assesses as being important in that situation. This, in itself, may reflect on qualifications for the position. The obvious disadvantage is that critical aspects involving the position may not be covered during the interview.

Regardless of the basic technique that is employed, each interview is somewhat unique. The most significant variables arise from the specific interaction between the interviewer and the applicant. This is why it is important to have the applicant interviewed by more than one person. Other variables are those involving time and place as well as the circumstances surrounding the specific position that is to be filled. As an example of the latter, one might be interviewing a prospective coach for a team in which there has been a problem involving team morale. This recognition is likely to guide the interview in that direction. In spite of all the variables, there are some general guidelines that tend to contribute to more effective interviewing.

1. *Do your homework.* Preparation tends to be very important in carrying out many of the mangerial functions; interviewing is no exception. The interviewer who knows quite a bit about the candidate before the interview is much more likely to be able to ask the key questions and to guide the discussion on a meaningful manner. In particular, the interviewer should review the letter of application, résumé, and letters of recommendation shortly before the interview. The review may be useful in focusing on a particular point of attention, or it may be used to establish a general frame of reference regarding the candidate.

2. *Establish and maintain rapport with the candidate.* The most obvious step in gaining rapport is to do whatever you can to make the applicant comfortable with the interview situation. The very nature of an interview makes this somewhat difficult to achieve. This is particularly true of an employment interview. Nevertheless the positive, but friendly, initial approach in the right kind of environment can be a big factor in working toward this rapport. Beyond that, both the candidate and interviewer must sense that they are communicating. The six basic questions—who? what? where? when? why? and how?—can be used effectively to guide the discussion in a meaningful manner and thus maintain the rapport.

3. *Beware of the stereotype assessment.* A fairly common pitfall in many employment interviews is when the applicant is assessed in terms of whether he or she fits the mold. There is a certain natural tendency to judge people in accordance with the image that we project from others who hold a similar position. Any limitation in this regard can be magnified in the sport enterprise, where we find strong images surrounding the athlete and the coach. An applicant might be considered to be highly qualified for a football coaching position because he or she fits the stereotype: the applicant looks like a football coach. The reverse could also apply. We reject an applicant because he or she does not meet our expectations in terms of appearance or mannerisms. In either case, the interviewer is trapped into superficial assessment. Beyond the stereotype as such, the interviewer should also beware of bias resulting from a single, dominant characteristic while overlooking other qualifications.

4. *Describe the position, the program, and the total situation as clearly as possible.* This is an area handled poorly in many interviews. Too often there is a tendency to present only part of the picture. Of course, it's not possible to cover everything in the course of an interview. However, that does not negate the basic need to present an accurate profile of the situation. If this is not done, the probability increases that subsequent staffing problems will occur. More specifically, the employer has an obligation to present the undesirable as well as the desirable features of the position. Many of the morale problems in various organizations can be directly traced back to false expectations stemming from the rosy picture that was painted during the interview. Things are never quite as we thought they would be. It is also true that we are inclined to hear what we want to hear. Yet many problems can be eliminated down the road if the employer is open and frank in his or her initial presentation of the circumstances surrounding the position.

These four suggested guidelines are by no means a panacea for the difficult task of interviewing. They are at least a start. As with many other aspects of effective management, the appropriate approach in interviewing will also be learned over a period of time. Administrators might be well advised to keep an employment "batting adverage," namely, a record of successful interviews versus successful employees.

Special Concerns in School and College Sport

Thus far we have considered procedures in the selection process that would be generally applicable to any organization that hires full-time employees. Is there anything about school or collge sport programs that points to exceptions in the general process? Basically, the answer is no; the basic process remains the same. However, some differences may be found in the special concerns that surround the process.

We noted earlier that school or college sport positions are likely to generate a large number of applications. Consequently, considerable work is involved in processing these applications. It is important to develop an efficient system of preliminary screening without omitting a potentially well-qualified applicant. Any pressure on the application process is likely to be compounded by the role of the media and subsequent public reaction to filling the visible positions within the department. Of course, this is particularly evident with respect to coaching positions. Everyone seems to know who is being considered for various coaching positions, but the public knows little about the selection of teachers or professors.

These circumstances are further compounded by what is called the "old boy" network, which has been a traditional favorite in filling positions in school and college sport. This is a network that relies on contacts: whom you know is the name of the game. Of course, that kind of operation is not limited to the field of sport. To some extent it is operative in most hiring practices. However, the strong public relations orientation in sport has resulted in an above-average tendency to employ those who have been close to the program. There is evidence that this is beginning to change to some extent. Nevertheless, it remains as a factor for consideration when assessing the staffing pattern in school and college sport.

At least one other item remains an area of special concern in the selection process for coaching positions. This relates to the transitory nature of coaches. Coaches come and go at an exceedingly high rate of turnover. Cady (1978) presents some data and interesting thoughts in that regard.

> The average tenure, for example, of Big Ten football coaches since 1901 is less than five years (considering current member schools only). Of the roughly 154 conference head football coaches during that period, however, about twenty-two have served ten years or more. Not considering that some of them served more than one institution but subtracting their numbers and years of service, the average tenure for the rest drops to three years. One in seven, it may be said, survived to become Coach.

> My guess would be that the national figures are rather more discouraging to the beginner. Are prospective coaches thereby discouraged: Very seldom. Why not? Because they are the sort of people they are, they have those qualities. Because they are in love with the game, the art and the life. Because the rewards of winning and the satisfaction of being coach are great. Because there have always been men, and they are the best in their way, who would rather be dead lions then live dogs. And because being part of a great college or univeristy is one of the vital adventures of the spirit in our time (p. 123).

Of course, Cady is referrring to high-level coaching positions. One might expect that there would be far less turnover in various other coaching positions in school and college sport. To some extent this is true. However, the coaching situation in general is characterized by considerable shifting of personnel. Although they may remain with the school system owing to their tenured teacher status, even high school coaches are frequently inclined to give up coaching after a few years on the job.

What has this to do with the special concerns in the selection of personnel? The implications are twofold. First, the selection process is more or less a continuous process for the director of the school or college sport program. It is not a simple matter of selecting a staff and looking forward to a stable personnel situation. Thus, the significance of the selection process tends to be heightened in this environment. In addition, the process frequently has to be accelerated. Any pressure in this regard is particularly evident at the college level owing to the need to provide an ongoing recruitment program. The result is a recurring need for a careful, but accelerated, selection process.

POSTSELECTION ELEMENTS OF STAFFING

Orientation

In general, orientation refers to those actions that are taken to familiarize the staff member with the total working environment. Such orientation is also an ongoing function. The basic difference between orientation and training is that orientation tends to cut across positional lines whereas training is aimed at the requirements for carrying out the responsibilities of a particular position. Within the school and college sport setting, two principal forms of orientation can be noted. These are the institutional orientation and the program orientation. The latter is the orientation for working in the basic unit structure, be that a program, department, or division. In other words, this is the orientation for working within the sport enterprise of that institution. The director of the sport program also has a responsibility to make sure that his or her staff is familiar with the general institutional policies and procedures. However, here we will be considering the orientation for personnel within the sport unit.

Policies. In our earlier discussion of policy development, two central thoughts were stressed: policies are developed from the general pattern of decisions within the particular program, and they evolve over a period of time. Consequently, it is virtually impossible to specify those policies that should be covered in the orientation of personnel in every school or college sport program. The particular situation and circumstances will determine the specific policies. Nevertheless, there are certain parameters that should guide the orientation in any context.

    1. *Athletes.* In general, the entire staff needs to know how the athletes are viewed and subsequently guided within the context of the sport program. How are they recruited? What restrictions are placed on the recruiting endeavors? What are the standards for admission? If there are athletic scholarships, how are they allocated among the various sport teams? What efforts are made to guide normal progress toward a degree? Are there provisions for tutoring athletes? What arrangements are made for meals and housing for athletes? How are athletic awards determined? What is the basis for disciplinary action?

    2. *Coaches.* In general, the new coach needs to know how he or she is expected to contribute to the development of the program; what the basic mode of relationships within the program, institution, and larger community is; and how he or she will be evaluated in the work. Those matters represent the broader territory for orientation of the coach. Within that scope, the following questions should be addressed: What are the objectives of the total sport program? What are the objectives for that particular sport? What has been the history of efforts to reach those objectives (strengths and weaknesses)? What are the relationships among line and

staff personnel? (In essence, how does the department conduct its business?) How is the coach expected to relate with faculty, students, and administrators in the school or college? What sort of interface is expected with the public? Is there a tenure system for coaches and, if so, how is tenure awarded? In either case, what is the basis for reappointment? What are the criteria for salary increases and promotions? How is the work load determined?

Answers to these questions will not complete the policy orietnation for the professional employees in a school or college sport program. However, the framework of such questions is a good place to begin. When one considers the continuous series of problems in college sport today centering around the standards for athletes and coaches, there is good reason to believe that there are marked deficiencies in the orientation process. Either that, or the policies have not been established in the first place.

Procedures. Much of the procedural information tends to be more of a training than orientation nature. However, the new staff member also has a need to know certain basic procedures for working in the program aside from those procedures that are focal to his or her position. It might be said that these procedures more or less represent the modus operandi for the program as a whole. What are some of the procedural points which should be covered through staff orientation in the school or college sport program?

1. *Financial.* Every member should have a basic understanding of the financial situation and the budget process. This form of orientation would include answers to the following essential questions related to finances and the budget.

- How is the program financed? (In other words, what are the major sources of revenue?)
- What are the major areas of expenditure?
- What are the possible sources for increased financial support?
- How are the funds allocated within the program
- When are budget requests submitted?
- Who authorizes expenditures?
- What is the system of accountability?

2. *Facilities.* In general, facility orientation revolves around the idea of who uses what and when? The staff must know the process that is followed in scheduling facilities. Beyond that they should also understand the priority system for use of the facilities. Several of the potential pitfalls in directing the program can be avoided if scheduling of and priorities for facility usage are adequately covered in the orientation process.

3. *Health care.* Basically, this aspect of sport program orientation includes a familiarization with the means of providing for the medical needs of athletes and other students. How are physical examinations scheduled?

What are the emergency procedures? What is required in the way of injury report? What kinds of health insurance are provided? What is the assignment of athletic trainers? Of course, as part of the larger orientation process, the staff members will also be interested in the provision for their own health care. However, that is generally part of the institutional orientation process.

4. *Travel.* Who makes the team travel arrangements? What options are available for team travel? How are individual travel requests handled? What are the restrictions involving travel? What are the general provisions for lodging and meals? What is required by way of travel expense reports? These are among a host of questions that should be covered in a complete orientation. Travel is a most integral consideration in all school and college sport programs because the need to travel extensively in interscholastic or intercollegiate sport is one of the major factors that tends to set these programs apart from most other activities in educational institutions. In most cases, travel costs represent a good portion of the expenditures for the sport program.

5. *Game management.* There is a general need for information concerning game management in some form or another. Game management usually involves several people working under different sets of circumstances. The new staff member should have a basic understanding of who does what in terms of "putting on" the game. The orientation should include information on the arrangements for officials, tickets, scorers, visiting teams, and security personnel. Obviously, the total game situation varies in each sport. Particular aspects of orientation will have to be geared to each staff member's kind of involvement in the game. Nevertheless, there is a general need for information concerning game management.

6. *Public relations.* Part of the orientation process should be directed toward providing a perspective on the public relations stance in the sport program. What image does the program strive to project because staff members are constantly relating to a multiple public under diverse circumstances? In varying degrees each staff member will have extensive contact with the media, other faculty members, athletes, other students, parents, and the public at large. In so far as possible, the staff should all be conveying essentially the same message as far as the direction of the total sport program is concerned. Each individual will have public relations concerns that are somewhat unique to his or her position. Nevertheless, it is important to provide the general tone of the public relations thrust.

Legal Considerations. Today there is hardly a single aspect of sport that is not touched by the law in some way or another. The recent court case involving Mark Hall and the University of Minnesota serves to dramatize that there is virtually no limit to the legal impact on sport. Hall, a basketball player at Minnesota, was declared ineligible because he was not in a degree-granting program. He brought suit against the university, requesting a temporary restraining order until the merits of the case could be heard. U.S. District Court Judge Miles Lord ruled that Hall should be allowed, at least for the time being, to resume his studies and his status as a player on the basketball team. In explaining the basis of his decision, Judge Lord said that Hall had been recruited to come to the University of Minnesota as a basketball player, not as a scholar. He went on to add, "It may well be true that a good academic program for the athlete is made virtually impossible by the demands of their sport at the college level. If this situation causes harm to the University, it is because they have fostered it, and the institution, rather than the individual should suffer the consequences" (*Hall* v. *University of Minnesota*, 530 F. Supp. 104, [Minn. 1982]. The university lost the case owing to the lack of due process afforded Hall. This is but one case that points to the relative importance of including some legal dimensions in the orientation process.

Potential litigation might come from any of the following sources: travel, injuries, good conduct codes, student protests, eligibility regulations, athletic scholarships, student fees, women's sport participation, and assessing athletics as being a right in lieu of a privilege. All of these have been sources for various court cases in recent years. In general, the staff should be oriented as to the policies and procedures that are in effect to deter the possibility of litigation in these areas. On the other hand, the legal orientation should not be designed as a scare tactic. Appenzeller (1975), the athletic director at Guilford College and the author of several books on sport law, offers solid advice in this regard.

> The courts have a history of deferring policymaking and management of athletics to those who conduct the programs. When policies are fair and reasonable, there is little to fear from the courts. When programs are run arbitrarily and rules are devised that are unreasonable, then, and only then, will the court take over. In too many instances, school administrators hesitate to take action because they are afraid of a lawsuit (pp. 28–29).

Appenzeller also points to the need for the staff to understand the legal responsibilities in their work when he states

> It appears that the court would prefer to return considerable authority to state and local regulatory bodies. It will not tolerate, however, rules and regulations that are arbitrary, capricious, or unreasonable. The key word in athletic litigation seems to be *reasonable!* The court expects and even demands action by school officials that exemplifies reasonable conduct, action, and judgment (p. 244).

Training

Training is an elusive topic to discuss within the context of a textbook because its very nature implies learning by doing in contrast to learning by thinking or reading. Yet training is also a critical aspect of staffing. Furthermore, along with the selection process and orientation, training should proceed from a sound theoretical framework if it is to be carried out in an effective manner. Therefore, the subject deserves some analysis in relationship to the staffing function in school and college sport programs.

Essentially, there are two major forms of training, on-the-job training and off-the-job training. It is generally conceded that the results of the former are clearly more evident or demonstrable than the results of the latter. Nevertheless, there obviously is a place and a need for both forms. In most cases, a large segment of the off-the-job training takes place prior to the acceptance of a position. That is the principal reason why we find various professional preparation programs in colleges and universities, including preparation programs in sport management. However, the need for such training does not cease with the acceptance of an initial position. An assortment of clinics, workshops, and seminars is available for the active professional person. More about that will be said in the last section of this chapter under the topic of development.

Any analysis of on-the-job training reveals a further breakdown into two principal varieties. What is most apparent is the training for acquiring the technical expertise to do the job. This is largely manifested in what we call apprenticeship training. Thus, in the sport contest we find that a young basketball coach learns the skills of coaching basketball under the tutelage of an experienced basketball coach. Similarly, the S.I.D. skills are learned in the sports inforamtion office, and the newly appointed business manager becomes familiar with the specific accounting procedures by working with someone who understands the accounting procedures of the institution. Such training is at the heart of the entire training process because without the technical expertise little will be accomplished. However, there is another form of on-the-job training that is also important. This is the kind of training that we principally have in mind when it is viewed as an aspect of the larger staffing function.

This training can properly be called management training. The extensive need for such training is well expressed by Fuoss and Troppman (1981) in the context of discussing effective coaching.[1]

There is a similarity between successful people in middle and executive management positions in industry, business, and government, and head coaches of athletic teams who are in organizational structures over subordinate personnel. All must be able to perform, to a high degree, specific management functions and skills in planning, organizing, staffing, directing, and controlling, and must be adroit decision makers. While each has his or her own particular technical or operational skills as the result of specialized training and education, to be highly successful each must possess management skills, too. A universally acceptable operational definition of management is "the accomplishment of predetermined goals and objectives through the efforts of others," which applies to every individual in a management position of a hierarchial organization structure regardless of one's technical or operation skills, including the coach-manager (p. 87).

---

[1]From Donald E. Fuoss and Robert J. Troppmann, *Effective Coaching: A Psychological Approach*, John Wiley & Sons, New York, 1981. Used with permission.

In this chapter we are considering management training as one form of on-the-job training and as the form of training that is a component of the staffing function. It involves different managerial concerns for each position in the sport program. However, the coach can be used as an example to provide a basic format for such training. What are some of the managerial concerns in coaching?

Planning. The coach learns to forecast by addressing basic questions related to the expected strength of his or her team and that of scheduled opponents. How many letter winners will be returning next year? What are the expected contributions of current members of the junior varsity? How might any newly recruited personnel fit into the team situation? Are there changes in the schedule or conference alignment that are likely to limit or enhance the team's success? What is known about the quality of returning players on the teams of scheduled opponents?

Having done some forecasting, the experienced coach should be able to arrive at realistic objectives for the forthcoming season. Such objectives should be established in consultation with team personnel. These would include individual as well as team objectives. Again we see the parallel between the coach as a manager and the broader scope of managerial positions. Just as there are institutional objectives and individual objectives for the total sport program, the coach must be able to provide the balance between team objectives and the objectives of the individual players. Such decisions are also reached through the experience of on-the-job training as a coach.

The coach's program planning takes a somewhat different slant in that he or she begins with a built-in structure as far as scope and priorities are concerned. It is clear at the outset that the general program is the sport that is being coached. Thus, the program planning involves the time segment for reaching the objectives in that sport. In addition to planning for the sport season, the coach must be prepared for the preseason, postseason, and out-of-season operations involving his or her particular sport. Program planning revolves largely around what is to be accomplished during each of those seasons. Although the sport season is the direct manifestation of the effective program, it is increasingly apparent that the successful coach is the one who has carefully planned a year-round program.

The role of the coach in scheduling epitomizes the need for careful planning. In many respects, much of the planning revolves around a schedule in some form or another. To begin with, of course, the coach has to give primary attention to the schedule of opponents for the season at hand. What steps should be taken to meet the demands of that particular schedule? Beyond that, the scheduling responsibilities of the coach extend to the preseason and out-of-season training schedules as well as to practice schedules and the schedule within a given practice session. It is safe to say that a good segment of management training for the coach revolves around the ability to arrive at suitable schedules in the total coaching situation.

Earlier in the text we suggested that Management by Objectives (MBO) could be used as the major format for budget planning. Within that context, the coach will also require training. Essentially, this will involve a familiarization with the MBO process from the identification of key result areas to the use of MBO as an evaluative medium. The coach will learn to identify his or her key result areas and to develop these into routine, problem-solving, and innovative objectives. When it comes to performance appraisal, MBO extends far beyond the budget process, as such. However, the relationship between MBO and zero-based budgeting, showing responsibility and accountability, is also an integral part of management training for the coach.

A good portion of the on-the-job training for the coach revoles around a familiarization with the procedures and policies that cut across the total program. Most important, the coach must learn the domain that is covered by policy. What are the policies that provide the parameters for his or her work, and what are the policies which guide the role of the athlete? These are up-front considerations in the training program. Beyond that, the coach also has to know which other procedures are formalized through the medium of policy. If a procedural area is not covered by a policy, as such, is there a modus operendi that is generally employed with respect to facilities, equipment, travel, scheduling, or any of the other procedural concerns. This aspect of training centers around a communication of how the department does its business. Needless to say, it is much easier to provide such communication within the context of a well-planned program. In other words, sound planning facilitates effective staffing. Once again, we note the strong link among the various managerial functions (Figure 4-1).

Organizing. The basic organizational challenge for the coach is quite clear: how can he or she most effectively organize the team? Like many other aspects of management, this can only fully be learned by doing it—through a process of trial and error. This is particularly true in sport management owing to the inherent diversity among sport teams. Organizing a golf team is very different from organizing a football team. From a training perspective, perhaps the best one can do is to provide an organizational frame of reference for the coach. Cratty and Hanin (1980, p. 10) point out the principal variables that will govern the specific structure of a sport team.

1. Divisible teams—athletes perform different functions.
   - track and field
   - football
2. Unitary teams—athletes perform same or similar functions.
   - volleyball
   - soccer (except goalie)
3. Coaction teams—scores combined artificially.
   - golf
   - bowling
4. Teams with close group interaction.
   - basketball
   - rugby

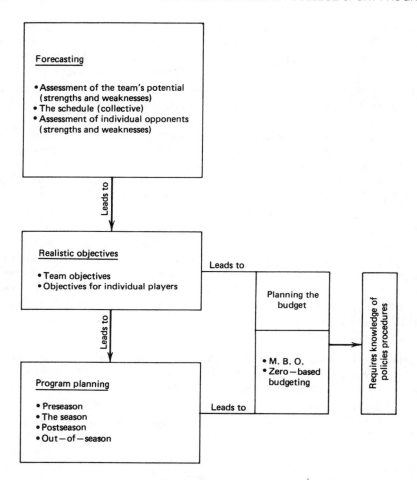

Figure 4.1. Management training for the Coach—learning to plan.

The coach must learn to organize within the basic structure that is delineated for his or her sport. The specific nature of that structure will largely determine the position qualifications. Beyond that any organization will flow from "grass roots" concerns on a daily basis.

Staffing. As noted earlier, staffing begins with the actual selection of personnel for the organization. How does the coach select the team? This is a most critical question at all levels of competition. Interestingly enough, little seems to be known about it from an external perspective. It seems to fall in the category of private knowledge. In other words, each coach knows how he or she proceeds with the selection process, but there is relatively little in the way of shared information or published guidelines. Several books on coaching have appeared in recent years. However, they tend to focus on working with athletes rather than selecting athletes.

In my opinion, the person who may offer the best advice in terms of team selection is Edwin Cady (1978). His work was referred to rather extensively in the first chapter. However, several of his ideas are also most applicable here in terms of a coach's training in the selection process. His advice is, of course, directed toward college athletics. However, the basic thoughts can be extended to high school sport as well. His ideas about the process for selecting athletes are found in the section entitled ''Student Athletes and Where They Come From.'' Cady begins by noting the overall importance of having the quality student athlete: ''If they are all right so is everything else that matters; but if they are not, it's all wrong'' (p. 144). In terms of general qualifications, he notes that ''successful athletes must be at a minimum, four things: gifted, hungry, intelligent, and tough-minded'' (p. 146). Every coach will probably have his or her own interpretation of what is specifically meant by each of those qualities, but they certainly offer the parameters for effective selection. Later, Cady is even more explicit in presenting seven reasons why the coach should not recruit those athletes who have a slim or no chance of surviving academically:

> You can list the reasons why a Coach ought not to try even that form of ringer: (1) Intellectually underqualified student athletes don't survive. I once studied an entering class of more than forty football players on athletic scholarship which happened to be characterized by a recruiting resolve to ignore academic promise. Almost half failed to survive the freshman year, and two-thirds were gone by the end of the sophomore year. Perhaps a quarter of them ever played at all. After one injury early in their senior year, none of the surviving 11 percent played. (2) Such losses wreck recruiting continuity and structure, which results in (3) ill-planned squads, out of personnel balance, without experience, and short on leadership. (4) Since athletes who survive for four years grow physically, learn much from coaching and competitive experience, you lose consistently to well-built, coherent, experienced teams with senior leadership. (5) On campus you alienate the players and your program from the academic communities and nourish the jock stereotype. (6) Off-campus you lose recruiting credibility in the field to the point where, eventually, you destroy the confidence of the college in all its elements, leaving yourself prey to the coach-burners. (7) Finally, you diminish the reputation of yourself, your profession, your game, and the institution (pp. 168–169).

I think that Cady has been most perceptive in pointing out the chain reaction that takes place when the selection process has not been aimed at obtaining the quality student athlete in the truer meaning of that concept. Earlier in this chapter, reference was made to the Mark Hall case at the University of Minnesota. Certainly, developments to date indicate at least a partial unfolding of Cady's scenario. This is not to suggest that Minnesota is alone in facing the problems associated with the selection process. That is far from the case; it just so happens that this particular situation has reached public attention. Can a coach be trained to select athletes who will also succeed academically? The answer may be yes or no, depending on precisely what one means by training. This much is more certain; at least the coach should be offered quidelines for player selection as part of the total personnel staffing function.

Directing. The directing function is the one aspect of management that is most directly related to the actual performance of the task. Much of the success in directing will depend on technical expertise plus general education and personality. For that reason it is a bit difficult to describe how a coach might be trained to direct his or her program.

Nevertheless, there are a few parameters that might assist the relatively inexperienced coach in carrying out the managerial function of directing. In any organization, but particularly the larger ones, directing begins with some delegation of responsibility and authority. A sense of approaching delegation can be gained by considering the six most basic questions: who? what? where? when? why? how? The first of these questions is largely answered for a coach. He will be delegating to assistant coaches (in the case of a head coach), captains, and managers. Beyond that, the other questions will be answered through assessment of the particular needs within that sport situation plus the relative strengths and weaknesses of the available personnel. The key to successful delegation is to avoid conflict in responsibilities. Much of it is learned through trial and error. Again, we note the relative significance of on-the-job training. However, the basic questions provide the basis for the decisions that have to be made.

Although the motivational efforts of the coach are intrinsic to that individual, he or she must learn to consider and, to some extent, balance, the various dimensions of the motivational concern. The athlete, the team, and the institution all require a different kind of motivational focus. Much of the success in directing will depend on the degree of blend in motivating these various constituncies.

As with motivation, the coach cannot be told how to coordinate his or her work. However, the coach must be alerted to the extent of his or her coordinating responsibility. Naturally, he or she will be most concerned about coordinating the team effort. However, the external dimension of coordinating is equally as important. The coach must learn to work with other coaches, other students, faculty, administrators, the booster club, alumni, the media, and the public at large. The role of the coach in game management is a classic example of how he or she must learn to direct his or her attention outward as well as inward (toward the team) in his or her coordinating effort.

Effective coaching actually epitomizes the ability to manage differences. From one standpoint that's what coaching is all about: the ability to manage differences. However, it would be a bit risky even to infer that a coach can be trained to mange differences. From the standpoint of overall management, the best one can hope for is to provide a frame of reference for dealing with this important topic. Fuoss and Troppman (1981) state the need in this regard quite well.

One of the most important concepts in a coaching philosophy is the respect for individual differences. Many coaches do not fully comprehend how important and how meaningful it is to recognize truly an individual's differences. Typically most coaches will recognize and make exceptions for individual differences in the skills and techniques of their atheletes, but a number of the same coaches may not recognize or tolerate individual differences in personality. Athletes have different backgrounds, arousal levels, and aspirations, and each reacts differently to situations and pressure (p. 143).

Coaching also dramatizes the need to manage change. In coaching, change is the name of the game. New rules, new strategy, revised schedules, new conference, new team members, use of reserves, and injuries all point in the direction of change. As with managing differences, the coach cannot actually be trained to manage change, but can be presented a basic posture in dealing with change. It could be said that the ability to manage change is something that is caught and not taught.

With respect to the entire function of directing, we noted that the training for the coach will take on a somewhat different form than that which is usually associated with the concept of training. Basically, the coach must be provided an emotional climate and a set of parameters that will enable him or her to do the job. He or she must learn to cope with differences and changes and must recognize that motivation and coordination are multifarious considerations and that delegation results from answering some key questions.

Controlling. As the final component of management training, the coach has to learn to control what has been established. Basically, control is carried out through the process of evaluation and the subsequent actions that flow from the evaluation. As one looks at a sport program, two essential forms of control can be noted—control of material resources and personnel control. Control of facilities and equipment is a prime example of the former. That aspect of control also requires some training for the coach or any other employee who is directly involved with the utilization of material resources. However, for purposes of management training, it is suggested that the focus should be on personnel control. As a person in a middle management position, the coach is most intimately involved in both sides of the controlling function. He or she must learn to operate within the context of performance standards that have been established for the entire program, department, division, school, or college. From the perspective of the coach, this could be called the external form of control. For example, if the decision is to go with MBO, the coach must receive training in the basic structure of MBO. Deegan and Fritz (1975) aptly describe how this relates to the controlling function.

The management process is completed through the function of *controlling*. It is commonly agreed that this function really includes two separate components: the act of making a judgment and any necessary corrective action that might be called for. If the college manager wishes his/her judgemnt about the work of the group to be not only a rational one but one which is accepted as helpful, he/she must evaluate on the basis of acceptable criteria. The only way to make an acceptable judgment is to evaluate performance against standards which have been agreed upon in advance with the workers. Without "par for the course" we are not in a position to make a meaningful approach. Management by objectives is a process which identifies in advance mutually acceptable standards of performance (p. 32).

The implication here is that the coach must be trained to function within the MBO framework. MBO is built on the concept of participative mangement. This is particularly critical in carrying out the controlling function. There must be mutually acceptable standards of performance. To achieve that requires a certain amount of training.

More specifically, the coach must understand the basic framework of the controlling process and the flow of events within that process. What are the sources of critical data within the athletic program? This would probably include information related to financial status, recruiting efforts, athletic eligibility, injuries, student participation, and public relations work. He will need to know what reports are required in reporting the status in those areas of concern. Such a data base leads to a discussion of the way in which performance standards are developed within the context of that information. How are routine, problem solving, and innovative objectives developed from the key result areas? Once these are developed, what are the steps in the evaluation of the coach? Also, when will it be done and who will do it? Finally, what is the reward system? What are the criteria for a merit increase or a promotion? On the other side of the coin, what are the possibilities for corrective action? The long and short of it points to the need for the coach (or any other employee for that matter) to know the general rules under which he or she is operating. Without such knowledge, there is no way in which real control can be manifested.

As stated earlier the coach is most intimately involved in both sides of the controlling function. Just as he or she works within a system of control, the coach must also provide control for the athletes. That is the kind of control that Edwin Cady stresses as a focal point in his work. This, too, will require management training for the novice coach.

The control by the coach can also be viewed in terms of its internal and external dimensions. To some extent, the internal aspect of control is built into the very nature of the sport that is involved. This kind of control revolves around performance standards for practice sessions and games. Every sport tends to have its own modus operandi in terms of the way things are carried out before, during, and after the games or matches. By virtue of his or her background in the sport, the coach will bring that sort of knowledge into his or her new situation. However, beyond that, the coach will also have to know what other standards need to be applied for the conduct of the activity, be it a practice session or the game. In terms of external control for the athlete, the coach is expected to work within the framework of policies that are set forth for the entire athletic program. This is part of the orientation process, as discussed earlier. Beyond that, any training for the coach's external control would take the form of any special circumstances that may apply to his or her sport.

Development

This is the one aspect of staffing that is most easily overlooked or receives little attention. The reason is fairly obvious: development is not essential to the immediate task at hand. Yet people have a basic need to grow and to have opportunities for advancement. Staff morale tends to be highly correlated with the extent to which such opportunities are available. At the school level, this may be manifested in the opportunity to move from a junior high or junior varsity coaching position to a high school varsity position. Of course, the move from an assistant to head coaching position is a principal sign of development at any level. In the colleges, development can be seen in the opportunity to become an assistant or associate athletic director. The possibility of becoming an athletic director always looms as a prime motivator in any efforts at development. Although, the possibility may be slim, coaches and other staff members should be alerted to and recommended for positions at other institutions. It is also very important for high school coaches to be provided with a medium to be considered for college positions.

How is development stimulated? The answer is to be found in those efforts that are directly aimed at professional growth. Advancement may ultimately result from having been at the right place at the right time. Nevertheless, staff members must be prepared for the opportunity that may become available. The developmental feature of staffing has both internal and external dimensions.

Internal. In general, the opportunity for internal development exists whenever one is able to move outside the confines of a position description or the normal scope of responsibilities. In other words, internal development really means professional growth within the program. There are at least four ways in which this is typically observed.

1. *Committee work.* Committee work is an area of professional involvement that represents both a source of irritation and a target for ridicule; some people deplore committee work whereas others are inclined to joke about it. Regardless of one's feelings toward committees, they are here to say. A certain number of them are necessary and important; the key is to choose the right ones. From a staffing standpoint, they can also be used as one of the means of contributing to internal development. New staff members can learn about the total program by getting involved with appropriate committees. Needless to say, having the opportunity to chair a committee can be even more significant for professional growth. Many people who work in school and college sport programs tend to isolate themselves from the broader academic community. Selected committee involvement can aid in narrowing the gap between the sport enterprise and the other areas of school and college life. Whenever feasible and applicable, the staff of a sport program should also be encouraged to volunteer for committees at the school or college level.

2. *Working as an understudy.* From time to time, most administrators can use some additional help owing to seasonable demands or a special set of circumstances. This is particularly likely to be true in a school or small college sport pro-

gram wherein we note the collapsing effect in the organizational matrix. In other words, the director generally has more than he or she can effectively handle. Another way to facilitate staff development is to select those with administrative potential and have them work in various administrative assignments that are outside the scope of normal responsibilities. In a way this is like an administrative internship; only the arrangements are made internally among existing staff with regular, full-time appointments.

3. *Working in an acting capacity.* Within any academic environment there is a periodic need to make acting appointments because of sabbaticals, other leaves of absence, or vacancies. The opportunity to serve as an acting administrator is another means of developing internally. The acting appointment may or may not lead to a regular appointment in that position but often opens the door to other appointments.

4. *A special assignment.* Personnel can also grow within an organization by being selected for a special assignment of a temporary nature. There are a host of such possibilities for special assignments within the context of school and college sport programs. Some examples would be (1) heading up a special fund raising drive, (2) conducting a feasibility study for a proposed facility, (3) developing a new security plan for the management of home contests, or (4) preparing a new format for the evaluation of sport instruction. Careful selection of personnel for such assignments can be a significant factor in professional development.

External. A large segment of professional development occurs outside the organization within which the individual is employed. Essentially, external development involves contact with the various facets of the profession at large. However, it can and should also include opportunities to use one's professional expertise in association with professionals in other fields as well as the general public. It might be said that external development amounts to stretching oneself beyond the boundaries of the immediate environment. How does it take place?

1. *Advanced degrees.* Within the educational sector this is the first and foremost form of external professional development. The only exception to that generalization would be that in certain academic areas, particularly in recent years, an increasing number of people have assumed their first professional position with the terminal degree in hand. In these cases, of course, advanced degree work is not part of staff development as such. However, within the sport management area, most individuals do not hold their doctorate degree at the entry level. This is particularly true in high school but is also true in the colleges. Consequently, the possibility of advanced degree work looms as a prime possibility when we consider the various avenues for external development in sport management.

When we explore the sources for advanced degree work, the developing academic programs in sport management become a principal consideration. Some of these programs are now quite well established. Others are still very much in the genesis stage. In the years ahead, the opportunities for appropriate degree work in this area should continue to increase as further steps are taken to develop meaningful and applicable curricula for those working in the field of sport management. Some institutions now offer the bachelor's degree in sport management. I feel that graduates from those programs should be encouraged to seek admission to M.B.A. programs when considering advanced degree work. In any case, administrators can take a major step in stimulating professional development by encouraging coaches and other staff members to pursue the most appropriate advanced degrees according to their future goals and needs.

2. *Clinics, workshops, seminars, and other short courses.* The entire area of nondegree, yet curricularly related, activities offers another potentially rich source for professional growth. The key here is for the staff member to make the right selection from the host of possibilities that are available. The pattern of coaches getting invovled with the various coaching clinics is already well established. Beyond that, the entire sport management staff should be encouraged to attend short-term sessions that might assist in developing their management expertise. As an example, at present many professional people in the field obtain considerable benefit from an exposure to the basics of fund raising or legal considerations in sport.

3. *Professional organizations.* When it comes to membership in professional organizations, the problem is not one of availability. In all fields, the proliferation of professional organizations is increasingly evident. The key is to associate with those that offer the potential for development based on one's particular interests and capabilities. The direction for the coach is relative clear-cut. He or she should begin with the coaches' association for the sport or sports that are being coached. Other organizational involvement of coaches and other staff members should be aimed at those organizations that represent the best opportunity for professional growth. Following are among the prime possibilities.

College Athletic Business Managers Association

National Association of Collegiate Directors of Athletics

State High School Athletic Directors Association (one for each state)

United States Collegiate Sports Council

National High School Athletic Coaches Association

National Athletic Trainers Association

National Intramural Recreational Sports Association

Getting actively involved prompts consideration of another aspect of professional organizations that is also part of the larger staffing function. Merely holding a membership card means relatively little. Attendence at professional meetings means just a little bit more. The more significant external development will take place when the new staff member serves on professional committees, presents papers, submits articles to the organization's journal, and eventually is considered for a position as an officer in the organization. From the standpoint of staff development, the administrative encouragement should be in that direction.

4. *Speaking engagements.* Those who work in school or colelge sport programs tend to be highly visible people. Consequently, the opportunities for speaking engagements of many types are likely to be numerous. Depending upon the particular position that is held by the individual, this may include banquets for youth sport groups, high school sport banquets, college sport banquets, booster club meetings, alumni gatherings, civic or church groups, and press luncheons, among several possibilities. As a result, the staff development in this area is not so much in the area of stimulation and encouragement as it is in the substance and form of public presentation. New staff members should be guided in the way that the objectives and functions of the total sport program are to be presented. This is not to infer that this aspect of development is aimed at restricting individual expression. However, it is important to assist in presenting the basic posture of the sport program.

5. *Visits to other schools and colleges.* Much can be learned through a more prolonged contact and discussion with those who work in other programs. What is meant is the kind of development that can take place when a high school coaching staff has the opportunity to observe and interact with a college staff or another high school staff. Or it might be a Division III or Division II staff giving insight from a visit to a Division I university. These are but two of several possibilities. There is no doubt that considerable professional development can occur when we have had the opportunity to visit other schools and colleges for an extended period of time on a more formal basis. Each program has its own way of doing business. An opportunity to observe that firsthand is often much more beneficial than any theoretical discussion of the topic.

Summary

In this chapter an attempt has been made to convey the central idea that the staffing function is much more extensive and complicated than would at first appear to be the case. Staffing is not a simple matter of obtaining people for the various positions; the real key is found in the actual selection process. If management can find the right people, be they athletes, coaches, or staff personnel, a major step has been taken toward achievement of a successful program. There is no substitute for "having the horses." However, so much can be lost when we think we can relax after obtaining the desired personnel. As with all the other managerial functions, staffing is also a continuous process. When we look at the successful coach, we can again see a vivid example of the need for total and continuous management. After selecting the players, every coach knows that he or she must orient, train, and develop those players. Likewise, administrators must be cognizant of the need for carrying out the complete staffing function. This entails appropriate orientation, sufficient on-the-job training, and providing the opportunities for professional development.

REFERENCES

Appenzeller, Herb. *Athletics and the Law.* Charlottsville, Va. Michie, 1975.
Berko, Roy M., Wolvin, Andrew D., and Curtis, Ray. *This Business of Communicating.* Dubuque, Iowa. Brown, 1980.

Cady, Edwin H. *The Big Game*. Knoxville, Tenn. U. of Tennessee Press, 1978.

Cratty, Bryant J., and Hanin, Yuri L. *The Athlete in the Sports Team*. Denver, Colo. Love, 1980.

Deegan, Arthur X., and Fritz, Roger J. *MBO Goes to College*. Clearwater, Fla. Deegan, 1975.

Fuoss, Donald E., and Troppmann, Robert J. *Effective Coaching: A Psychological Approach*. New York. Wiley, 1981.

CHAPTER 5

Directing a School or College Sport Program

CONCEPTS AND PROBLEMS

Leadership Is the Key to Effective Directing

Basic Questions Determining the Nature of Delegation

Distinction Between Intrinsic and Extrinsic Motivation

Applicability of Maslow's Need Hierarchy for Work in School or College Sport Programs

Motivation to Become "The Coach"

Winning and Losing—A Two-edged Sword

The Basic Disjunctive Nature of School and College Sport

The Stratified Dimension in Sport Groups

Differences Between Men and Women in Sport Programs

Key Questions in Managing Differences Among Sports

Differences Among the Three Components of a Total Sport Program

Vast Differences in the Ability to Manage Change

The Pervasive Influence of Financial Limitations in Managing Change

Litigation—Change Is More A Matter of Degree than Kind

Cable TV—The Epitome of Change

The directing function signals the action point. Directing involves getting the job done from the perspective of management. Planning, organizing, and staffing are all aimed at carrying out the directing function. On the other hand, control is an outgrowth of the results of directing the program. Thus, directing is pivotal in terms of what precedes and follows in the managerial cycle.

Before we proceed with our analysis of this function, further clarification of the general nature of directing may be helpful. Taken literally, the term *directing* may convey false signals. A certain authoritarian air surrounds the concept of directing. It implies "calling the shots." Depending on one's leadership style, that may or may not be the case. One need not be authoritarian to direct a program succesfully.

That will depend on the person and the situation. It just so happens that many coaches have been very effective in the employment of an authoritarian leadership style. However, from there one cannot jump to the conclusion that the entire directing function in school of college programs is or should be in the authoritarian mode.

Reference to leadership prompts the need for a further point of clarification. Leadership is actually a very pervasive ability that cuts across all the managerial functions. However, when a person is directing a program, he or she probably shows then the most concrete evidence of leadership ability. Various definitions of leadership have been advanced. Fuoss and Troppmann (1981) say that one of the more meaningful definitions of leadership might be the one that was presented by the late President Eisenhower: "He said leadership was the ability to get a person to do what you want him to do, when you want it done, in a way you want it done, because he wants to do it " (p. 273). This reinforces the thought that leadership is most clearly linked with the directing function.

In addition to the many definitional attempts to describe leadership, various theories or approaches to leadership have also been presented. Along with other authors, Stogdill (1948) stressed the situational approach that points to the variables in leadership that extend beyond the traits of the leader. Fuoss and Troppmann (1981, p. 280) utilize that concept in presenting the "Leadership Fusion-Interaction Triangle," which depicts the variables surrounding the leader, the followers or group members, and the situation. Variables involving the leader include personality, attitudes, skills, interests, values, and general abilities. The leader interacts with group members who reveal variables in these same categories. Both sets of variables are fused in a situation that is determined by social, political, economic, and physical variables as well as those variables stemming from the idea that leadership ability is a situationally defined capacity.

I am of the opinion that this is the sort of conceptual framework that should guide our thinking as we analyze the directing function in school and college sport programs. There is no magic formula to determine the precise way in which a sport program should be directed. In this chapter, we will be considering the processes of delegation, motivation, coordination, management of differences, and management of change. The way in which each of these processes is carried out will depend on the variables involving the leader, the group members, and the specific situation. In other words, what works in one school or college sport setting might not be at all successful in another. However, there are certain prime considerations and parameters that can generally assist in effective directing of a school or college sport program. These are presented for consideration.

DELEGATION

There is no particular mystery surrounding the general idea of delegation. The meaning is fairly clear; to delegate is to entrust to the care or management of another person. Any uncertainties involving delegation stem largely from some very basic questions. What should be delegated? To whom should it be delegated? When should this take place?

Broyles and Hay (1979) identify six principles of delegation that can be helpful in carrying out the entire process of delegation.

> Delegation can be more efficiently performed if the preceding principles—clarity of delegation, coincidence of authority and responsibility, unity of command, clearly defined chain of command, fixed responsibility, and feedback—are followed. If responsibility (the obligation to perform a function) and accountability (the measurement of how well the function is performed) and authority (the right to perform a function) are understood, chances are good that delegation can be efficiently performed (p. 36).

What is involved in an attempt to fulfill each of these principles?

1. *Clarity of delegation.* Delegation is a two-way street. Both parties, the delegator and the subordinate, must have a mutual understanding as to what is being delegated. This brings us back to some matters that were discussed in Chapter 3. To a large extent, the clarity of delegation is provided by an organization chart and position description, assuming these are properly conceived. The one major exception to this would be a special assignment. In that case, it is particularly important that the nature of the assignment be mutually understood.

2. *Coincidence of authority and responsibility.* The principle of coincidence of authority and responsibility was referred to in discussing the organizing function. There must be delegation of authority as well as responsibility. Otherwise, the subordinate cannot take action without permission on relatively routine matters.

3. *Unity of command.* Only one person should delegate to another person in regard to any particular activity. In other words, it is difficult to have two bosses for the same function. This potentially could be one of the limitations in having both a director of the sport program and an athletic director, as proposed under certain structures in Chapter 3.

4. *Clearly defined chain of command.* A clearly defined chain of command is actually a corollary of the previous principle. A clearly defined chain of command will assist in establishing unity of command. Again the organization chart is the key in facilitating the process of delegation. As an example, if the chart clearly shows that the sports information director reports to the athletic director, a step has been taken to facilitate delegation.

5. *Fixed responsibility.* The scope of what is delegated should be delineated as carefully as possible. As an example, the athletic business manager would likely be delegated the responsibility for the actual preparation of the budget.

6. *Feedback.* This would usually be in the form of written reports or actual observation of results, showing how well the delegated responsibilities are being carried out.

As we look over these six principles of delegation, we again note the very close link among the various functions of management. It is obvious that sound organization is the key to effective delegation. It is also clear that feedback brings us into the controlling function of management. Nevertheless, the six principles should guide the process of delegation, and they set the stage for the entire directing function. What, then, are some of the prime considerations in the delegation of responsibilities in school or college sport programs?

General Areas of Delegation

As is true in many organizations, a certain amount of the delegation in school and college sport programs is fairly automatic. In general, this tends to be more true with regard to the line positions although the role of the athletic trainer is clearly an exception to that generalization. We begin with the coaches and sport coordinators. With them, the basis for delegation is clearest. This is particularly true of the coach. Essentially he or she is responsible for the team; the parameters are not too fuzzy. To a large extent, this is also true in terms of delegating responsibility to a sport coordinator. This is one distinct advantage in appointing sport coordinators; the managerial territory is rather clearly defined. Simply stated, the coordinator is delegated the responsibility for a particular sport. The only time we are likely to encounter the gray area of delegation here is when the program has an organizational structure that has a coach reporting to the sport coordinator. In that situation, the director of the sport program will have to give special attention to the "fixed responsibility" principle.

For the most part, the real decisions involving delegation will have to be made with respect to the staff positions and those activities that cut across the program (e.g., contest management). The athletic trainer has already been noted as an exception in that regard. His or her responsibility is quite clear-cut before any delegation takes place. To a somewhat lesser extent, this is also true of the sport information director and the ticket manager. By and large, the other staff positions (business manager, director for sport promotion; and manager of facilities) will require further thought in delegating the scope of responsibility. However, it is clearly the positions of associate athletic director and assistant athletic director that offer the greatest latitude in terms of what is or is not delegated. Regardless of who is responsible for a given task, the following are areas that call for decisions in the process of delegation.

Budgetary Control. There is no single area that calls for more important decisions regarding the kind and degree of delegation than budgetary control. The reason is obvious; if the budget is not in good shape, there are bound to be problems somewhere along the line. Every household realizes the significance of delegation in budgetary control. The basic idea is the same in school and college sport programs. The only real difference lies in the complications surrounding the delegation. The most basic decision relating to budgetary control revolves around the extent to which the budget will be controlled at the top level of management. In other words, to what degree will each subunit or individual be responsible for direct control of the allocated portion of the budget. For example, a subunit, such as the baseball program, might be allocated X amount of dollars for the program. With that allocation there is a delegation of authority and responsibility for budgetary control of the baseball expenditures. The coach or baseball coordinator would be making the decision as to how much is spent for equipment, umpires, uniforms, travel, and so on. Delegation of budgetary control in that manner would stand in contrast to a budgeting system in which requests for expenditures are submitted to the director of the sport program (or the business manager) according to the category of expenditure. Thus, there would be an overall equipment budget, controlled at the central level, with individual units making requests for expenditures from that budget. Of course, there are also various possible combinations of these two extremes. Later in this chapter we will be considering the variables in kind and degree of delegation. The size of the total sport program is obviously a most significant variable in delegating budgetary control.

This type of decision regarding the delegation of budgetary control will have to be made regardless of whether the program is large enough to employ a business manager. The only further decision in this case involves the delegation of responsibility from the director of the sport program to the business manager. In general, it would be expected that the director would retain the primary responsibility for financial planning and acquisition. The accountability for the budget would be delegated to the business manager.

Facilities. The actual management of facilities (exclusive of facilities planning) basically involves decisions concerning usage, maintenance, and security. Aside from school programs or relatively small college programs, we generally find a large amount of delegation of everyday facility control. This is why the facilities manager is often a distinct position in the large programs. In the absence of a facilities manager, responsibility in this area is likely to be delegated to an assistant or associate athletic director. As a general rule, one would expect the director of the sport program to retain the principal responsibility for long-range planning of facilities, with the actual decision involving usage, maintenance, and control being delegated to a facilities manager.

The role of the coach or the sport coordinator or both can be a significant factor in carrying out this aspect of directing the program. This is particularly true if the facility is not basically of a multiple-use nature. For example, the baseball coach is likely to consider the baseball field as his or her domain. In such cases, the director of the sport program will have to pay close attention to the principle of "fixed responsibility" in carrying out the process of delegation.

Game Management. Game management is one of the grayer areas in terms of delegating responsibility. As pointed out earlier in the text, many people tend to be involved in contest or game management in one way or another. With some sports, contest management is a relatively straightforward matter and does not require the involvement of several people. An interscholastic or intercollegiate tennis match would be an example of a situation in which the management of the contest could more or less be left with the coaches. In general, the need for careful delegation in contest management is with the more popular spectator sports.

One possibility is to delegate a single person as being responsible for all facets of game management. In the larger programs, this could be a separate position, or the responsibility might be delegated to an assistant or associate athletic director. The limitation of such an assignment is that it is virtually impossible for a single individual to keep track of everything that has to be done in a complex game environment. For example, Chalmers (1971) suggests a check list of 50 items as a guideline for precontest arrangements for football. Parkhouse and Lapin (1980) offer an elaborate contest management checklist of items to be covered before the contest, during it, at halftime, immediately following the contest, and the day after the contest. As one looks over the various checklists, it is apparent that certain categories emerge that provide the core of game management. Among the more common concerns are tickets, seating, security, parking, scoreboard, facility maintenance (including cleanup), locker rooms and equipment, concessions, emergency procedures, media, and officials. A number of items can be identified as checkoff points under each of those categories.

In light of the extensive scope of the operation in the "big game," it might be best to delegate responsibility according to one of the more general categories. To some extent, this is already accomplished through positions such as ticket manager and manager of facilities. The important thing is that the so-called loose ends be picked up in delegating responsibility for game management.

Sport Coordinators. Throughout the book we have stressed the need for appointing sport coordinators. This is the only logical way to go when one is managing a diversified program like those we find in schools and colleges. The most basic reason for this is that each sport tends to have its own modus operandi. Aside from that one can have a much more efficient system of managerial control by channeling the scheduling, equipment usage, and other procedures through a single person.

However, in terms of delegation, the only real complication involving sport coordinators is when the program is large enough to call for both a sport coordinator and a coach in the same sport. In the relatively smaller programs, this should be no problem because we would assume that the coach or one of the coaches would be the coordinator for that sport. However, in the larger programs, the director will have to delegate responsibility carefully between the coach and the sport coordinator. Adherence to the principles of "clearly defined chain of command" and fixed responsibility becomes increasingly important in that context.

Sports Information and Sport Promotion. Within the past few years we have noted that a relatively large number of Division I universities and some Division II colleges have established a separate position for sport promotion. Obviously, this arises from a pragmatic need to extend the fund-raising capacity. Where separate positions as sports information director and director of sport promotion do exist, there is once again a need for careful delegation of responsibility. The sports information director is also involved with sport promotion. The same could be said for any member of the total sport staff. However, the sports information director's direct contact with the media brings him or her closer to the area of promotion as such.

One general way to delegate responsibility between the two positions is to begin with the idea that the sports information director is essentially responsible for reporting the activities of teams and athletes. With that, of course, goes the accompanying responsibility of providing support service for the media coverage of these same team athletes. By contrast, the director of sport promotion is much more involved with the gestalt—the promotion of the entire sport program. He or she is first and foremost a marketing person in contrast to having principally journalistic expertise like the sports information director. This also gives the director of sport promotion a direct responsibility for fund raising. That kind of distinction should be useful when it comes time to delegating specific responsibilities. Nevertheless, the "clearly defined chain of command" principle will be a challenge in making assessments in that area.

NCAA and Conference Regulations. NCAA and conference regulations have increasingly become one of the prime areas of delegation in college sport programs. The reason is obvious; the steadily increasing bureaucratization of college sport makes it necessary. It has become almost a full-time job just to keep abreast of the rules that emanate from the governing bodies. In fact, this area represents one of the greatest challenges currently facing the small college athletic director who does not typically have the advantage of being able to delegate in this regard.

Furthermore, it's not a simple matter of knowing the regulations. Even more important, there is the ever-pressing need to maintain control in an effort to adhere to the regulations. The Sunday, March 21, 1982, edition of *The New York Times* highlights the problem as follows.

> Seventeen schools are on the National Collegiate Athletic Association's probation list, equalling the highest number for a single period, and the list will go higher before it goes lower, according to David Berst, the director of the association's enforcement department.
>
> At a time when costs are escalating rapidly in college sports, at a time when lucrative television dollars are available for successful football and basketball teams and at a time when increased outside involvement from alumni and boosters have led to excesses and embarrassments in recruiting and, in some cases, outright scandal, educators are being forced to consider whether the athletic system is out of control.
>
> The violations against the 17 schools range from illegal transportation to illegal entertainment and illegal financial inducements for recruiting prospects. . . .
>
> In addition, other schools are on probation for violations involving forged academic transcripts and unearned credits and administering improper financial aid to athletes. As many as 35 more schools are under investigation by the NCAA for possible violations. . . (p. 15).

It is not to suggested that an athletic director should or can delegate the responsibility to control the program with respect to NCAA regulations. However, the magnitude of the problem certainly points to the fact that the athletic director will need help. There is every reason to believe that there is invariably a need for some kind of delegation in that area with the "feedback" principle looming as a top consideration. Where the size and resources of the program permit, an associate or assistant athletic director is usually delegated responsibility for thorough familiarity with NCAA regulations.

Travel Arrangements. The situation with travel arrangements is not unlike that with respect to game management in that several people are likely to be involved in providing for travel arrangements in one way or another. Again, the question is largely one of the extent to which the responsibility for travel arrangements should be centralized with an individual. If resources permit, a travel coordinator is a logical focus for one of the areas of delegation. Short of that, most athletic directors are likely to delegate the responsibilities for pretravel arrangements with the business manager. This would leave the logistics of travel and the report of travel as delegated responsibilities for the coaches. Even though it is difficult to provide blanket answers for how delegation should proceed in this area, there is little doubt that the director must be certain that the responsibility for each aspect of travel is covered from beginning to end. As with game management, the checklist become the most effective tool for carrying out this aspect of the directing function.

Variables in Kind and Degree of Delegation

Thus far we have examined what would appear to be some of the principal areas for delegation in collegiate sport programs. By and large these tend to be areas that are major owing either to the scope or depth of the activity. In terms of scope, they represent activities that cut across the program—involving various people with various roles. With respect to depth, it is an area that is critical owing to the complexity of the consideration (NCAA regulations as a prime example). However, as with the broader topic of leadership, delegation is also a situationally defined function. Moreover, it is almost impossible to offer a formula as to what should be delegated to whom under what circumstances. The general areas can be useful in providing a frame of reference for the delegating process. However, it is just as important to be cognizant of the variables that influence the kind and degree of delegation.

Size of the Program. This variable has already been referred to several times in the previous discussion. By all accounts it has to be the number one variable in any considerations involving delegation because the extent of delegation is almost directly proportional to the size of an organization. That is the primary reason why secondary group leaders must have different abilities from the primary group leaders. The higher one moves up in the organizational ladder, the more important it becomes to carry out the process of delegation effectively.

Nevertheless, one should bear in mind at the same time that delegation does not begin and stop with the relatively larger organizations. Even the director of the school sport program should recognize that there is a need for some delegation. The size variable points directly at differences in degree and kind of delegation. Indirectly, Bronzan (1981) reinforces this idea very well in his stress on communication as the key to "managing" people.

> The prudent athletic director recognizes these conditions and seeks help to control them. The greatest potential source of help can be found within his own department personnel. Yet, this source is seldom tapped. Ideally, staff personnel will be invited to give assistance on a regular basis; they will be better prepared to give assistance and more willing to do so (p. 16).

Actually, Bronzan's discussion relates to the need for communication in problem solving. However, beyond problem solving per se, the implications for delegation of responsibility are also evident. One is more likely to get involved in seeking a solution to a problem if he or she has been involved through the delegation of some kind of responsibility. For this reason, even though size remains the principal variable in determining the kind and degree of delegation, we should not be trapped into any tendency to overlook delegation in the relatively smaller programs.

Strengths and Weaknesses of the Director. There is little doubt that certain managerial responsibilities, such as budgetary planning, lie first and foremost with the director of the sport program. However, beyond those more basic responsibilities, there is a considerable advantage for the program if the director goes with his or her strengths and delegates those areas of relative weakness. The significance of this variable is most evident, but it is also one that is not so readily accommodated. When a college has both a director of the sport program and an athletic director there is an obvious need to provide balance with respect to qualifications. This, in turn, will determine the general areas of delegation. Much the same can be said in terms of the relationship between an athletic director and an associate athletic director.

As an example, the athletic director could be a person who is a well-known, former athlete and coach. His or her extensive sport experience, including considerable contact with the media, has enabled him or her to develop public relations skills. At the same time there is evidence that the athletic director experiences some difficulty in directing the activities of personnel on a primary group level. In such a hypothetical situation, there is good reason to believe that the athletic director would retain the primary responsibility for the external affairs of the department and that the day-by-day management of internal activities would be delegated to the associate athletic director. The key to the variable is increased self-awareness of relative strengths and weaknesses.

Strengths and Weaknesses of the Personnel. Not much more need be said about the variable of strengths and weaknesses of the personnel in the process of delegation. It is obviously as significant as that involving the director. There is only one other dimension that should be considered. This brings us back to organizing and staffing, particularly the matter of selecting staff who meet the qualifications for position descriptions. We should assume that an individual is selected for a position primarily owing to his or her strengths in being able to carry out the duties of that position. This might be called predelegation, or it may be outside the scope of delegation as such. However, one's work in any organization does not stop with the position description as such. There is always work to be done in any organization that extends beyond the scope of position descriptions. This is the basic area for assessing relative strengths and weaknesses of personnel in the process of delegation. For example, a particular staff member may have unique ability in chairing a committee whereas another will work much more effectively on an individual assignment. In such extremes, the basis for delegation is rather clear.

Focus of the Program. What is the highlight of the total program? This, too, will determine the kind and degree of delegation. Of course, there are also sport programs in educational institutions that show no particularly strong focus. That is, there tends to be a balance among the intercollegiate, intramural, and instructional components, as well as a balance among the various sports. Within such a program one would expect that other variables will determine the kind and degree of delegation. However, as pointed out throughout this book, other programs clearly reveal a focus that indicates a priority within the total program. For a given school, it might be basketball. Should that be the case, the head basketball coach might be delegated responsibility that extends well beyond that normally assigned to a basketball coach. Currently, we are noting some examples of this when a basketball coach receives an appointment that in title or in essence makes him or her the athletic director for basketball. This can be viewed as a variable involving program focus that represents an extreme form of delegation.

Of course, it can also work the other way. Possibly the athletic director is a former football coach with a particularly solid reputation in that sport. The focus of the total program is clearly on football. Such an athletic director may choose to be more directly involved with the football program and delegate the management of the other sports to an associate athletic director. I am not here arguing that this is the way it necessarily should be, but it would also be naive to overlook the fact that this kind of situation does exist. Regardless of the pros and cons, such examples clearly demonstrate that the program focus can be another significant variable in determining the kind and degree of delegation.

Special Circumstances. In a way all the preceding variables could be called special circumstances, particularly if they fall in the category of being a most significant variable. However, beyond the usual determinants, other circumstances may point to the need for delegations that exceeds the normal limits. It is a bit difficult to discuss special circumstances in a general treatment of this topic because they are special. Nevertheless, a few examples might assist in conveying the idea.

Occasionally, we find an athletic director or another member of the sport staff who is asked to assume an additional responsibility at the school or college level. Any number of possibilities exist. It might be an additional administrative responsibility in an acting capacity or other type of temporary appointment, or the athletic director may be asked to coordinate a special fund-raising drive for the college.

Likewise, the director might get involved in extensive external responsibilities such as an important office in the NCAA or serving as the commissioner of a newly formed conference. As the bureaucracy of intercollegiate sport increases, these kinds of involvements are increasing daily. All this points to a further need for delegation, a need that is still another variable in the entire process of delegation.

Conclusions Regarding Delegation

Delegation is an initial step in directing a school or college sport program. As with all the management processes, it is also a continuous activity. The size variable still looms as the most significant factor in the degree of delegation. Yet some kind of delegation is always necessary. The day of the traditional and completely authoritarian sport or athletic director is no longer effective or even possible. There are areas that clearly point to the need for delegation. Beyond that, delegation is also very much situationally defined, depending on a consideration of those variables that have been discussed.

MOTIVATION

Numerous motivational theories have been advanced. For purposes here, it does not seem appropriate to evaluate the various theories. In general, one can conclude that there is relatively little consensus regarding the nature of and the means toward motivation in spite of the extensive research on the topic. However, there are a few propositions that at least provide a frame of reference when we analyze motivation as a component of the directing function of management.

One of these is the distinction between intrinsic and extrinsic motivation. The words themselves actually convey the essential difference between these two forms of motivation. Intrinsic motivation comes from within the individual who is motivated. Basically, one performs the task as a result of the satisfaction that is gained from the performance. By contrast, extrinsic motivation is tied with the rewards that are to be obtained from the performance. Extrinsic motivation comes from the outside. Money perhaps represents the clearest, if not the best, example of extrinsic motivation. If a person works solely for the purpose of making money, he or she is extrinsically motivated. As is true of many attempts at classification or categorization, there frequently is some middle ground. In other words, ones motivation may be both intrinsic and extrinsic. It becomes a matter of the degree to which one is intrinsically or extrinsically motivated.

When we consider the management of school and college sport programs from that perspective, it is apparent that the director is generally supervising people who have a relatively high degree of intrinsic motivation. The reason for making such an assertion is at least twofold. To begin with, we would assume that those who enter the field of education as a whole tend to be on the intrinsic side of the motivational continuum. At least it would be difficult to imagine that money would be the external stimulus. In the case of sport program personnel, we have to add the dimension of being involved with an activity that has a great deal of built-in appeal. Thus, the motivational challenge for the director is largely one of retaining the intrinsic motivation and providing whatever additional extrinsic motivators are important in that particular environment.

This latter thought prompts attention to another proposition that is persuasive among the various motivational theories. This is the continuing need for motivation resulting from changing conditions in the individual's environment. It's not simply that if one is motivated, then everything will fall in place. Along with other professions, sport management offers dramatic evidence of this proposition. If that were not the case, we would not find so many examples of "burned out" coaches, as well as professors and teachers who fall into the same category.

There is at least one other enduring element that emerges from the assortment of modern theories of motivation. That is the relationship between motivation and the satisfaction of certain needs. The concept of goal-directing behavior is a corollary of this proposition. An individual's needs are met in the effort to achieve certain goals, and this becomes the basis for being motivated. Any disagreement among psychologists, sociologists, and other scholars of the subject stems largely from the classification of such needs and the relative importance of the various categories of needs. However, the work of Maslow (1954) is probably the principal reference in showing the relationship between need satisfaction and motivation. Maslow's Need Hierarchy has become a premium guide in the attempt to understand motivation better. Although it does not directly explain how we can motivate others, it offers an appropriate frame of reference for anyone who is in a leadership position. Here it seems to offer a starting point when one assesses motivation as an integral component in directing a school or college sport program.

Maslow's Need Hierarchy

Maslow identified five general levels of human needs: (1) physiological or physical; (2) safety or security; (3) belongingness, social, and love; (4) esteem or ego; and (5) self-actualization or self-realization. One notes here a progression from the most basic or primary needs to those that are secondary in the sense that they are more abstract and not as integral to every individual. The first two levels could also be classified as largely needs of the body whereas the upper three levels bring us more into the realm of the mind and spirit.

The most basic physical needs stem from the principal physiological functions: hunger, thirst, breathing, rest, exercise, and sex. They are largely instinctive and thus further removed from motivation in the typical sense of that concept. The safety or security needs extend beyond the physical realm per se to include psychological factors involving protection from threatening situations. Obviously, this would include job security. More about that will be said later in terms of its applicability to the management of school and college sport programs.

There are several dimensions to the third level of needs, but the key concept is probably the social dimension. Although we here note greater differences among individuals, there is a general need for some kind and degree of acceptance. Although this level can be considered as less basic than the physical needs, there obviously is a fine line when we categorize the social needs as being somewhat more secondary. It could easily be argued that the need for love and affection is also extremely basic.

The relative significance of motivation in the professional environment is particularly evident in the highest two levels of needs. That is not to suggest that either the ego or self-actualization needs are exclusively related to professional careers, but such needs are certainly very evident in that realm. In terms of esteem ego, Maslow actually identifies two subsets of needs. The more basic needs are adequacy, confidence, independence, and freedom. We would have to assume that such needs are more generally shared with a larger segment of the population. Within the second set we note an extension of ego satisfaction stemming from the need for status, prestige, importance, dimensions, and related concepts. The second set clearly brings us more into the professional or political environment or both.

The more purely professional needs are even more evident at the highest level in the hierarchy, the self-actualization or self-realization needs. These needs largely relate to the idea of reaching one's potential. The need to make a significant contribution is an important aspect of this level. The motivation to be competent and to achieve are corollaries that can be identified. There is little doubt that both the fourth and fifth level needs offer fertile ground for an analysis of motivation in the management of school and college sport programs.

Although Maslow's Needs Hierarchy offers a most appropriate launching pad for assessment of motivation, the subject is much more complicated then appears on the surface. In general, it could be said that an individual progresses from lower-level to the higher-level needs. However, no level or particular need exists in isolation. Thus, motivation might stem from a composite need for security, social acceptance, and ego satisfaction. As another example, the physiological needs are always present even though one's direct attention might be focused on the fulfillment of a higher-level need. It's never a simple matter of leaving one level and moving to the next.

Another important point to keep in mind is that a satisfied need does not mark the end of the motivational concern. The healthy individual is in a continuous state of motivation. Once a particular need is satisfied, we are motivated toward new horizons. This is even true of the highest level of needs related to self-actualization. An example from college sport should assist in reinforcing this point. A college basketball coach might be successful in winning an NCAA championship for the first time. Beyond a doubt, that is a mark of competence and achievement, associated with Maslow's fifth level. However, the potential always looms as the possible next step in the motivational drive. It might be the next NCAA championship or a new challenge in the sport career or some other career. There is also an age factor. For many individuals, some of the lower-level needs may again become much more evident in the twilight of a career or in retirement age. From a management perspective, the key is to recognize the composite of needs that appears to be evident among employees at any given time.

General Bases for Motivation in Sport Management

It seems appropriate to begin with the general recognition that those who work in sport management programs are typically motivated through the same needs that characterize any person in a professional career. Thus, we can look toward personal advancement, program development, and development of the profession as the principal bases for motivation. In line with Maslow's Hierarchy Need, this points to the fourth and fifth level needs as being the motivational source for work in this area. To carry this one step further, it would appear that the second set of needs in the fourth level is particularly prevalent among those who occupy the various sport management positions. The needs involving dominance, importance, prestige, and status are very evident in many of the sport management positions. By contrast it could be argued that the relatively undefined nature of the sport management profession leaves it somewhat short of other professions in terms of the fifth level, self-actualization needs. However, such an assertion needs the test of further scrutiny. Perhaps an opinion will be clearer after we consider some of the more specific motivational concerns in the management of school and college sport programs. At least, the general bases for professional motivation offer a point of departure.

Personal Advancement. In almost all work situations, the opportunity for personal advancement has to be considered as a prime motivator. Thus, this motivational base extends well beyond the scope of professional fields. The underlying common denominator in all personal advancement in the working environment is the pay or salary increases. Beyond that the personal advancement of professional people tends to be very much related to promotions or the assumption of new responsibilities that may or may not include salary increases. In the academic environment, the awarding of tenure is yet another dimension of personal advancement. Ironically, even through tenure may assist in facilitating a security need, in some cases it serves as a deterrent in meeting needs at the fourth and fifth level of Maslow's hierarchy.

The desire to become a head coach or athletic director looms as a major motivational factor in school or college sport programs. However, this is clearly a case of "many are called, but few are chosen." Once again, the words of Edwin Cady (1978) express the motivational challenge. Referring specifically to Big Ten football coaches, he noted: "One in seven, it may be said, survived to become Coach" (p. 123). Beyond that specific situation, he points to the additional challenge involving personal advancement in college sport.

> My guess would be that the motivational figures are rather more discouraging to the beginner. Are prospective coaches thereby discouraged? Very seldom. Why not? Because they are the sort of people they are, they have those qualities. Because they are in love with game, the art, and the life. Because the rewards of winning and the satisfaction of being Coach are great. Because there have always been men, and they are best in their way, who would rather be dead lions then live dogs (p. 123).

Personnel advancement in college sport tends to be somewhat further limited through the typical lines for advancement. To a large extent this involves a differentiation between line and staff functions. The record shows that the vast majority of athletic directors are former coaches or are still active as coaches. Furthermore a large percentage of these are football or basketball coaches. There are those who argue that it shouldn't be that way and that things are changing in that regard. On the other side of the coin, as noted earlier in this text, others will argue that "it takes one to know one." Without taking a side on the issue, with respect to motivation it seems more important to recognize the situation at the present time. Athletic department personnel cannot necessarily look to equal opportunity for advancement. This is a factor in deciding on the degree to which the extrinsic motivation should be directed toward need satisfaction, associated prestige, and status.

The matter of academic rank presents another complicated dimension in terms of personal advancement as a motivation in sport management. Superficially, it would appear that academic rank should serve as a positive motivating factor for a person in a sport management position as well as any other professional position at the collegiate level. In some situations this may indeed be the case. On the other hand, it is well known that in many colleges the awarding of academic rank carries with it the accompanying responsibilities for teaching, research, and service in the more traditional sense. From a personal advancement, motivational standpoint, this could actually place a coach (or other sport manager employee) in the unfavorable position of competing from a different performance standard. Any difficulty in achieving promotion in rank could be a most negative factor in need satisfaction. The reverse can also present a problem. The decision may be to recognize sport management personnel as a special kind of professional employee in the academic setting in a category in which personnel advancement is not linked with academic rank. That may be the most appropriate decision except that tenure and certain status considerations are also very much associated with academic rank. At this point the motivational concern involving coaches may well switch to the second or fourth (or both) levels of Maslow's Need Hierarchy, security and status needs. Thus, it can be seen that the entire area of personal advancement represents a complex decision regarding motivation for work in sport management.

Program Development. Those who manage school and college sport programs begin with a certain built-in advantage in the attempt to motivate toward program development. As mentioned earlier, the program for the coach is really quite clear-cut. It is a case of his basketball or her field hockey program. In other words, there is no lack of focus for the coach. As a matter of fact, personal advancement and program development tend to be very closely related in this context. Generally speaking, they go hand in hand. The only real motivational problem is likely to result from a situation wherein the coach feels that he or she does not have sufficient resources or support for developing his or her program.

This points to the administrative challenge in using program development as a basis for motivation in school and college sport. It has been noted that the director is actually managing a whole series of programs. In most cases, something has to give; it is almost impossible to provide equal support for all programs. The key is to establish an environment in which the staff is motivated toward the development of the total sport program. Obviously, that is easier said than done. Nevertheless, there must be an effort to show that the welfare of the entire department is to some extent dependent on mutual support of the various programs. This does not necessarily mean that each program should expect equal resources. If the school or college is primarily known for its basketball program, the other staff members must be led to appreciate how that program can assist in meeting some of their needs.

Development of the Profession. The particular aspect of motivation known as development of the profession brings us into the general territory of Maslow's fifth level of human needs—those associated with self-actualization or self-realization. It is a fairly major step to move beyond program development to the development of the profession at large. As noted, program development tends to be tied in quite directly with personal advancement. However, fewer people will be motivated to work toward the development of the profession. Generally speaking, they must be able to recognize the link between the profession and their particular program.

When we look at school and college sport in this context, a complication is immediately evident. In a sense, there is no profession as such. On the other hand, it could also be agreed that there is a whole series of professions. One might begin by noting the coaching profession. However, there is reason to doubt whether even coaches are unified in a single professional group. Then we also note the S.I.D.s, business managers, facilities managers, trainers, and others, each with his or her own kind of professional affiliation. Some of the sport leaders, particularly at the high school level, would be inclined to identify physical education as being their professional home. However, as stressed earlier in this text, that also presents various limitations owing to the diversified and unfocused nature of the physical education field.

The answer seems to lie in working toward the development of a sport management profession. Even though the sport enterprise is extensive and a highly significant cultural factor, it is not reaching its potential owing to its splintered base. Many of the current problems in the conduct of sport might be alleviated if a truer professional status could be achieved. That is not to suggest that everyone who works in sport should do things the same way or even work from the same perspective. Nevertheless, there would be much to be gained by working from the centrality of sport. The medical and legal professions might serve as worthwhile examples to be followed. There are all kinds of doctors and all kinds of lawyers. In both cases, some are in private business, and others are public employees. In spite of any diversification, the core element is always medicine or law. There is strength in a focus and in numbers. The motivational implications are clear. Those who work in the various sport programs should be led to appreciate the advantages of "getting their act together."

Specific Motivational Concerns in School and College Sport

If you are involved with the management of a college sport program, it will not take long to realize that there are certain special concerns in that environment that are primary in meeting the challenge of attempting to motivate those who work under your direction. These concerns are not completely unique to college sport, but collectively they present a particular kind of challenge. The director who fails to appreciate the nature of these concerns is likely to fall far short in any effort at motivating. I note the specific concerns as being at least seven in number.

Winning and Losing. Winning and losing are clearly a case of a two-edged sword. We would have to assume that the desire to win is often the motivating force for coaches and athletes. Furthermore, in sport, the result (winning or losing) is so concrete, so evident. Therefore, those who manage college sport programs begin with a certain motivational advantage, starting from the basic drive to win. However, we all know that for every one winner there is a loser. The losing season or the loss of a key game may just as easily serve as a negative condition in the motivational efforts. Consequently, the director must be prepared to work with coaches and athletes who are losers as well as winners. Cratty (1981) offers some appropriate advice in describing the coach's role with respect to team motives and aspirations.

Moreover the coach, like leaders of other work groups who perform under stress, may heighten the team's success by giving them an accurate idea of the difficulty of the tasks. Disorientation in either direction, determining that the competition is overly difficult or easy, is likely to lessen the team's appetite for the contest as well as lower their satisfaction with success. For the most success to be felt by a team, the coach should (1) ascertain the real strength of forthcoming opponents and (2) help the team believe that the task of overcoming them is difficult, but achievable. . . .

Realistic goal setting by the coach, with the help of the team, should also lead to fewer and less marked shifts in aspiration after both failure and success experiences. That is, the team as a whole, like the individual, is less likely to markedly shift aspirations upward after success and downward after failure, if prior to the competition realistic group aspirations have been set and agreed on by all (pp. 152–153).

Although Cratty's discussion centers on the implications for the coach, it is clear that the advice is also applicable for the director who is attempting to guide coaches' motives and aspirations. Coping with both winning and losing is an important part of motivational success in school and college sport.

Intercollegiate—Intramural—Instruction. Throughout the text, the need for an integrated sport program has been stressed—one that includes the intercollegiate (or interscholastic), intramural, and instructional components. In spite of the overall advantages of such a program, one limitation should be noted with respect to motivation. Those who work primarily in intramural sport or sport instruction do not share the same built-in advantage of the coach in directing an activity that has the team success as the motivating force. Furthermore, in terms of Maslow's fourth level of needs, the recognition and status are almost exclusively with the intercollegiate or interscholastic program. Staff members who work in the intramural or instructional components have to be more intrinsically motivated in order to be effective in their work.

Another factor also bears on motivation for work in these areas of the total program. Rather frequently we find a coach who also has responsibilities for intramural sport or sport instruction or both. The very nature of the situation points to the fact that he or she is likely to be much more highly motivated to the task of coaching the team. The built-in factors associated with winning, success, recognition, and status again prevail. In such cases, the director will have to make a special effort to motivate toward total program development. It also appears that the only realistic way of dong this is to establish appropriate performance standards that extend to the intramural and instructional components. This brings the director into the controlling function of management. Once again we note the close connection among the various managerial functions.

Line and Staff Personnel. From a motivational perspective, the situation with regard to line-staff differentiation is not unlike that involving differences among the intercollegiate, intramural, and interscholastic components. The staff personnel are also outside the main flow of the motivational thrust in college sport. In most cases, they hold those positions that are the least visible within the department. They also have the general mission of providing support services for the various aspects of the total program. Much of the motivation will again have to be of an intrinsic nature. Appropriate performance standards again offer the key to any external efforts at motivation. Some extrinsic motivation can result from identification with the success of the various teams. However, administrators must do whatever they can to establish performance standards that are aimed at the welfare of the total program.

Major and Minor Sports. In the final analysis, the issue of major and minor sports may be the most critical motivational problem in school and college sport. The "second-class citizen" syndrome seems to be particularly evident in this regard. The theoretical proposition is to suggest that there are no minor sports—that they all should operate on an equal basis. In some settings, that may be true. However, in the cold light of reality, one would have to be an ostrich to ignore the basic differentiation between those sports that are tied in with extensive gate receipts per se. The mere popularity of school and college football and basketball points to a different category of sport. Obviously, in certin sections of the country, ice hockey has to be included in that category.

In spite of any tacit recognition of these facts, any coach is likely to feel that his or her sport deserves a more legitimate "place in the sun." This is a natural reaction on the part of every person who is dedicated to a particular program. The total motivational problem in school and college sport departments is heightened in those situations in which there is even further differentiation among the so-called minor sports. One or more of these sports may become particularly popular at a given institution owing to local or regional interest or for other reasons that are not totally explainable. This can be the case in spite of what is or is not done by the coaches in the other sports.

Thus, it is not at all unusual to find a hierarchy of sports within the total program in either a school or college. What does this mean in terms of any efforts at motivation? To begin with, there must be a realistic appraisal of the objective for each aspect of the program or, in other words, for each sport. This brings us back to the potential significance of MBO. Beyond that, the only real hope lies in the establishment of appropriate performance standards and an equitable reward system. At best, this particular feature of school and college sport is likely to test the most capable administrator in carrying out the directing function.

Former Coaches on the Staff. Earlier reference was made to the relatively high turnover of coaches. Much of this can be attributed to external pressures or the pure demands on the time and energy of a coach or both. Regardless of the reasons, the coaching turnover is a fact of life in school and college sport. As a result of tenure, longevity, and other reasons, a certain number of these former coaches remain on or in the department in another capacity. Whenever this occurs, another motivational problem looms on the horizon unless the talents of the coach can be used in some other meaningful capacity. We noted earlier that coaches are likely to have received considerable reinforcement in terms of Maslow's fourth level of needs. It's a different ball game when the coaching days have ended. From the standpoint of the department and the former coach, nothing can be more detrimental than having him or her shoved off into a corner. As with the challenge of coping with major and minor sports, the management task will not be easy in this case. But the mutual search for appropriate redirection in assignment must continue.

Academic Versus Nonacademic Appointments. At the college level, the sport or athletic department tends to be one of the few units on campus that includes both academic and nonacademic appointments. This is not true of all college athletic departments, but the dual system of appointment (with and without academic rank) is quite prevalent. Where it exists, another motivational problem may arise. This area may also contribute to the idea of "second-class citizens." In this case, much will depend on the attitude that is established within the department. There are coaches who are relatively indifferent about the need for academic rank. They are content to do what they do without being concerned about this form of recognition. Again, so much will depend on the reward system. If the possibilities for reward are clearly slanted in favor of academic rank, a motivational problem may be in the making. The key here is that all those with similar responsibilities must be given equal opportunity to achieve academic rank when it is considered to be applicable to the sport program. Obviously, this is no longer one of the special concern areas when academic rank is not factored into the college sport structure.

Facilities. There is at least one other area that can be earmarked as a special concern in attempting to motivate those who work in a school or college sport program. The truth of the matter is that facilities can be a motivational problem or asset in almost any organization. However, the situation tends to be heightened in sport programs owing to the unique dependence on facilities. A fine facility can be a most contributing factor to program development. Likewise, an inadequate facility can stand in the way of any other factors that may be on the positive side in developing the program.

It is natural to expect that coaches and instructors will be very inclined to make two kinds of comparisons with respect to their facility. They will make external comparisons with other school or college facilities for their sport. Internally, they will be assessing the facilities for the other sports in the total program. Right or wrong, the quality of the facility is usually marked as an indicator of program support.

From a motivational standpoint, the key consideration for management is to establish individual program objectives that are realistic within the facility limitation. The director should also be conscious of all interests and communicate extensively in facility planning. Occasionally, one notes fine programs that develop in spite of an adequate or above average facility. That may become a positive motivational factor in itself. However, such exceptions cannot be used as a general guide in attempting to motivate coaches and instructors wherever they are employed.

COORDINATION

Basically, coordination is the process of bringing a group into common action. This immediately prompts attention to the fact that communication is a key factor in all efforts at coordination. Without the communication, any common action is likely to be more by chance than design. However, before proceeding with any meaningful consideration of coordination as a managerial function, it is important to recognize that a group is not a group and communication is not communication. That means that groups differ considerably in their nature, and communication occurs in various ways. Thus, there is no simple formula for effective coordination. It can probably be best approached by understanding the parameters involving groups and communication.

One way to understand a group is to note the tasks that are performed by the various members of the group. Stech and Ratliffe (1976) note that five dimensions are involved in analyzing group functioning from a task perspective.

1. Is the task *simple* or *complex?*
2. Does the task involve *conjunctive* or *disjunctive* efforts?
3. Is the task *routine* or a *new* program?
4. Is the group in *control* of most of the factors involved in the task, or does the program involve *uncertainty* and high *risk?*
5. Does the task involve *information processing* or taking *action?* (p. 38.)

Further insight into the nature of a group is added through the authors' discussion of group atmosphere. They note that a group can be categorized on "a stratification versus equal participation" dimension as well as the dimension of being "close versus distant" (pp. 90–91). The two dimensions yield a quadrant in which we note that "some groups are stratified but close; other groups may be stratified yet distant; it is also possible to have groups that are equal but distant; equal and close groups are also possible" (p. 92). A stratified group is "regulated, restricted, closed, controlled, one-way, impersonal." An equal group is "participatory, free, open, interactive, personal." A distant group is "risky, conflictual, competitive, critical." Finally, a close group is "trusting, friendly, supportive, cooperative, cohesive" (p. 91). When we look at various groups involved with school and college sport programs in that context, it becomes apparent that by and large there is a mixture of stratified-close groups and stratified-distant groups. The "equal dimension is not as evident. This, in turn, will have a definite bearing on the process of coordination.

That also brings us to a consideration of the various ways in which communication takes place in a school or college sport program. To begin with, there is always the most basic distinction between formal and informal communication. The "grapevine" is a particular manifestation of the latter type. Communication also varies according to its proprietary or confidential nature, as contrasted with open communication. With respect to both of these contrasts, there is communication within the total program, between units in the program, and outside the program.

The relative effectiveness of the coordinating effort will thus initially depend on the selection of the appropriate mode of communication to meet the task demands of the total group as well as the various subgroups. In addition, an assessment of the groups atmosphere will influence the process of coordination. It seems appropriate to analyze school and college sport programs within that threefold context: tasks, atmosphere, and communication.

Tasks in School and College Sport

Throughout the text we have called attention to the relatively unique nature of a school or college sport program in that in one respect it is actually a whole series of programs, involving the various sport teams. This immediately calls attention to the basic disjunctive effort of the total group. However, under that disjunctive structure one finds a mixture of activities that are very much on the conjunctive side of the ledger. The functioning of the team is the prime example. However, the following are also classic cases of conjunctive efforts in sport programs that call for a different kind of coordination.

Game management.

Facilities planning, scheduling, and control.

Travel arrangements.

Public relations.

Somewhat the same mixture applies to the distinction between simplicity versus complexity of group tasks. From one standpont, the task is quite straightforward—to coach the team, teach the sport, manage the ticket sales, or provide the athletes with injury care. However, any coach of a major team sport is acutely aware of the complexities in coaching that team. Game management and the other conjunctive efforts noted earlier serve only to reinforce the complexity for the school or college sport group.

Is the task of managing a sport program routine or new? That, too, represents an interesting, but complicated, question in the coordinating effort. The natural inclination might be to approach this consideration with the feeling that one is dealing with a fairly routine program. However, it doesn't take long to recognize that every season is very different for every sport. This is aside from the addition of new sports or the dropping of sports from the program. Recent modifications in school and college sport programs only serve to dramatize the new quality. Any thoughts about the routine nature tend to fade in the shadows of tradition. More about that will be said in terms of managing change.

In terms of control versus uncertainty, the sport director is beyond a doubt managing a group that is well toward the uncertainty side of the continuum. The hazard involving the won-lost record is the pivotal concern. But, in addition, the entire enterprise is replete with uncertainty. Sport injuries and the extreme dependence on the weather are two other classic examples. Beyond that, the very existence of programs is frequently threatened by the uncertainties involving financial support.

The final group task variable is also most clear-cut. First and foremost, the school or college sport program is an arena for action. Any information processing is likely to be only of a supportive nature. This factor is a prime determinant with respect to the entire coordination effort. There is often little time for deliberation.

Any committee work that does exist is more than likely to be of an ad hoc nature to cope with an action concern. Furthermore, the action component is heightened by the multifarious nature of the action. Sport seasons overlap; one game follows another in rapid sequence; teams and athletes move in and out of the tournament picture. All this provides a great test in the process of coordination.

The Group Atmosphere in School and College Sport

Earlier it was suggested that the school and college sport groups tend to be either of a "stratified-close" or "stratified-distant" nature. However, such an assertion requires clarification and certain qualifiers.

The central, stratified dimension stems primarily from the basic functioning of a team and its coach. By and large the team structure is a closely regulated environment. Part of this may be attributed merely to tradition. Yet further consideration is likely to yield a firmer rationale. Sport is a rule-bound activity. Therefore, in the simplest terms, the athlete is taught to play according to the rules. With that basic start, the control factor emerges primarily in the strategy for preparing for the game and the tactics of playing the game. It is also very much of a closed environment in that everything is focused on the contest and the preparation for that contest. The "closed practice session" merely epitomizes the stratified nature of the sport group. It is not at all surprising that the coach and the athletes have typically come to the mutual understanding that the coach "calls the shots"; the very nature of the sport is geared in that direction.

When we move beyond the sport team per se, we find that the stratified atmosphere tends to permeate the entire sport or athletic program. The coach is likely to be most comfortable working in a broader environment that is somewhat parallel to the closed, controlled, one-way environment of his or her team. Acceptance of the stratification even extends somewhat to the student body at large in their contacts with the sport program. An example here is that it is not at all uncommon for students in a class to address the sport instructor as "coach," regardless of whether he or she actually works in that capacity.

This is not to suggest that everything involving coordination in the sport program is or has to be of a stratified nature. Quite obviously, the very concept of intramural sport is couched in a participatory, free, open, interactive, and personal environment. When it comes to coordinating the total program, adjustments will have to be made to maintain the basic intent of intramural sport. It's also quite probable that even the interscholastic or intercollegiate program should be less stratified than is frequently found to be the case.

Today the need for some degree of stratification in the sport program is even being felt from another perspective. Economic inflation points to steps in that direction. Tully (1979) made this point in discussing the impact of inflation on athletic facilities planning and project success.

Inflation is a rate. If you cannot change the rate, change the time. Accelerate. The impact of inflation can be blunted by aggressive project leadership in project planning, together with an awareness of the changing rules.

Project success in this context means rational decisions made in motion without stopping to consider all options. Only those options that seem urgent. The cost of the stop may far exceed the benefit gained by the careful option study. This is analogous to a ball carrier making a decision in motion. Stopping to consider his options would cost him his gain. . . .

It is a difficult task, but your administrators must be constantly reminded of the impact of delay; the game rules have changed. When the project goes into committee, try to get the committee reduced to one person. If not one person, select a leader who is aggressive, who will set decision making target dates and keep them (pp. 25–26).

Tully's remarks were initially presented to a group of college athletic directors. It would seem that they should have little difficulty in making the transfer in their mind from the stratified dimension of the sport team to the need to cope with inflation in a similar vein.

The close versus distant dimension is one of the most critical considerations in any effort at coordination. In many situations, the athletic or sport director is managing an environment that is distinctly risky, conflictual, competitive, or critical. This side of the group atmosphere spectrum may be manifested in any one of several ways. To begin with, there is usually some form of competition among the various sport teams for financial resources and other forms of support. For example, the soccer team may well feel that it is not receiving its share of support owing to the overpowering presence of the football team. Likewise, there may be conflict between the men's and women's programs. It is not at all uncommon to hear criticism from the intramural and instructional components that they are being ''short-changed'' owing to the emphasis that is placed on the intercollegiate program. These are a few of the more common ways in which the ''distant'' group atmosphere permeates school or college sport.

On the other hand, the ''close'' group dimension may also be evident in varying degrees. Within a sport there is usually some evidence of the close quality. However, the research shows that successful teams may be either quite close or relatively distant in their relationships. The same may be said for those teams that are less successful. Nevertheless, in the final analysis there remains a tendency to be supportive within the sport, as contrasted with external cooperation. At times and in certain situations, the close characteristic may extend to the sport program as a whole. This is likely to be most evident when there is a need to justify the status of the total program in comparison with other units on campus. Regardless of the balance in the distant-close dimension in any given institution, it is obvious that the most appropriate means of communication must be selected at least in part from that perspective.

Communication

We began our discussion of the coordination aspect of the directing function by noting that communication is the key. However, it should now be apparent that effective communication will very much depend on the insight in assessing the group atmosphere and the tasks to be performed. Although each situation will be different owing to the personalities involved, the following ideas may serve as general guidelines for effective communication in many school or college sport programs.

Departmental meetings should be kept to a minimum, both in terms of frequency and length. History and English professors (among others) may take satisfaction in extended discussions about departmental affairs. This is much less likely to be the case with respect to coaches and other personnel in the sport program. Part of this may be attributed to the dominant action aspect of the group tasks. In essence, often there is little time for deliberation. Any natural reaction against extensive and prolonged departmental meetings is reinforced by the generally stratified dimension of the sport group. In many cases, the staff is waiting for the answers; they are not there to solve problems. This is not to say that there is no place for meetings in a sport program. A certain number of meetings are necessary and important in almost any program. However, when they are held, they should be action-oriented. There should be a carefully planned, straightforward agenda that should be followed as closely as possible. By and large these departmental meetings should be used as a medium for establishing policies as well as considering other important matters that cut across the total program.

A program handbook can be a most useful means of communicating in the context of school or college sport. Part of the need for a handbook stems from the basic, disjunctive nature of program tasks. In particular, the handbook should be used to disseminate a core of information that is of mutual concern. Any established policies should be included in the handbook. It can also be used to solidify other procedural information related to game management, travel, and public relations, as well as personnel procedures. In most cases, it is necessary to revise such a handbook on a yearly basis.

Much of the communicating in a school or college sport program will be done on a one-to-one basis. The disjunctive nature of the tasks again points in this direction. Exactly how this is carried out will depend on a perceptive assessment of the "close-distant" group dimension, which was discussed earlier in this chapter. In the larger programs, an effective reporting system is also critical in facilitating this kind of communication. More about that will be said when we examine the controlling function.

There may be a feeling that one-to-one relationships are somewhat in opposition to the whole idea of coordination. After all, we began our discussion of this topic by noting that coordination is the process of bringing a group into common action. The key is to schedule only those meetings that are appropriate, whether they involve the entire staff or subgroups within the total program. Routine business is conducted on the one-to-one basis. When properly handled, that too can be a facilitator of common action.

MANAGING DIFFERENCES

Every experienced administrator has learned that no situation is the same for all those who work in the organization. Two principal sources of variables can be noted. The first is the people who are involved. Every individual approaches the situation with his or her own blend of background, abilities, and attitudes. To that is added the second set of variables, involving the tasks that are performed by the members of the organization. These composite differences are very evident in school and college sport programs. Most of the major areas of difference have been alluded to throughout this book. However, some of these differences should be analyzed in greater detail, particularly in terms of how they influence the directing function.

Men and Women

The topic of men and women is paramount and pervasive with respect to two aspects of the directing function, managing differences and managing change. We will consider it here with the understanding that it is equally significant in terms of managing change. The changes that have taken place in sport programs for women during the past 10 years are most evident. By and large, these changes have reinforced the differences that are involved in providing an appropriate sport program for both men and women. The differences are manifested in all the principal variables: background, abilities; attitudes, and tasks.

It is well known that sport has traditionally been first and foremost a male domain. In fact, it was one of the most distinguishable areas of male domination. Gilbert and Williamson (1973) expressed the situation most succinctly.

> There may be worse (more socially serious) forms of prejudice in the United States, but there is no sharper example of discrimination today than that which operates against girls and women who take part in competitive sports, wish to take part, or might wish to if society did not scorn such endeavors. No matter what her age, education, race, talent, residence or riches, the female's right to play is severly restricted. The funds, facilities, coaching, rewards and honors allotted women are grossly inferior to those granted men. In many places absolutely no support is given to women's athletics, and females are barred by law, regulation, tradition or the hostility of males from sharing athletic resources and pleasures. A female who persists in her athletic interests, despite the handicaps and discouragements, is not likely to be congratulated on her sporting desire or grit. She is more apt to be subjected to social and psychological pressures, the effect of which is to cast doubt on her morals, sanity and womanhood (pp. 88, 90).

Although that statement would no longer be accurate today, it is obvious that differences continue to exist. The background differences are the most apparent. Some of these are of a philosophical nature and can be seen in the recent conflict between the NCAA and the AIAW.

Differences between the sport abilities of men and women also tend to be largely of an experimental nature. As a group, the women do not begin to have the type of experience that is found among most of the male candidates for the various coaching and staff positions. The reason for this is obvious: a 1973 *Sports Illustrated* article provides the answer. Until recent years, women's experience was largely limited to the field of physical education, where they did little or no coaching and by and large did not work in promotion, sports information, and the business aspects of sport. Although qualified women coaches are not being attracted from various academic backgrounds, they still fall far short of having the cumulative coaching experience found among the men. At the same time, the number of available coaching positions for women has increased considerably. The net result is that the market condition for male candidates is very different from that of the women. From the management perspective, this results in an assessment of different sets of credentials. Needless to say, this has a direct bearing on the staffing and controlling functions as well as the directing function.

Being what they are, attitudinal differences are more difficult to pinpoint. Nevertheless, this still represents a third area of difference between men and women in sport, which is undergirded by the experiental factor. Parkhouse and Lapin (1980, pp. 5–8) list 23 inadequacies that are common to many women in management. The inadequacies run a range from those that are action-oriented to those that are more in the attitudinal vein. The following appear to be in the latter category.

1. Women want to be liked.
2. Women believe they are inferior managers.
3. Women feel that they cannot trust anyone else to do the job right.
4. Women are not willing to take risks.
5. Women do not understand the concept of the inner circle and the related game of politics.
6. Women view their jobs as just a way to make a living.
7. Women are reluctant to get involved.

Although probably any one or more of the seven could be off-target in the assessment of women's attitudes, collectively they represent a point for consideration in carrying out the directing function in school and college sport. The women who work in these programs have assumed a new role. They are almost certain to bring with them attitudes that have been shaped from years of being in a subordinate position. The manager who fails to recognize this large area of difference is almost certain to encounter some difficulty in directing the program.

Finally, all the differences between men and women cited earlier clearly point in one direction—the task differential. In general, the women are involved in building new programs whereas the men are working in the context of established programs. The ramifications of this general differential are extensive. For the women, there is a new set of procedures to be learned. For the men, there is likely to be a need for modification of procedures that have been in existence for some time. Athletic scholarships represent a classic case in point. What are the most appropriate scholarship sports for women? Almost every major collegiate sport program has had to face that question during the past few years. How is that question tied in with the matter of revenue-producing sports? As a result, what changes will have to be made in the total athletic scholarship allocation for men? These are questions that only serve to dramatize the task differential.

The publicity dimension is another prime consideration when assessing the difference in task. Any new program requires considerable publicity if it is to have a legitimate opportunity to be recognized. Such a general need is heightened in the context of women's sport programs owing to the traditional tendency to overlook the fact that women can also compete in sport in a most meaningful kind of way. The challenge of the task here is to provide the most appropriate form of publicity for women's sport. What should be stressed? How should this be different from what is commonly advanced for the men's sport program? At the same time, there is an accompanying need to advance the idea that the men's sport program is not headed for decline as a result of Title IX and associated social changes.

In the final analysis, the task differential may appear in any one of several forms, but the key is to recognize that the men's sport program is not necessarily the prototype. Some objectives, policies, procedures, and actions may be most appropriate for both men and women in sport. Others will have to be tailored to meet the current needs of both sexes.

Among Sports

Even though this book is designed around the common denominator of sport, from another standpoint it is equally as important to recognize that sport is not sport. Many differences can be noted among the various sports. We have the revenue-producing sports and the nonrevenue sports, spectator sports and participant sports, team sports and individual sports, ball games and form sports, seasonal sports and year-round sports, popular sports and developing sports. Beyond that, football coaches and players are different from their counterparts in basketball. Each group, in turn, is different. We could continue with an extended listing of the various forms of differentiation among sports, but we hope that the point has been made. In essence, each sport has its own modus operandi.

How does one manage differences within this context? It is not an easy question to answer. Part of the answer is to be found in the disjunctive nature of the task that was discussed with respect to coordination. In other words, it is important to begin by understanding that certain of these differences are natural. Another part of the answer lies in the establishment of separate performance standards for each sport under the M.B.O. framework. That possibility will be explored in greater detail in the next chapter. In terms of more direct steps to manage differences among sports, it seems that the following questions have to be given some consideration.

1. What is the public image of the sport? By *public* is meant the entire constituency that is external to the actual conduct of the sport program. This would include students, parents, faculty, administrators, alumni, and the general public. The answer to the question posed is likely to be an important factor in determining the kind of support that is given to that particular sport. When this question is considered for each sport, quite a range of differences is almost certain to be found.

2. What types of athletes tend to be attracted to each sport? Just as a sport is not a sport, an athlete is not an athlete. Distinct differences can be noted among basketball playes, wrestlers, and tennis players. Much the same can be said for comparisons of athletes in other sports. Such differences arise from a composite of cultural, physical, and attitudinal factors. Those who manage school and college sport programs must recognize those differences and make the necessary adjustments in terms of effectively carrying out all of the managerial functions.

3. What are the special facilities and equipment needs for each sport? Although all sports tend to have a relatively unique dependence on facilities and equipment, vast differences are evident among the various sports. For example, soccer and gymnastics stand in sharp contrast in this regard. Gymnastics will rank high on the list of expenditures for equipment. Aside from gymnastics, all sports will show quite a range in terms of expenditures for equipment. Such differences have to be weighed against the relative popularity of each sport, as evidenced in the response to the first question noted earlier.

4. What is the overall competitive situation for each sport? This is an extremely important, but complicated, question involving several different considerations. If the school or college is a member of a conference or league, there may well be a vast difference in terms of the level of competition among the various sports that are sponsored by that conference. Some conferences are primarily known for basketball, golf, field hockey, or some other sport. In other cases, a conference may be particularly strong in two or more sports. When this situation exists, it is not reasonable to expect that the performance standard will be the same for each sport. In another situation, a sport team may have to travel relatively extensive distances in order to have a suitable schedule. With travel costs ranking high on the list of expenditures, this may be an important factor in making decisions about that sport. Once again, this factor has to be weighed against the first question posed earlier. While we are discussing travel costs, the number of players involved in travel also is a prime consideration. This factor adds considerably to the composite differences among sports. For example, it might mean that a school has to drop a baseball team in favor of retaining a tennis team. Some sports also have unusual arrangements in terms of tournaments for which they are eligible or the manner in which these tournaments are conducted. In other words, each sport tends to have its own kind of tournament structure.

When all these questions are considered, it is apparent that the modus operandi varies from sport to sport. The key to managing differences in this context is to know the peculiar demands of each sport and to make the necessary adjustments within the perspective of benefit for the total sport program. The director has to "get inside" each sport, so to speak. This may not be totally possible within a large program, but that brings us back to the importance of appropriate delegation in such an environment.

Instruction—Intramural—Intercollegiate (Interscholastic)

An integrated sport program (one involving all aspects of sport) points to another dimension of managing differences. Even though such integration seems highly desirable owing to the reason cited earlier, the differences must also be taken into account. As indicated throughout this work, the differences between the instructional and intramural components have typically been exaggerated through an artificial organizational division. The appointment of sport coordinators would help to alleviate some of the differences that are found in that regard.

The important consideration is to recognize and effectively manage the differences between the intercollegiate or interscholastic program and the sport program for the student body at large. These differences will be primarily manifested in the support for these programs, the motivation for working in them, and the reward system for the work that is performed. The motivational concerns stemming from this basic difference have been discussed earlier. There is no way in which an intramural sport program can expect or hope to achieve the kind of visibility that is associated with an intercollegiate program. That, in itself, poses no problem. However, any problems arise in the natural tendency to provide more support for what is most visible. This is the key consideration in terms of managing differences in this area. It also brings us back to a consideration of objectives for the total program. If the objectives tend to be in the direction of balanced intercollegiate and intramural participation, a special effort must be made to support the intramural component. By support is meant not only to financial support. Without that, of course, other problems involving differences will continue to exist. Beyond that, the intramural component (including instruction) requires daily attention from those who are responsible for the total sport program. If the intramural program continues to exist, but without due recognition, administrators have not begun to manage differences with respect to the total program.

MANAGING CHANGE

If there is a single aspect of directing that stands out from all the others, it is the managing of change. The basic reason for this is that change is largely external in its origin. In most cases, an organization needs to make internal changes to meet the demands of external changes. By contrast, those four aspects of directing that we have just considered are considerably more internalized. For the most part, delegation, motivation, coordination, and managing differences are intraorganizational concerns. Those who are in management positions must look beyond their program if they are to be successful in managing change. The natural inclination is to focus on internal affairs to the exclusion of external factors. It is also well known that many people tend to resist change. The net effect is that we find vast differences in the ability to manage change. When the ability is there, it tends to be one of the most distinguishing characteristics of effective management. It might be said that effective management of change epitomizes one's success in carrying out the directing function. In a sense, directing is providing direction. There can be little direction if administrators are not sensitive to those external conditions that indicate the need for change.

As one considers those external conditions that bear on school and college sport today, the need to manage change is more evident than at any time in recent history. It is not at all surprising to find that much of the need is financially based. Although changes often occur as a composite of several factors, finances invariably provide the precipitating agent to transfer thought to action. There are at least six areas that can be readily identified as major areas of change in school and college sport at the present time. Each of these will be considered in some detail because the total implications for management are extensive.

Financial Limitations

As noted earlier, the place to start is at financial limitations because all the other changing conditions have some kind of relationship to finances. Inflation, unemployment, and the declining birth rate are the chief factors in reducing the institutional support for school and college sport programs. These more basic factors have also resulted in changing attitudes about the support for such programs. In a time of severe financial limitation, it is not surprising that many educators readily turn to the sport program as a place to begin the cutback. Actually, it becomes a two-edged sword. On the one hand, sport can be viewed as being outside the mainstream of educational life and thus is a target for an early reduction in funds. On the other side of the picture, the visibility and general popularity of sport make it a useful tool in the attempt to gain more public support for the total educational program. If the football program is dropped, the taxpayers will probably really begin to pay attention to the financial plight of the school. By contrast, the elimination of biology courses might go relatively unnoticed. Those who manage school and college sport programs must constantly be aware of the tenuous situation resulting from the educational assessment of sport and the public enthusiasm for sport.

Much of the attention to the financial limitations has resulted from state legislation that calls for a reduction in property taxes. Naturally, the public schools have been the institutions that have been most threatened by such legislation, but the messages have been clear for the entire educational sector. Variances can be noted in the different regions of the country and from state to state, but the general impact is more or less nationwide. The legislation in California and Massachusetts particularly served to focus on the public intent for reduced funding for school programs. However, some 20 states have pending legislation of a similar nature.

California sounded the warning with its highly publicized so-called Proposition 13. This legislation called for a 57 percent cut in property taxes as of July 1, 1978. The effects of this legislation have not been nearly as devastating as initially feared, but it does provide dramatic evidence of the need to manage change in school sport programs. It also clearly shows how external change brings about the necessary internal changes. Soon after Proposition 13 went into effect, Bronzan (1978b) looked in the positive direction with respect to the resulting changes in sport programs.

> Some athletic directors and physical educators believe that no good will result and that harm may occur. Many other athletic directors, coaches, and physical educators believe that Proposition 13 will serve to motivate schools and colleges to take inventory of their operating philosophies, policies, programs, and practices. This self-evaluation will serve as a catharsis. Outdated elements will be cast aside or changed; those policies, programs, and practices that remain will be improved to meet current and future needs. Improved program content, better utilization of personnel, elimination of wasted funds, more selective equipment and supply purchases, increased attention to maintenance and issue of equipment, coordinated planning of sport schedules so as to allow more than one team and male and female teams to share transportation, and increased efforts to provide every student with positive athletic and physical education experiences. . . .

> In summation, when an existing program is threatened with curtailment or termination, often this serves to move one to reexamine and re-evaluate existing conditions. For this reason alone, the adoption of Proposition 13 may well prove to be a constructive, rather than destructive measure for the interscholastic and community college athletic and physical education programs in California (p. 19).

In an interview some three years later, California's superintendent of public instruction, Wilson Riles, noted the traumatic effects of Proposition 13. He was quick to point out that the public schools in that state had managed to survive only because the state had increased its support for the local schools from about 40 percent to 70 percent. This could be done only because of a surplus in the state treasury, and that was now running out. Much as Bronzan did, he stressed the need for a strong philosophical base for sport programs. "A lot of people say interscholastic athletics have been overemphasized. The problem is that intramural sports have been underemphasized. We need to provide more opportunities for participation" (*Athletic Purchasing and Facilities*, May 1981, p. 12). In terms of the approach that is taken in this text, this is exactly why we need a well-planned, integrated sport program for the schools and colleges.

The changes brought about by reduction in property taxes in Massachusetts are more recent. Effective July 1, 1981, the so-called Proposition 2½, in essence, required that local property taxes would be limited to no more than 2½ percent of assessed value, compared to the 6 to 8 percent level that was the rate in many communities. In that state, the reaction also demonstrates differences in the ability to cope with change, as shown in this excerpt from *Athletic Purchasing and Facilities* (July, 1981).

> Naturally, public officials across the country are keeping a close watch on the situation in Massachusetts, much as they did when California's Proposition 13 was passed several years ago. With the apparent "taxpayer revolt" intensifying across the country, many of them realize that their state could be the next to pass a drastic measure affecting state support of municipal services, including schools.
>
> In Massachusetts, there is a wide range of reaction to Proposition 2½ among administrators of school athletic and municipal recreation programs. Feelings range from predictions of gloom and doom, resignation and if that's what the taxpayers want, that is what they'll get to a "roll-up-the-sleeves-and-let's-get-to-work" attitude. . . .
>
> But if there's anything positive to come out of their experience, it's the example that Proposition 2½ can give to the rest of the nation—that the era of the tax revolt is upon us, and the traditional sources of funding for school athletics and municipal recreation programs simply can no longer be relied upon.
>
> It's the schools and park systems that recognize this fact and begin actively seeking alternate means of financing and operating their programs that are going to be healthy in the long run (pp. 44, 47).

Numerous examples could be cited in terms of the various ways in which schools and colleges are beginning to make the changes in terms of financing and operating to meet the financial limitations from normal budget sources. At the college level in the private sector, Babson College offers a good example of what can be done in this regard. A few years ago that small college built a multi-use sport facility, which was jointly financed by the college and small private investors. The investors were local sport enthusiasts who were also interested in serving the needs of the community. They also realized that the Babson Recreation Center offered moneymaking potential. The idea was generated through the search for a location to build a hockey rink in Wellesley. It resulted in an athletic complex for Babson "which includes eight indoor tennis courts, a 200' by 85' ice hockey rink with seating capacity of 1500, men's and women's locker rooms, saunas, pro-shops, a snack bar, a first aid room, a nursery, and waiting rooms" (Bauman, 1978, p. 63). Babson would not have such a facility were it not for the fact that someone was willing and able to manage change.

On the other side of the ledger, the financial limitations also point to the need for innovation in saving as well as financing. As an example here, Bronzan (1978a) offers appropriate advice on how equipment supervisors, either full- or part-time, can also be used at the high school level. Although the equipment supervisor has typically been employed at the college level, high schools have been slow in moving in that direction. Bronzan estimates that the decrease in expenses resulting from loss of equipment through improper care, damage, and theft would more than cover the salary for a full- or part-time supervisor, depending on the size of the school program.

The examples that have been given should be sufficient to make the point that the financial situation is the logical place to begin when one is to be effective in managing change. Most of the other major changes in school and college sport today are related to it in one way or another. The link with the area of promotion and fund raising is most evident.

Promotion and Fund Raising

Aside from the changes involved in the development of women's sport programs, it is safe to say that no other aspect of school and college sport has been so much affected by change as that involving the broad area of promotion and fund raising. These changes are evident in terms of both the scope and the depth of the enterprise. Either directly or indirectly, colleges have been promoting their sport programs for many years. The very act of selling tickets is in itself a form of promotion. However, it is only within the past 10 years that colleges have significantly advanced their promotional efforts beyond the ticket realm per se. Selling tickets is still the name of the game in spectator sport, but the associated merchandising is now also an integral part of many promotional efforts in college sport. We also note some significant changes in terms of how college programs have proceeded in increasing their ticket sales.

Don Canham, the athletic director at the University of Michigan, has been one of the leaders in the multifaceted promotion of college sport. The impetus was provided through the use of direct mail to increase ticket sales. His assistant athletic director, Will Perry (1981), describes in part how this was accomplished.

The University of Michigan was a pioneer in the massive, direct mailing of athletic ticket brochures. In 1972, Michigan sent 500,000 brochures to special mailing lists and increased the mailing to one million in 1973. Average attendence rose from the 70,000s to 80,000 and 90,000 and finally to sellouts. Despite the success of the program, Athletic Director Don Canham did not neglect the special markets, even though the emphasis on a seven-county area contributed keenly to Michigan's steady rise in attendance.

Also in the early 1970's, a special mailing went to high schools and elementary schools throughout Michigan, northern Ohio and northeast Indiana as part of youth ticket plan. At its peak, the youth ticket plan was bringing 70,000 youngsters annually into the 101,701-seat Michigan Stadium to watch wolverine football, which was exactly what Canham had planned. . . .

Canham recalled meeting a group of young adults one Saturday after a football game. "They all had season tickets now, but two of them said they had first attended Michigan football games with their high school groups and then just kept coming." Canham said, "I think that proves a point about promoting youth ticket sales." (p. 26).

Michigan's promotion of athletics does not stop with football ticket sales. Canham and his staff have also been leaders in the total merchandising effort. Palmisano (1980), the director of promotions, marketing, and special events, identifies both the usual and unusual items that are sold with the mark of Michigan Athletics. These include: T-shirts, sweatshirts, caps, glasses, cups, bumper stickers, oil paintings, rugs, clocks, western wear, wallets, key chains, neckties, belt buckles, sport bags, scarves, mittens, tams, beach towels, playing cards, Christmas ornaments, cloth dinner napkins, and sports dolls dressed in the Michigan uniform. The list is not inclusive, but it should convey the idea regarding the scope of the marketing enterprise. They are constantly introducing new items and changing those that have been previously sold. Obviously, not every college athletic department would choose to get involved with such an extensive merchandising effort. However, the principle should be clear: in times of financial restraint, promotion must extend beyond ticket sales.

The Univeristy of Maryland has also been one of the leaders among those institutions that are now pursuing special fund raising efforts for support of athletic programs. Tom Fields (1980), the executive director of Maryland's Terrapin Club, stresses the importance of a positive attitude in meeting the challenge: "The first requirement in fund-raising is attitude. Don't listen to the negative person. Remind yourself that it can be done. There's not an institution in the country where you cannot develop a support base, fund raising program adapted to your particular needs and circumstances" (p. 20). Fields's promotional design is an extension of the direct mail idea. Maryland places the emphasis on personalized mail and the follow-up personal contact. It is constantly adding to its list of donors through an extension of the prospect list. In turn, each donor receives about 35 letters a year showing appreciation for support of the program. Through such efforts, the Terrapin Club support for Maryland athletics now amounts to more than $1 million a year.

Another aspect of sport promotion is that involving special efforts to increase ticket sales for individual games. Jane Zailskas (1982) was formerly the sport promotion director for Boston College, and she is now a consultant in sport marketing and promotion for school and college programs. She notes that many programs fall short in the ideal of selling most of their tickets to season ticket holders. In the effort to fill the stadium, the answer may be found in special promotions for individual games. High school band days, youth football clinics, family days, scouts day, and a day to honor players from nearby communities are among the possibilities cited by Zailskas. She also points out how local merchants can be effectively tied into the promotional effort through advertising and by serving as ticket outlets.

The extent of some of the recent developments in sport promotion and fund raising is indicated to some extent in the series of articles that appeared in the March 1981 issue of *Athletic Purchasing and Facilities*. A successful high school booster club, promoting girls' sports, and working with "corporate partners" all point to the extensive nature of the promotional thrust.

The idea of booster clubs certainly is not new. As with ticket sales, booster clubs have been around for a long time. What is new is the scope and depth of booster club activity. That also calls attention to the need for careful control in booster club activity. However, more about that will be said when we examine the controlling function in school and college sport. The need for fuller development of high school sport booster clubs is particularly indicated owing to the financial limitations resulting from reduced property tax support, as noted earlier in this chapter. The *Athletic Purchasing and Facilities* article examines some of the ingredients in a successful high school booster club. The J-Hawk Booster Club in Urbandale, Iowa, was offered as an excellent example of what can be done to meet the challenge of change in support of high school sport programs. The keys there are noted to be membership, organization, and activities. As part of the latter, the Urbandale Booster Club has been responsible for hosting more than 50 invitational tournaments per year. Benefits, in terms of admissions and concessions, have aided considerably in the total support to the school's sport program.

The state of Iowa is also used as an example of what can be done to promote girls' sports. Although Iowa has an advantage in this regard owing to the advanced status of its sport programs for girls, the executive secretary of the Iowa Girls High School Athletic Union, Wayne Cooley, noted that it still requires work to maintain that status. Among his suggestions are the development of coaches followed by the development of players, original writing by getting the information from the school to the media, reduced admission for girls' sports, and high-quality invitational tournaments. In spite of the relatively unique situation involving girls' sports in Iowa, it is evident that some successful elements there can be used to meet the demands of changing conditions in girls' and women's sport throughout the nation.

The "corporate partner" dimension of sport promotion involves working with businesses to generate added revenue for the program. This might be through advertising, contribution to a building fund or other special fund, or sponsorship of various other activities. Marlene Anderson is a promotion director for a large financial institution. She offers numerous examples of how sport programs can come up with unusual ideas to assist in the promotional cause. Here is an example: "In addition to seeking sponsors for your athletic trophies and awards, try to sell the centers of the tables at the team banquet. For a donation, a sponsor can have decorations that signify his company placed at the center of each table. 'The center of the table is sitting there anyway,' says Anderson, 'Why not get $150 from it' " (*Athletic Purchasing and Facilities,* March 1981, p. 26).

At the college level, special factors in promoting sport programs for women have also been considered. Lopiano (1980) analyzed both the realities and the potentials in "selling women's athletics." She stresses an idea that is very similar to that advanced by Cooley with respect to the promotion of girls' sport at the high school level. The first step is to establish program credibility; in other words, there must be something to sell. Lopiano also notes the differences involved in the tactics for promoting underdeveloped sports as contrasted with the established sport programs. Her four suggestions for underdeveloped sports are particularly indicative of how one might manage change in the context of a large program:

1. Establish a support group for each sport.
2. Hosting one major annual event to highlight each sport.
   (would probably be outside of national caliber.)
3. Hosting a minimum of one national championship a year. (For recruiting and developing public interest.)
4. Highlight individual athletes as opposed to the entire team (p. 10).

The advice that is offered by Lopiano points to another dimension that should not be overlooked with respect to the total effort of promoting school and college sport programs. Thus far, we have more or less integrated the ideas of promotion and fund raising. The latter is actually a subset of the former. Promotion is indeed a much broader concept. Much of the promotional effort is directed toward the raising of funds, but we also promote to gain support for the program in various other ways. The underdeveloped sports and the nonrevenue sports both reflect the need for an extension in the promotional design.

Michigan's Palmisano (1982) also presents some useful ideas for "developing an overall promotions program for an individual 'non-revenue' sport." He suggests the following: (1) get a theme, (2) develop a group following, (3) recognition day, (4) special clubs, and (5) alumni events (p. 84). The idea of the support group is perhaps the most common denominator in all the thoughts about promotion. This is particularly applicable to the nonrevenue sports because the support has to be developed through means that are outside the normal promotional thrust. It is relatively easy to gain support for the winner in the popular team sports. By contrast, support for the swimming team or softball team will require a special twist, something innovative.

Before leaving the general topic of promotion and fund raising, one other development should be noted. Those who seek further guidance in meeting this element of change can now benefit through membership in the recently formed National Association of Athletic Marketing and Development Directors (NAAMDD). Also, sports promotion clinics have been sponsored by the University of Michigan at various sites in the United States during the past few years. At these clinics one can receive up-to-date information from the national leaders in sport promotion who are up front in meeting the needs for sport programs in the 1980s.

Part-Time Coaches

Another area of change in school and college sport that is clearly financially based involves part-time coaches. The number one reason why part-time coaches are being employed in increasing numbers is that schools and colleges lack the resources to employ the desired number of full-time coaches. This is due in part to the results of Title IX, but beyond that the broader financial picture has forced the change in this direction. At the high school level, at least two other factors lie behind the change. Declining school enrollments have resulted in a reduction of the teaching staff. At the same time, the need for coahes has risen owing to the overall increase in sport participation by boys and girls. Also, there is evidence of a growing tendency among staff members to give up their coaching duties while retaining their teaching positions. The net effect is that administrators now must be prepared to manage change as it relates to the staffing function. What can be done to meet the challenge in this area of change?

Before we attempt to answer that question, it is important to begin by recognizing that there are several dimensions to this total problem that currently faces many administrators. In the simplest terms, there are part-time coahces, and then there are part-time coaches. Not all part-time coaches fall into the same category. Much of the recent concern has focused on the need to employ coaches from outside the school system—businesspeople, salespeople, fire fighters, homemakers, and so on. Some of those people may have the professional qualifications; others lack the educational background that is generally sought or required in a school system. Within the school system, we also find a whole assortment of part-time coaches with varying kinds of qualifications. Most of these are classroom teachers who are also involved in coaching. That type of part-time coach has been in existence for a long time. One possibility for change is to make even fuller and more effective use of the classroom teacher. More about that will be said later.

The difference between the situation in the schools and that in the colleges also has to be noted. By and large, part-time coaching is more of a school problem than a college problem. There are several reasons for this. A much larger number of people aspire to coach at the college level. Consequently, many well-qualified applicants for college positions will accept a part-time position in order to "get their foot in the door." Also, at the high school level many of the coaching resignations occur among physical educators; there tends to be less of this at the college level. Colleges are also not nearly as bound by state legislation with respect to who is qualified to coach; this, of course, is particularly true of private colleges. Many of the state universities are also in the advantageous position of being able to employ relatively well-qualified graduate students in the part-time coaching positions. All of this makes the total situation quite different in schools and colleges. Nevertheless, colleges must also be prepared to make the necessary adjustments in the management of a program with several part-time coaches.

Part of the answer for the schools may be found in generating more interest in and greater attention to coaching certification. However, much of that is outside the direct control of any given school system. State legislation and the development of additional academic programs in coaching certification or coaching minors or both are the keys in that direction. From the school perspective, more extensive lobbying efforts may be of the most assistance. There is a fair bit of irony here resulting from certification as it affects the physical education–coaching relationship. Along with other teaching positions, physical education in the public high schools is heavily tied in with certification requirements. Many of the physical educators in the system are the ones who choose to relinquish their coaching duties in favor of full-time teaching. That is not to fault any physical educator–coach for taking such action. The fallacy lies in the system. Possibly the schools have spent years in gearing their sport certification efforts in the wrong direction; certification is not found where it is really needed. Incidentally, this is one of the reasons why this book is directed toward the idea of an integrated sport management program for the schools and colleges.

Samuel Adams of Washington State University has been one of the most articulate spokespersons on the topic of part-time coaches from the perspective of paraprofessionals, volunteer coaches, and all related concerns involving quality control factors. He is a strong advocate of coaching certification.[1]

> There is a great need for coaching certification. The evidence that certification would upgrade coaching is overwhelming. . . .
>
> Coaching is a specialized area of education. It is an area that must be regarded as an entity in itself. It is different although similar with some basic qualities and characteristics of physical education. Being a good physical educator doesn't assure one of being a good coach. There are specialized knowledges needed for coaching expertise; in sports medicine, sports psychology, sports technique, sports administration, sports physiology, public relations, sports facilities and equipment, and sports problems that include law and liability and assessment of personnel and programs. A curriculum which includes these areas can be assimilated into a coaching major or minor and certification. . . . Any plan must include the above areas and include a means of certifying the coaches that are presently coaching in the public schools. It may also include on-going or in-service training for paraprofessionals and laypersons (p. 22).

It seems to me that Adams is very much on target with respect to the particular need for managing change. The further change might be to forget about physical education certification and move toward sport management certification with coaching certification as a sub-set of that domain. Physical education certification still controls the public school sport environment. Aside from that, Adams has clearly identified the need with respect to preparation for coaching.

One of the better possibilities for meeting the need for more and better-qualified part-time coaches is to make fuller and more effective use of other teachers in the various subject matter areas. Generally speaking, the private schools have done a better job of this than is evidenced in the public schools. That may also be attributed to the general public school relationship with physical education. The classroom teachers could also be utilized as part-time sport instructors in their area of specialty. What is needed here is the incentive. Such incentive could be provided from at least two directions. The first involves the hiring process. School adminis-

[1]*Athletic Purchasing and Facilities,* November 1978.

trators could increasingly look toward the employment of teachers who also have coaching capabilities. With the current surplus of teachers expected to continue in the near future, this becomes a real possibility in the selection process. In many cases, coaching could be included as part of the contractual arrangement with the provision that a teacher does not relinquish coaching responsibilities except under extenuating circumstances. The second incentive would be increased compensation for coaching. At present most high school coaches are nowhere near being adequately paid for the amount of work performed and the extent of their responsibility. If the communities value interscholastic athletics as highly as appears to be the case, then they should be prepared to allocate an equitable amount of funds in this direction. It may seem that this is not a realistic suggestion in a time of financial cutback. However, it is important to keep in mind that the employment of additional, qualified, part-time coaches means that there is an accompanying savings in the employment of full-time coaches.

At both the school and college levels, the rapidly expanding master's programs in sport management offer a rich, potential source for obtaining well-qualified, part-time coaches at a relatively low salary. My experience in working with such students shows that many of them come from exceptionally fine academic backgrounds (in a variety of undergraduate majors) and with extensive backgrounds as college athletes. All they need is the experience of working in an apprenticeshiplike situation under the guidance of an experienced coach. Furthermore, most of the programs require some form of internship for completion of the degree requirements. In essence, here is a ready pool of the kind of talent that is sought for entry-level coaching positions. In the long run, everyone stands to benefit: the school and college athletes, the apprentice coach, and the administrators of the sport programs. When this type of arrangement can be worked out, one sees dramatic evidence of what it means to manage change.

School and Community Recreation Cooperation

An aspect of sport that offers some of the most fertile territory for constructive change is school and community recreation cooperation. It also represents an area in which we note considerable variance in the progress that has been made to date. As is true of the other manifestations of change, this change element is also financially based to a great extent.

> Cooperative relationships between financially-strapped school districts and park/recreation departs are gaining momentum across the country.
>
> Nowhere is this more evident than in post-Proposition 13 California, where cost-cutting programs are being initiated by assessing community needs, and analyzing public agency resources to see how the needs can be met (p. 20).[2]

[2]*Athletic Purchasing and Facilities,* June 1982.

The reasons behind the traditional gulf between sport programs in the school and those sport programs offered by the department of community recreation are too complicated to discuss here in detail. Much of it may be attributed to conservative thought about the nature of the school in relationship to the recreational enterprise. Professional preparation programs can also be blamed for providing sharp differentation between the preparation of physical education teachers and recreation leaders. Of course, it could also be argued that such programs only reflect the public desire. Suffice it to say that the gap has existed and more or less continues to exist. The need for an integrated community sport program is paramount. In this case, the financial restraint could actually turn out to be a "blessing in disguise."

It may take a long time to reach the ideal of having a completely integrated sport program in the community, or we may never achieve that goal, but in the meantime much can be done in that direction. Facility sharing is a good place to begin. That is where the most progress can also be noted to date. Much can be accomplished through joint facility planning, Iddins (1980, p. 24) furnishes data that show that a community might save $24,200 by developing a 13-acre school park site. Separately acquired and developed park and school sites would cost the two agencies $100,050. This is contrasted with the $75,850 for a joint development.

Beyond the realm of facilities per se, education and recreation agencies could do much more in terms of coordinated program development. One can find considerable overlapping of sport programs offered by the schools and community recreation groups. Some of this may be justifiable. In many other cases, it is not only wasteful but does not contribute to the offering of the best quality program. Iddins also stresses some other points that are applicable to meaningful coordination of programs. One of these is the need for formal agreements between the cooperating agencies. Many school-community cooperative relationships originate on an informal one-to-one basis. That's a good place to start. However, owing to personnel turnover, such relationships should eventually be formalized. Obviously, communication is the ultimate key in coordinated program development. Joint policy statements, coordinating committees, and joint publications are all steps in that direction.

The personnel area is likely to be the most difficult if one is striving to bring about real extensive change in the school-community sport context. The simple reason for this is that it is very much a case of "protect your turf." Invariably, integration of programs will be interpreted as meaning loss of positions. Even coordination of programs may be viewed as a step in that direction. The future lies in professional preparation programs that are designed to prepare people to teach or coach sport or both, be it in the school structure or some other component of the total community sport program. As an interim measure, steps should be taken to upgrade the qualifications of all those who are involved in teaching, coaching, and management in nonschool youth sport programs. Once again, Bronzan (1982) succinctly points to the need for change:

Today the number of young people involved in organized nonschool sports competition is greater than ever, and there are no signs to indicate anything but continued growth. Meanwhile professional physical educators and school athletic administrators refuse to acknowledge these facts.

Particularly, departments of professional physical education and athletics in colleges and universities continue to ignore the presence and impact of youth sports programs. It is rare for these departments to offer even a survey course to familiarize their students with the scope, structure and operation of these out-of-school organized sports programs (p. 12).

Bronzan also presents some most significant data in terms of the total sport involvement of youth in the United States.

- 20 million young people, 6 to 21 years, involved in out-of-school sports.
- 17 million participating between 6 and 16 years—40 percent of that population.
- 2 million participate in baseball, 8 to 18 years of age.
- More than 100,000 girls compete in softball.
- Little League Baseball, Inc., lists more than 40,000 teams.
- More than 1 million boys play tackle football in organized leagues.
- Soccer has more than 1500 organized teams for boys and girls—projected that the number of participants will double within 5 years.
- More than 1 million youth involved in age-group swimming.
- The Youth Basketball Association increased from 50,000 in 1976 to 200,000 in 1979.
- More than 1 million each in organized youth programs in golf and bowling.

Talk about change and the future for the development of sport management programs! The preceding data should reveal plenty in itself. Until we can reach the point of having more complete preparation in appropriate sport management curricula, colleges should at least begin to develop courses for the training of in-service personnel on a part-time basis. At the same time, school and community leaders should exercise more careful screening in the selection of teachers and coaches who have the qualifications, and steps should be taken to initiate a certification program for work in school and community sport.

Litigation

The change that can be observed with respect to litigation is more a matter of degree than one of kind. Since the 1950s educators have not generally been protected by the doctrine of ''sovereign immunity.'' Consequently, the increase in legal action against the schools and colleges has been with us for some time. Of particular concern today is the matter of tort negligence in sport injuries, both in terms of the nature of the court interpretation and the increasing amounts awarded to plaintiffs in cases of negligence. Two areas appear to be particularly vulnerable: (1) facility design and maintenance and (2) supervision, including instruction in techniques and safety precautions. There is little doubt that administrators must take steps to protect their programs against the new wave of legislation.

The sport facility concern centers around contributory negligence as manifested in secondary assumption of risk, when one party negligently creates a dangerous situation, and another party knowingly and unreasonably subjects himself or herself to risk of injury from the condition. Penman (1981) offers most appropriate advice for those who are responsible for the management of sport facilities.

1. Use recommended standards when designing a sports facility. If deviation from recommended standards has been made, have documentation as to why your deviation is safer.

2. Use common sense when designing facilities. Don't place glass surfaces, guy wires, poles, sprinkle heads, sharp or blind corners near areas where vigorous activity is conducted.

3. Anticipate potential safety problems at the design state. Have a safety officer and sports facility design consultant review plans, looking for potential safety problems.

4. Purchase quality building products and accessories, such as bleachers and standards, from reputable dealers who are noted for guaranteeing their products and providing good services to their customers.

5. For all existing facilities, designate a safety officer. Develop a clear written policy for establishing responsibility for inspection, maintenance and reporting of safety related to sports facilities.

6. Conduct periodic safety inspection and correct unsafe situations by either taking those facilities out of use or placing warning signs in appropriate areas or both.

7. Keep accurate records of safety audits, correction of potentially unsafe facilities and accidental injury sustained relating to a sports facility.

8. Work for legislative changes related to tort liability which would decrease unrealistic settlements and predatory attorney fees by:

    a. Elimination of a dollar amount in a suit.
    b. Limitation of awards in specific types of cases.
    c. Requiring plaintiff to assume responsibility for all defendants' costs related to unfounded suits.
    d. Limitation on contingency fees (p. 32).

The second major area of concern may be even more threatening owing to the inherent limitation in being able to take the necessary steps to prevent litigation in this regard. Adams (1982) brings attention to a February 1982 court decision in Seattle, Washington, in which $6.3 million was awarded to a high school football player who was injured while playing in 1975. "The primary allegations of negligence were in two areas: failure to properly instruct and failure to warn sufficiently. Nearly all other allegations were directed toward liability in these two areas. The allegations of negligence were directed toward the Seattle School District and the football coach and high school football coaching staff'' (p. 12). Adams points out how this is further evidence of the need for coaching certification. Beyond that, the case demonstrates the considerable responsibility that is being placed on administrators for the proper selection and training of coaches. There was also stress on the idea that coaches have an obligation to teach safety practices in addition to the instruction in proper techniques. The court ruled that the latter is not sufficient. Athletes must be made aware of the inherent dangers in using incorrect techniques. From the management perspective, the Seattle case points to the need for documented evidence of what coaches are covering in their instruction to the players.

The total scope and impact of the sport litigation indicate the need for one other major area of change. In addition to the orientation and training on the job, much more has to be done in covering the legal aspects of sport in the professional preparation curricula. All sport management students should have at least one course on sport and the law. There may not be sufficient resources to employ a trained lawyer on every sport management faculty. However, at least one member of the faculty should be responsible for developing a course that utilizes the up-to-date material prepared by a professional lawyer. A considerable amount of this material is now being published. Like it or not, familiarity with sport litigation is a significant factor in the future of effective preparation for positions in sport management.

Cable TV

Cable television epitomizes the need to manage change, particularly in terms of the applicability to college sport. At this writing, the impact of cable television on college sport is already very extensive. By the time this book is in print, we will have observed considerable more develoment in the relationship between cable television and college sport. The expanding NCAA involvement speaks for itself.

During the 1981–1982 academic year, The Entertainment and Sports Programming Network (ESPN) provided a cablecast of 23 NCAA men's and women's championships. Championships in all three divisions were included. The rights fee for the entire package was $550,000. Beginning with the 1982 football season, the NCAA signed a supplemental football television package via cable with the Turner Broadcasting System, the parent company of WTBS-TV in Atlanta, Georgia. The cable series was designed to supplement NCAA football telecasts on ABC and CBS. It was also aimed at broadening the base of participation in television appearances. For example, any team appearing in a nationally broadcast network game in 1981 was not eligible for an appearance on the supplementary package in 1982. Totally, 163 Division I-A and Division I-AA institutions were eligible to appear under the terms of the package. Under the contract, Turner Broadcasting System paid rights fees totaling $17,696,000 over two years: $7,408,000 in 1982 and $10,288,000 in 1983. Needless to say, the total impact of this arrangement is incredible. Statements at the time of the signing are indicative of the significance of this step, as indicated in this quote from *NCAA News* (Feb. 15, 1982).:

> "The NCAA looks forward to the series," said Wiles Hallock, chair of the NCAA Football Television Committee. "Coupled with the ABC and CBS packages, it will constitute the highest level of intercollegiate television income to NCAA member institutions in history—about two-and-a-half times the revenue over the previous four-year period."
>
> R. E. "Ted" Turner III, chairman of the Turner Broadcasting System, also viewed the agreement as a boom for college football as well as the cable television industry. Not only does the series represent the first supplement package ever administered by the NCAA, but it will also mark the first time for regular-season college football to be carried live by a predominantly cable television carrier.
>
> "This is a great milestone for cable television," Turner said. "These additional football telecasts will aid greatly in the continued growth of the cable industry and Turner Broadcasting. We are delighted with this arrangement and what we feel will be a long-term relationship with the NCAA" (p. 1).

That was the assessment in 1982. Who knows what further developments will have taken place by 1985? The cable coverage is expanding so rapidly that it is difficult to keep abreast of the up-to-date status. Even though the "big money" is in Division I football, it is obvious that all college athletic directors and even high school athletic directors should be cognizant of the potential for involvement with cable television. It's important to become familiar with the terminology in this rapidly expanding communication business. This can help in presenting the right kind of approach to a cable system representative. For the nonrevenue sports, exposure may be the key. The contest will be held regardless of any cable coverage. The sport program might as well take advantage of any opportunity for additional exposure. This may be the incentive for the cable operator to initially cover an event. On the other hand, the sport director should also be alert to any opportunity, including conferencewide agreements, which will maximize the revenue potential. Basically, there is now a need for every sport or athletic director to be cable television-oriented.

Summary

As we reexamine the directing function, we note that it encompasses a wide scope of endeavors in the total management process. The simple reason for this is that directing represents the brunt of the action. It is a long way from delegation to the management of change. Nevertheless, the job of directing is not complete unless some attention is given to all five aspects of directing. It is also difficult to say where the priorities lie for the manager's most effective use of time in carrying out the total function. Much will depend on the local and immediate situation. Obviously, motivation has to be an up-front consideration in any program. In the larger programs, delegation looms as an area of considerable significance. Coordination and the management of differences tend to be aspects of special concern in school and college sport programs owing to the multifaceted nature of the enterprise. Change always appears over the horizon. However, some periods of time are particularly highlighted by change. This could be said for school and college sport in the 1980s. It is also important to keep in mind that the effective management of change will offer the most severe challenge for many individuals. Regardless of variances resulting from different situations or changing times, the manager will in the long run be judged by his or her ability to direct the program. This function represents the bottom line in the management process. It also reminds us that the controlling function offers the means for assessing how well the job has been done.

REFERENCES

Adams, Samuel. "Certification in Coaching: A Sorely Needed Aspect in Education." *Athletic Purchasing and Facilities*. Vol. 2, Nos. 1, 6, November 1978, pp. 20–23.

————. "Court Decision Hits Hard With New Liability Twists." *Athletic Purchasing and Facilities*. Vol. 6, No. 5, May 1982, pp. 12–16.

Amdur, Neil. "Problems are Mounting in N.C.A.A." *The New York Times*. March 21, 1982, Section 5, p. 1.

"Athletic Promotion and Fund-Raising." *Athletic Purchasing and Facilities*. Vol. 5, No. 3, March 1981, pp. 17–40.

Athletic Purchasing and Facilities. Vol. 5, No. 7, July 1981.

Bauman, Marty. "Unique Financing Provides Babson College with a New Athletic Complex." *Athletic Purchasing and Facilities*. Vol. 2, No. 5, October 1978, pp. 63–64.

Bronzan, Robert T. "Communication Is the Key to 'Managing' People." *Athletic Purchasing and Facilities*. Vol. 5, No. 4, April 1981, pp. 14–18.

————. "Equipment Supervisors Ar Money Makers for High Schools as well as Colleges." *Athletic Purchasing an Facilities*. Vol. 2, No. 7, December 1978a, pp. 28–34.

————. "Preparing Leaders for Non-School Youth Sports." *Athletic Purchasing and Facilities*. Vol. 6, No. 3, March 1982, pp. 12–16.

————. "Proposition 13—A 'Bust'?" *Athletic Purchasing and Facilities*. Vol. 2, No. 5, October 1978, pp. 16, 19.

Broyles, J. Frank, and Hay, Robert D. *Administration of Athletic Programs: A Managerial Approach*. Englewood Cliffs, N.J. Prentice-Hall, 1979.

Cady, Edwin H. *The Big Game*. Knoxville, Tenn. U. of Tennessee Press, 1978.

Chalmers, Gordon H. "Administration of Athletic Events." In *Administration of Athletics in Colleges and Universities*. Edward S. Steitz (ed.). Washington, D.C. National Education Association, 1971.

Cratty, Bryant J. *Social Psychology in Athletics*. Englewood Cliffs, N.J. Prentice-Hall, 1981.

"Education in the '80s: The Fight for Adequate Resources." Interview with Wilson Riles in *Athletic Purchasing and Facilities*. Vol. 5, No. 5, May 1981, pp. 10–22.

"Examples of Outstanding School/Park Cooperation." *Athletic Purchasing and Facilities*. Vol. 6, No. 6, June 1982, pp. ?

Fields, Tom. "Attitude is Important in Fund-Raising." *Athletic Purchasing and Facilities*. Vol. 4, No. 10, October 1980, pp. 20–21.

Fuoss, Donald E., and Troppmann, Robert J. *Effective Coaching: A Psychological Approach*. New York. Wiley, 1981.

Gilbert, Bil, and Williamson, Nancy. "Sport is Unfair to Women." *Sports Illustrated*. May 28, 1973, pp. 88–98.

"How to Work With a Corporate Partner." *Athletic Purchasing and Facilities*. Vol. 5, No. 3, March 1981, pp. 24–30.

Iddins, Carol. "Carefully Organized School—Public Agency Partnerships Mean More Facilities, Programs." *Athletic Purchasing and Facilities*. Vol. 4, No. 1, January 1980, pp. 21–24.

Lopiano, Donna A. "Selling Women's Athletics: Realities and Potentials." *Athletic Purchasing and Facilities*. Vol. 4, No. 10, October 1980, pp. 8–14.

NCAA News, February 15, 1982.

Maslow, A. H. *Motivation and Personality*. New York. Harper & Row, 1954.

Palmisano, Michael. "Merchandising Can Mean Added Revenue for You." *Athletic Purchasing and Facilities:* Vol. 4, No. 10, October 1980, pp. 22–24.

Palmisano, Michael. "Promoting Your Non-Revenue Sports Takes Work." *Athletic Purchasing and Facilities:* Vol. 6, No. 4, April 1982, pp. 84–86.

Parkhouse, Bonnie L., and Lapin, Jackie. *The Woman in Athletic Administration*. Santa Monica, Calif. Goodyear, 1980.

Penman, Kenneth A. "Sports Facility Litigation — A Growing Problem." *Athletic Purchasing and Facilities:* Vol. 5, No. 1, January 1981, pp. 28–33.

Perry, Will. "Using Direct Mail to Sell Tickets, Raise Revenue." *Athletic Purchasing and Facilities*. Vol. 5, No. 11, November 1981, pp. 26–30.

Pickle, David. "New Cable TV Series to Broaden Exposure." *NCAA News*. February 15, 1982, pp. 1, 5.

"Promoting Girls' Sports: It's Working in Iowa." *Athletic Purchasing and Facilities*. Vol. 5, No. 3, March 1981, pp. 20–23.

Stech, Ernest, and Ratliffe, Sharon A. Working in Groups: *A Communication Manual for Leaders and Participants in Task-Oriented Groups*. Skokie, Ill. National Textbook Company, 1976.

Stogdill, Palph M. "Personal Factors Associated with Leadership: Survey of Literature." *The Journal of Applied Psychology*. Vol. 25, 1948, pp. 64–65.

Tully, Daniel F. "Inflation: Its Impact on Athletic Facilities, Planning and Project Success." *Athletic Purchasing and Facilities*. Vol. 3, No. 6, June 1979, pp. 22–26.

Zailskas, Jane. "Special Promotions for Ticket-Selling." *Athletic Purchasing and Facilities*. Vol. 6, No. 1, January 1982, pp. 37–40.

6

Controlling a School or College Sport Program

CONCEPTS AND PROBLEMS

Personnel Control Is the Key that Unlocks the Entire Controlling Function

Further Utilization of Management by Objectives

Key Result Areas for Developing Performance Standards

The Key to an Effective Reporting System—Who Is to Submit What, How, and When?

Evaluation Is Pivotal in the Controlling Function

Purposes of Evaluation

General Criteria for an Evaluation: Objectivity Reliability, and Validity

The Reward System Is Not Terminal

Two Sides to the Reward System

Status Is a Two-Headed Consideration for Those Who Work in School or College Sport Programs

The Emotional Ambivalence in Coaching

Any standard dictionary is likely to provide somewhat diffuse definitions of the word *control*. We tend to use that word in various contexts with different meanings. However, in general, the idea of control conveys thoughts about restraint, regulation, a check, or keeping within limits. Such thoughts are also applicable to the managerial function of controlling, but in a sense they only reveal half of the picture. From a management perspective, certain things must be kept in check, within limits. Yet is equally as important to provide the stimulation for moving beyond existing limits in an effort toward improvement. Evaluation is the key concept in the managerial controlling function. It is the pivotal process between performance standards and the reporting system, as initial components in controlling, and the reward system, the culmination of the controlling function. This also indicates the matural progression in carrying out the controlling function. In that respect, it is much like the organizing and staffing functions.

The concept of control is actually a very pervasive factor in school and college sport programs. There is a need for some kind of control with respect to each of the following considerations in the total program: budget, facilities, equipment, game management, recruitment, eligibility, and personnel. In this chapter we will be focusing on the latter, personnel control. The reason should be apparent. Personnel control is the key to carrying out all other aspects of the controlling function. It is the personnel performance that will determine the relative effectiveness in controlling the budget, facilities, or any of the other control factors. Some of the performance standards are aimed directly at those factors. For example, one would certainly expect that budgetary control would be a principal area in setting performance standards for an athletic business manager.

DEVELOPING PERFORMANCE STANDARDS

Management by Objectives (MBO) was discussed in Chapter 2 with respect to budget planning. It is equally applicable in the development of performance standards. The key result areas offer a most appropriate base in determining what is expected by way of personnel performance. This is particularly true in light of the central pillar of MBO, participative management. Supervisors and subordinates arrive at mutually acceptable goals, which are developed from the key result areas. These goals are used as guidelines in monitoring the progress of the subordinate in carrying out the responsibilities of his or her position. That is a direct manifestation of the controlling function. In presenting the benefits of MBO, Deegan and Fritz (1975) show how MBO can contribute to effective controlling.

MBO benefits the individual *supervisor* by the following.

1. Providing a good coaching framework.
2. Strengthening weak appraisal methodology.
3. Strengthening the supervisor-subordinate relationship.
4. Motivating subordinates.

Perhaps the most important benefits accrue to the *subordinate* as follows.

1. His or her authorities and responsibilities are clarified.
2. He or she is aware that he or she will be measured by performance and results rather than personal characteristics.
3. He or she knows what is expected.
4. He or she experiences increased job satisfaction (p. 37).

In this chapter we will be considering some of the more likely key result areas for various positions in a sport program. The specific performance standards would be developed from this general territory. They would be developed between the supervisor and subordinate within the context and needs of the particular sport program. Although there are standards of performance that are generally applicable to all school and college sport programs, the specifics must be developed to meet the demands of the particular situation.

Athletic Director

Coaches. Much of the success of an athletic director (A.D.) will depend on his or her ability to recruit, guide, and retain a qualified coaching staff. This brings us back to the staffing function. In other words, the A.D. should be effective in carrying out all aspects of the staffing function as it relates to coaches. The A.D. should have a sense of what to look for in the way of coaching qualifications. Thus, the turnover rate on the coaching staff becomes an important criterion. The A.D. should be able to select coaches who function effectively in the program. Of course, the reverse can also be true. Some of the better coaches will be prime candidates for more attractive positions at other insitutions. This factor has to be taken into account when assessing the turnover rate. Nevertheless, the percentages of dismissals and resignations loom as prime indicators of success in the staffing process.

As is true within many other organizations, low morale tends to be a problem with many coaching staffs. In terms of setting a performance standard, this will be a difficult area to assess within the MBO context. Some effort should be made to assess the flow of communication between the A.D. and the coaches. To what extent are the coaches familiar with departmental procedures and policies? What are the critical incidents that indicate a lack of communication? Is there evidence that the A.D. communicates with all the coaches? These are questions that might help in connection with getting a firmer handle on this somewhat nebulous, yet very important personnel area.

Athletes. The policy domain is a good place to begin in establishing performance standards for the A.D.'s relationship with the athletes. Owing to the very nature of his or her position, much of the athletic director's contact with athletes is indirect. The measure of effectiveness will in large part depend on the development of appropriate policies to govern recruitment, eligibility, living arrangements, disciplinary action, legal questions, and awards. If the school or college is not able to attract and retain quality student athletes, something may be amiss in the policy area. For example, what percentage of athletes receive their degrees? That could be an important criterion in arriving at a more specific performance standard.

In spite of the more indirect contact with athletes, the athletic director should also show evidence that he or she makes efforts to increase his or her familiarization with athletes on all the teams. Does the A.D. appear at a reasonable number of home and away contests? If so, do these appearances tend to be more or less balanced among the various sports? Does the A.D. have a general profile on the athletes who are representing the program? Is he or she available to consider individual cases when the need arises? These questions will probably go along way in developing some kind of performance standard in this regard.

Finances. The relative success of an athletic director in the management of finances usually can be analyzed by considering three principal components: planning, acquisition, and control. To what extent does the A.D. show evidence that he or she has been able to look ahead in anticipating financial needs? Is there a one-year plan? a five-year plan? What factors have been taken into account in the planning process? Is there evidence that the financial planning is consistent with program objectives?

With respect to acquisition, what evidence is there that the A.D. has made efforts to increase the amount of external funding for the program? What is the extent of the alumni contributions? At the high school level, what is the amount of potential support? What steps have been taken to organize a booster club? In turn, how is it controlled? What efforts have been made to increase ticket sales?

In terms of finances, control refers to control of the budget. What type of budgetary analysis is employed? What is the comparison of actual revenues and expenditures to budgeted amounts? What is the system of budget accountability within the department? These financial questions resulting from the third key result area will also assist in providing parameters for the evaluation of an athletic director.

Facilities. The A.D.'s effectiveness in managing facilities will often depend on factors that are outside his or her control. Therefore, any performance standards in this area have to be developed with considerable reason and care. Appropriate policies again provide the key in determining levels of expectation. Is there a long-range planning policy? How has it been developed? To what extent have the facilities been used to their fullest potential? What provisions have been made to provide for safety in facility usage?

The facilities area generally offers ample opportunity for the development of problem solving and innovative objectives. There is scarcely a program that does not have some kind of facilities problem. Also the planning and utilization of facilities make a rich territory for innovation. Many athletic directors demonstrate considerable ability in solving facility problems or being innovative in facility development or both. When there is a general deficiency in the facilities situation, performance standards might be developed from the problem-solving and innovative perspective.

Public Relations. Public relations also has to be near the top of the list of key result areas for any athletic director. Needless to say, there is some overlap here between effective public relations and financial acquisition. However, each area encompasses a broader territory. Even though the total staff is involved in public relations, the athletic director holds prime responsibility for what is done in this regard. Performance standards should be developed to control the scope of the endeavor. A checklist would include specific steps taken by the A.D. to facilitate positive communication with each of the following groups.

Students	Alumni
Parents	The media
Faculty	Visiting teams
Other school or college employees	Colleagues in other athletic departments
The administration	The public at large

Such a list, with appropriate specifics, actually provides a most significant control factor for the A.D. If there is evidence of a deficiency in terms of the quantity or quality of contact with any of these groups, remedial action must be taken.

Coach

When it comes to establishing performance standards for a coach, many people are inclined to think that this is a very clear-cut matter—number of games won. Beyond a doubt this is *the* performance standard for professional sport and many large university teams. The fallacy lies in thinking that the same kind of standard should be extended to all school and college coaches. It is all too apparent why we find this undue proliferation of the winning standard. Victories are the most measurable element. Actually, they are a classic example of MBO in action. Also, victories tend to be the central concern of many people who are external to the sport program. For these reasons, the sport administrator must work hard to establish more comprehensive performance standards for coaches. The following key result areas may serve as guidelines.

Athletes. Athletes are the people who ultimately count in the interscholastic or intercollegiate sport program. Although we earlier noted that the work of the A.D. should be assessed in this area, for the coach it is the principal consideration. In spite of any difficulties in precise measurement, effort must be made to determine the extent to which the coach holds the respect of his or her athletes. How well have they adapted to the coach's style of play? What kind of discipline problems and how many can be observed on the team? What is the dropout rate among the players? Do former players demonstrate support for the team? Some of the answers to these questions might not be as quantitative as one might hope, but at least they provide some sort of frame of reference for developing this important performance standard.

Some kind of performance standard should also be developed in terms of the coach's guidance of the academic progress of the athletes. Although he or she cannot be held completely responsible for everything that occurs on the academic side, there are signs that indicate the degree to which the coach is making an effort at control. What percentage of the athletes receive their high school diploma or college degree? How many honor students are there on the team? How many athletes are declared ineligible for one or more seasons of competition? Answers to these questions will also reveal something about the work of the coach.

Knowledge of the Sport. There is some overlap here with the previous area because part of the player's respect will be derived from what the coach knows about his or her sport. However, in both areas there is more involved in terms of a standard. Part of the coach's technical performance can also be judged by the reputation of the coach among fellow coaches. Is he or she up-to-date in the latest coaching strategies? Does he or she receive honors from groups that are external to the program? In essence, one might ask how highly the coach's expertise is assessed in the total coaching fraternity in that sport.

Knowledge of Medical and Legal Aspects of Coaching. Knowledge of medical and legal aspects of coaching represents a broad key result area. It includes training and conditioning: preparing the athlete for competition. The teaching of safety precautions is also part of this domain. Is the coach up-to-date with the latest training methods and use of the most appropriate equipment? How well does he or she understand the various physical factors that influence athletic performance? Although there are some general medical considerations, part of the knowledge here will also be reflected in the knowledge of the sport. This area will influence the degree of respect that the athletes have for the coach. Also, from a legal standpoint, such knowledge is critical.

Public Relations. Next to the athletic director, the coach is the one individfual who holds a major responsibility in public relations. Consequently, it is reasonable to expect that some kind of performance standard should also be developed in this context. Visibility is the key factor in making this a critical role for the coach. In general, the coach should be assessed as to how well he or she reflects a positive image that is consistent with the goals of the sport program. The contacts with parents and the media are particuarly significant for the coach. However, he or she also must be sensitive to the many-sided public. This is difficult for a coach because of a certain amount of inherent role conflict. In many respects, the work of the coach in public relations epitomizes the need for the controlling function.

Management. At least one other area should provide a strong indicator of the relative effectiveness of a coach. In Chapter 4 we stressed the importance of management training for the coach. With respect to control, there must also be some effort to determine how well the coach is carrying out his or her duties as a manager. In essence, the performance standard will be aimed at completeness in the total management process. Does the coach give attention to all five management functions? Any marked deficiency should be fairly apparent. In this case, the various aspects of each function actually provide the criteria for determining the performance standard.

Sport Coordinator and Instructor

Much the same standard of performance can be expected of either a sport coordinator or an instructor. The only real difference is that the sport coordinator has a wider scope of managerial responsibility. Whether or not we customarily think of an instructor's position in those terms, he or she also plans, organizes, staffs, directs, and controls the class. The abilities of the coordinator may be more of a focus in this area owing to the extended scope of responsibilty. In either case, the performance standards should not be that different from those that are developed for a coach. Essentially the same kind of performance should be expected in relationship to demonstrated knowledge of the sport and the medical aspects of teaching sport activities. This frequently seems to be one of the areas of greatest deficiency in many sport programs. We seem to be willing to settle for less when it comes to instruction. By contrast, the coach is on the line; any deficiencies in his or her knowledge are more apparent to a wider constituency. Efforts should be made to upgrade teaching standards along a similar vein.

It could also be argued that an instructor has somewhat the same responsibility to the students as a coach has to his or her athletes. Any difference here lies in the more in-depth and extended contact of a coach with his or her athletes. In both cases, measure of respect might be used as a standard of performance. The nature and extent of the coach's contact provides the differential in priorities. Much the same can be said for the public relations area. Although the responsibility here extends to the entire staff, including instructors, this area does not have the same kind of priority as noted for the athletic director and the coaches.

Staff Positions

It is difficult to be as definitive about the performance standard for staff positions in school and college sport programs. The difference is largely due to the very nature of a staff position. It exists to provide support for other personnel who are in the main line of managerial responsibility. For this reason, the performance standards are largely built into the position description. However, any difference does not negate the need to also develop some kind of performance standard for each staff position. As we consider these positions, it becomes increasingly evident that the key result areas can be identified with one or more of the total functions of management. By and large those who hold staff positions are not involved in the complete management process. Yet they contribute significantly to certain aspects of management. Performance standards can be developed within that framework.

Business Manager

Financial Organization. After the program is funded, much of the success in managing a financially sound program will depend on the way in which the financial arrangements are organized. This is the first of two key result areas for a business manager. He or she has the primary responsibility for organizing the procedures to be followed in budget development, cash flow, and financial reports.

Financial Control. In the case of finances, control is a direct outgrowth of organization. The work of the business manager is in essence a microcosm of the larger controlling function. Some of his or her major tasks involve setting the financial standards, obtaining the financial data and evaluating the financial system. In a lesser sense, the business manager also provides reward through a system of budgetary accountability. His or her work should be judged accordingly. If the financial arrangements are well organized and controlled, there is little more that one can expect in the way of performance standards for this position.

Director for Sport Promotion

Marketing Procedures. Much of the work of the director for sport promotion relates to the planning function. More specifically he or she is the one individual who is most directly involved in establishing the procedures for marketing the total sport program. Thus, performance should be assessed both in terms of the scope and depth of the marketing endeavors.

Coordination. The other key result area for this position is a component of the directing function. As we review the position description for the director for sport promotion, it is apparent that he or she must have extensive contacts with many different individuals and groups both within and external to the program. A considerable amount of success in fulfilling the duties of the position will depend on the extent to which he or she can get people to work together in the promotional effort. Consequently, the results here should also earmark the level of performance.

Sports Information Director (S.I.D.)

Procedural Planning. Much of the work of the S.I.D. is of a procedural nature. He or she is responsible for a vast array of procedures, related media contacts, press releases, press guides, compilation of statistics, game arrangements, photography, and the speakers' bureau, along with many other details. An initial indication of success on the job can be found in the extent to which all facets of sports information are covered.

Coordination. The performance standard here is much like that which applies to the director for sport promotion. The key is to be found in completeness and consistency in approach in working with both internal and external constituencies.

Reporting System. The S.I.D. also plays a key role in the controlling function. More specifically, he or she is one of the major contributors to the reporting system. The extent of complete and accurate data on the totoal sport program should serve as an important measure of the S.I.D.'s performance.

Manager of Facilities

Facilities Planning. The role of the manager in long-range planning for new facilities may be somewhat limited. His or her effectiveness in facilities planning will be largely judged by the degree to which there is evidence of optimum and safe usage of existing facilities with a minimal amount of conflict.

Ticket Manager

Planning Ticket Sales. The keys here are largely those related to the proper pricing and seating strategies. Are those strategies generally meeting the needs of the diverse constituencies that support the various sports? The specific performance standard will very much depend on the particular ticket situation for the major sports at the given institution. For example, the performance standard would obviously be different at a college that has a need to stimulate ticket sales for individual games than it would be for a program that generally sells a high percentage of season tickets.

Controlling Ticket Distribution. Controlling ticket distribution covers the entire flow of ticket distribution from the time the tickets are printed and sold until they are collected and seating is complete. Any deficiency in this regard points to the need for some type of corrective action. In essence, the ticket manager's position is mainly one that centers on planning and control; his or her performance should be evaluated accordingly.

Athletic Trainer

A head trainer is actually very much involved in carrying out all of the managerial functions, not unlike those who hold the line positions in a sport program. However, in contrast with the other four functions, the controlling function represents the raison d'être of the athletic trainer's position. It is here suggested that the performance standard should be set primarily from that perspective.

Standards for Participation. The trainer is the one person who is in the best position to know when and to what extent an athlete is physically ready to compete. The direct responsibility in this regard should reside with the trainer, and he or she should be evaluated in terms of his or her decision making in this area.

Reporting System. In the preceding chapter we noted the growing concern about sport litigation. Responsibilities for many of the safety factors center on the trainer. He or she must maintain an accurate, consistent, and regular account of all injuries. Beyond that, the trainer should be involved in preparing more general reports on the conditioning of all athletic participants.

Evaluation. Evaluation ties in directly with the standards for participation. Through his or her ability to evaluate the physical status of the athletes, the trainer is in a position to make decisions regarding standards for participation. Basically, how acute is the trainer in the evaluation process?

Reward. With the work of the trainer, reward is first and foremost manifested in the area of corrective action. It is *the* key result area for the trainer. Does he or she demonstrate knowledge of the most up-to-date methods in the care of athletic injuries. This represents the bottom line for the trainer.

A Final Note on Performance Standards

Performance standards are specific to the situation. Thus, we cannot easily make external judgments as to what is expected of a coach, a trainer, a facilities manager, or one in any other position. However, it is clear that in each position there is a certain kind of territorial responsibility. This can be used to set forth key result areas under which the more specific standards can be developed. An attempt has been made to identify what appear to be some of the more likely key result areas for selected positions in college sport. Some of these positions, particularly those of a line nature, will also be found in school sport with comparable key result areas. The major difference between line and staff positions is evident in terms of performance standards. Those in line positions tend to have more complete managerial responsibility for a segment or component of the program. Staff personnel generally contribute more in depth to one or more of the managerial functions in a cross section of the program.

ESTABLISHING A REPORTING SYSTEM

Establishing a reporting system is not necessarily a follow-up to the development of performance standards. As a matter of fact, these first two steps in controlling more or less take place concurrently; either one may precede the other. More importantly, both steps must precede the actual evaluation process. Performance standards and the reporting system provide the base for evaluation.

The key to any effective reporting system is determining who is to submit what, how, and when. Among these four questions that guide reporting, the question of how tends to be the most local determinant. The reason for this is that each institution generally has its own kind of reporting format, and the mode of reporting has to follow that format more or less. Consequently, there is no need to present a series of forms that can be used in a reporting system in school or college sport. These should be developed to meet the requirements within the context of the specific institution.

Primarily we will be focusing on the questions *who* (namely, who is responsible for submitting the report?) and *what*. In some cases, the question *when* is also of some significance. In the final analysis, the question *what* is perhaps the most significant in any reporting system. This points to the differences in the kinds of information that can be received: critical or vital, useful, nice to know, and superfluous. Obviously, the reporting system should be aimed at emphasis on the critical and on providing as much useful information as possible within the constraints of time. The question *who* is also quite significant in that it delineates the responsibility in the reporting process.

Annual Report of Individual Performance

Each professional employee in the program (line and staff personnel) should be required to submit an annual report that reflects his or her professional activity during the previous year. Such a report can serve the dual purpose of appraising result-oriented performance and assessing personal development. In other words, the report should show what has been accomplished both for the program and the individual during the previous year.

As an integral part of this report, the individual should provide a comparison of results achieved for each objective that was agreed upon between the employee and the supervisor at the beginning of the year. This is part of the MBO framework (Deegan and Fritz, 1975, p. 236). In some instances, there may be a marked discrepancy between the objective and the result. That requires an explanation of any extenuating circumstances. At this point we can really see the controlling function in action. The report should also provide opportunity for the individual to note any accomplishments that exceed the objectives or moved the employee into new territory.

Routine, problem-solving, and innovative objectives should be used as a base for this type of reporting. They provide a framework for assessing the accomplishment. The report should also reflect those areas of personal growth during the past year as well as areas for improvement in the same position or in future career development. In essence, this report is an annual indicator of what the individual would contribute, did contribute, and might contribute to the program and his/her own professional advancement. This individual, professional progress report is at the very core of the controlling process.

Other Elements in the Reporting System

The other part of the reporting system should be designed to provide a steady and consistant flow of information that is essential to the effective management of the program. Internally, this information is used to facilitate the actual operation of the program. Externally, it is used for institutional control and public relations purposes.

Athletes. The reporting on athletes should include the following.

1. *Record of scholastic or academic background or both*. This should be kept up-to-date on a semester or term basis. Ultimately, this is the re-

sponsibility of the athletic director. In the larger college programs, this responsibility will probably be delegated to an assistant athletic director. Some of the responsibility may also be delegated to coaches.

2. *Physical status.*The essentials here are a record of up-to-date physicals with a doctor's signature and complete reports of all injuries. The atheltic director should have a checklist for each team. Most of the specific accountability is delegated to coaches and the athletic trainer. Part of the checkoff process includes adequate coverage by health insurance.

3. *Parental Information.* The athletic director is also responsible for maintaining a record of essential information involving the family. This includes the statement of parental approval for participation and an emergency data card indicating the athlete's legal address and the person to contact in the case of an emergency. In some cases at the college level it is also necessary to have information on the family's financial status for financial aid purposes. When there is a tender of financial aid, the letter of intent also requires a parent's signature. Another checkoff item is the "consent to release information."

4. *Familiarity with regulation.* The athletic director should also maintain a record that indicates that each athlete is familar with the applicable regulations governing the program, be they local, conference, state, or national in origin or a combination.

Other Sport Participants. The following factors are important.

1. *Participation Figures.* These are an important factor in the control of the instructional and intramural components of all school and college sport programs. Internally, these figures are used to determine work load and priorities. Externally, they provide a principal source of information in obtaining support for the total sport program. These data should initially be prepared by the sport coordinator for each sport.

2. *Injuries.* There is too often a tendency to overlook the need to report all the significant injuries that occur among the varoius sport participants. A record of such injuries should be maintained by the athletic trainer. In most cases, a trainer is not present when the injury occurs. It is the responsibility of the instructor or supervisor to report these injuries to the trainer.

Finances. In the larger programs, financial reporting is a primary responsibility of the business manager. Depending on the relative size, this may be the responsibility of an assistant athletic director, administrative assistant, or the athletic director in the smaller programs. In any case, financial reporting should at least include the following elements.

1. Up-to-date record of every purchase. This includes a receipt for each cash payment.

2. Daily ledger on expenditures and balances.
3. Monthly statements. Most institutions send departments or programs monthly statements of their accounts. These should be checked against departmental records, and any discrepancies should be worked out. Each coach and sport coordinator should also be given a monthly account of the financial status for their sport.
4. Annual comparative report between the budget and actual expenditures. Needless to say, this is the bottom line in the financial aspect of control.
5. End-of-year audit. This should be conducted by an external source.

Facilities. The reporting responsibility here is similar to that involving finances. In the larger programs there is likely to be a facilities manager who has the responsibility for facility control. Otherwise, this reporting area is handled by an assistant athletic director, the athletic director, or an administrative assistant. Some of the critical reports are these.

1. *Facilities Utilization.* This would usually be submitted on a yearly basis although it also might be required for each term or season. Essentially, this report should provide a complete profile on how the facilities are used: when, by who, and for what purposes. The report can be a useful document in long-range planning. More immediately, it serves as a principal organ for corrective action in assigning facilities for the following year.
2. *Facilities Maintenance.* This is also likely to be an annual report, but it might be submitted on a more frequent basis. Basically, two parts are needed in such a report. The first would be a listing and any special notations of maintenance work completed during the past year. The second part is a schedule of work planned for the next year or two. This would include special reference to those aspects of the facilities that are safety concerns.
3. *Critical Incidents.* The critical incident form of reporting is actually a key element in the reporting system for all aspects of the total sport program. Such reporting provides ready documentation for subsequent decisions. It is mentioned here because the facilities area is a prime target for critical incidents. Special problems related to facility conditions and usage should be noted when they arise. This is one of the more continuous features of control.

Promotion, Fund Raising, Public Relations. The area of promotion, fund raising, and public relations is a broad reporting area that might be divided into a number of separate reports. Regardless of how the reporting is specifically carried out, there should be some type of accountability of the work that is done with the external constituency on a yearly basis. Again, depending on the size of the program, any one or more of the personnel in the following positions might be delegated responsibility for reporting on these items: director for sport promotion, ticket manager, assistant athletic directors, business manager, or athletic director.

1. *Media Contacts*. This would include a summary of the extent of regular media coverage through newspapers, radio, and television. At the college level, it would include a statement of any revenue generated through television contracts.

2. *Alumni Relations*. At the college level, the report should include documentation of the extent of involvement with the alumni. How many members belong to the alumni association? How many new members have been added during the past year? What is the amount of the alumni contribution to the program? What efforts have been made to gain additional alumni support?

3. *Parental Contacts*. At the high school level there should be notation of the kind and degree of parental involvement with the program. If the parents are assessed for travel, equipment, or any other program expenses, what is the amount of such contributions? To what extent and how are parents kept informed about the vairous activities in the total sport program?

4. *Booster Clubs*. Any booster club activity should be reported. Again, this should include the amount of any financial contributions as well as a notation of other kinds of support. There should also be an indication of efforts that are made to control the booster club involvement to keep it in line with the total objectives for the sport program.

5. *General Fund Raising*. In addition to the preceding, what other efforts have been made to generate additional revenue for the program during the past year? What is the amount of revenue in each of the fund raising areas?

Line Personnel. Both the athletic director and the director for sport information should present a summary of personnel actions and status for the year. This would include the following.

1. A Listing of coaches, coordinators, and instructors for each sport.
2. Additions and deletions from the coaching or instructional staffs.
3. Changes in assignments or responsibilities, including any promotions.
4. Notation of any special personnel concerns.

Director's Report

In addition to his or her own, individual report, the director of the sport program is responsible for submitting an annual report that reflects the state of the program. Much of this will be a composite and summary of the various areas that have been outlined for the complete reporting system. This is also the opportunity for the director to comment on any outstanding or deficient contributions among staff members as noted in the reports of individual performance. Aside from its reference to personnel, the director's report should also be used to specify any particular needs for the program as evidenced in the summary of the current status of the program. This report would be submitted to the next level in the administrative structure of the institution. At the high school level this would in most cases be the principal of the school. In the colleges, the report would probably be submitted to a dean, academic vice-president, or provost.

EVALUATION

Earlier in this chapter we noted that evaluation is the key concept in the controlling function. As used here, evaluation is the direct action of comparing the performance standards with the results that are manifested in the individual and program reports for the year. Sometimes evaluation is also interpreted in a broader sense to include the performance standards, reporting system, and the actual assessment. However, we have already covered the first two steps. We are ready for the process of putting these steps together in an appraisal of performance. Evaluation is a complicated topic. It is an activity that can be approached from many different angles. There is no perfect system of evaluation. There is a never-ending search for a more effective means of evaluating. In spite of any pitfalls, three questions loom as critical when we consider the evaluation process: why? who? and how?

Why Do It?

The question "Why do it?" tempts simple answers. One could merely respond by saying that we evaluate to provide a basis for reward or to carry out the controllng function. However, such answers fall far short of the fuller intent of evaluation. They also do not begin to explain why evaluation is so integral in the process of control. We need a fuller explanation: evaluation is carried out for several reasons.

1. *To improve individual performance.* This answer actually undergirds the entire evaluation process. From the perspective of both management and the individual, it is the major reason for conducting the evaluation. This reason is also one of the pillars in the MBO framework, which is aimed at result-oriented performance appraisal. The evaluation directs attention to the past, present, and future. What were the objectives at the beginning of the evaluation period? How well were those reached? In other words, what were the results? Regardless of the level of performance, what can be done to produce even better results in the future? Evaluation does not stop with an assessment of previous plans with present results. There should be a strong motivational thrust in the evaluation effort. Evaluation is first and foremost aimed at improved performance that stands to benefit both the individual and the organization.

2. *To coordinate program development.* Evaluation can also assist in the developement of the total program. The composite of individual performance evaluations should shed considerable light on the relative strengths and weaknesses in the sport program. Thus, evaluation might lead to adjustments in program assignments. It might also point to areas that are unmet in terms of existing assignments.

3. *To provide a basis for external critique.* No program in an educational institution exists in isolation. There is a constant need to provide data that can be used to make comparisons among the various programs. Sometimes such data are also used to make decisions regarding decreased, streaky, or increased support for a given program. Within the program this reason for evaluating may often be viewed with concern or skepticism, but it cannot be overlooked. It is much better to be prepared by having available data for an attempt at objective evaluation than it is to have the decisions made by whim or prejudice.

4. *To stimulate individual development.* This reason has a strong relationship to the first cited. Improved performance will likely lead to development, but the latter connotes an extension beyond the performance in the immediate position. The nature of development was discussed in Chapter 4 as a component of staffing. Evaluation can also help here because the results are available for presentation when the individual is being considered for other positions or new opportunities associated with the present position.

5. *To fulfill a basic need involving status.* How do I stand? How am I doing? These are basic and frequently asked questions in almost any educational or working environment. There is a certain natural curiosity that calls for feedback about the quality of one's performance. One of the potential morale problems in any organization is to be found in the lack of such feedback. As a result, evaluation is also directed toward the fulfillment of this personal need.

6. *To determine appropriate personnel actions.* This is the one reason for evaluating that is closest to the reward system per se. Unfortunately, it may also be the only reason that is recognized by many people who are involved with either side of the evaluation process. Although it is an important reason, it is not the only reason. It is also important to keep in mind that any complete and effective reward system includes more than personnel actions. Nevertheless, evaluation is a most direct tool in determining promotions, retentions, dismissals, tenure, and salary increases.

Who Should do It?

The question "Who should do it?" is not as easily answered as the first one. At one time it was much simpler. The traditional answer was "the boss." It is obvious that such a response or decision is no longer appropriate in many organizations. This is particularly true in the educational sector owing to the diverse nature of the constituency.

In terms of organizations generally, we can begin by identifying four basic choices: superiors, peers, subordinates, and employee self-evaluation. Then, of course, there is the possibility of multiple assessment involving any combination of two or more of these basic sources. There may also be a personnel or evaluation committee that is to some degree representative of these sources. Aside from the more basic choices, sometimes there is even a need to have, or interest in having, input from personnel who are outside the program. Within the larger programs, the picture is further complicated in terms of the choice of superiors.

Specific decisions regarding who should be the evaluator or evaluators will depend very much on the size, particular needs, and prescribed circumstances of the sport program. Some institutions have definite guidelines that must be followed in conducting the evaluation. For instance, there may be a requirement that each department or program has to have a personnel committee that is involved in the evaluation process. In a similar vein, there may be a requirement that student evaluations must be included. Consequently, we will be considering here some of the pros and cons involving the various categories of evaluators. Decisions for each program can be made within this framework. In general, it would seem that some form of multiple assesment is appropriate for most programs.

Superiors. The possibilities under this category in school and college sport programs include those who hold the following positions: director of the sport program, athletic director, director of sport instruction, head coaches, and sport coordinators.

The director of the sport program has to be involved in the evaluation process in some way or another. The only real question here involves the kind and degree of involvement. In a real large program it is reasonable to assume that his or her evaluation work will be largely in a coordinating and review capacity. The extent of his or her direct involvement will also depend on the organizational structure for that program. If one or more of the staff personnel report directly to him or her, he or she has direct responsibility for evaluation in those cases. He or she would also have direct responsibility to evaluate the athletic director and the director of sport instruction whenever these exist as separate positions. Other than that, he or she would be receiving and reviewing evaluations that are submitted from other sources within the total program.

The most basic controlling responsibility of the athletic director is to evaluate the performance of the head coach for each sport. The extent of his or her involvement in evaluating assistant coaches will depnd on local arrangements. Other direct evaluative responsibilities would include any staff personnel who report directly to the athletic director.

Much the same can be said regarding the role of the director of sport instruction. His or her principal responsibility is to evaluate the sport coordinator for each sport. In most cases he or she would be reviewing the evaluations of all sport instructors. The degree of direct involvement in the latter would again depend largely on the size of the program.

The roles of the head coaches and sport coordinator are perhaps the most straightforward in the entire evaluation process. The head coach is the key person in evaluating any of his or her assistants. In a very parallel vein, the fundamental controlling responsibility of the sport coordinator is to evaluate the performance of each instructor for that sport.

In summary, it can be said that superiors have to be involved in the evaluation of those who work in school and college sport programs. The only questions are those that relate to the degree of direct involvement for any given position and the extent to which the superiors receive evaluative input from other sources. Answers to these questions will largely depend on a consideration of the other sources that may be included in the evaluation process.

Peers. Peer ratings are generally considered to be a most useful instrument in many evaluation systems. However, the validity of peer assessment is determined by a couple of basic considerations that should be taken into account before a decision is reached regarding the degree to which peer evaluation is to be factored into the total evaluation process. One of these is the extent of mutual involvement in the task performance. The other is the nature of the competitive environment in the peer situation. Are the peers competing for reward under a limited structure? Merit pay raises or a limited number of promotions would be examples in this category. The competition may also be heightened through limited financial support for various components of the total program. In general, these considerations are applicable to the situation in school or college sport.

For the most part, the peers in these sport programs will be fellow coaches or fellow sport instructors. The sport coordinators also comprise a peer group. Some of the people holding staff positions may also be working on a level with peers who hold other staff positions. When considering the valdity of peer assessment for the sport management personnel, we must take into account the basic disjunctive nature of the school or college sport program, as discussed in the preceding chapter. By and large the coaches do their own thing in their own sport. Much the same can be said for the sport coordinators and the sport instructors. The fact that the entire program actually operates like a whole series of sport programs is also a factor in enhancing the competition for limited financial support. For these reasons, it is probably not too surprising that many coahces do not show a lot of enthusiasm for getting involved with personnel committees.

Nevertheless, it would appear that the professional employees in a sport program should at least be given the annual opportunity to elect a personnel committee. If a personnel committee is required by the institution, that, of course, is another matter. It may well be that peer evaluations will receive less weight or be handled somewhat differently in school or college sport programs. But at least the possibility should be considered, and options should be presented.

Subordinates. The category of subordinates tends to be a somewhat elusive one in an educational institution. In a working organization, a subordinate is typically one who reports to a person who holds a higher level position in terms of responsibility and authority. In schools and colleges, we actually have two categories of subordinates: employees and students. It could also be argued that students are not really subordinates in the true sense of that term. Regardless of any definitional uncertainty, it is clear that they are not on a peer level with coaches or instructors. Within sport programs, the picture is further complicated by the distinction between athletes and other students. In a sense, each of these categories comprises its own peer group and is subordinate to those who manage the program. At any rate, how should the various subordinates be involved in the evaluation process?

It would seem that much of the subordinate evaluation does take place and probably should take place at the informal level. There is need for steady feedback regarding the performance of superiors. Such feedback has to be assessed in terms of source and limited perspective. Nevertheless, it can be very valid in terms of that perspective. Aside from the informal evaluation, employees should be given an opportunity for some type of systematic review of performance of those who hold the higher level managerial positions. In many cases, a three-year review seems appropriate for this purpose.

Student evaluation of instruction is also frequently conducted on a formal level. That is much more customary than having the athletes do a formal evaluation of the coach. This may be attributed in part to the traditional coach-athlete relationship. The other difference is that student evaluations should be factored into the total evaluation of instructors. There is no blanket answer. Perhaps the best one can say is that formal student evaluations should be given some consideration in the ultimate assessment by superiors or peers or both.

Self-Evaluation. Under the MBO structure, self-evaluation is an integral part of the controlling function. It does not replace any of the other sources of evaluation. Also, it does not stand by itself. The employee is involved in a systematic appraisal of his or her annual performance in order to facilitate the complete evaluation process. More about that will be said in terms of the means for conducting the evaluation. Here it is sufficient to note that one of the sources of evaluation should certainly be the individual who is the subject of the evaluation.

How Should It Be Done?

Part of the answer to this question can be found in the criteria that are generally recognized for any form of evaluation. These are objectivity, reliability, and validity. Objectivity is the first intent in the process. Every effort must be made to ensure that the evaluation is relatively free of prejudice, bias, distrust, previous opinion, or judgments. I say relatively free because it is most difficult to attain complete objectivity. This is particularly true with respect to previous judgments when the same employee is evaluated year after year. Nevertheless, the search for objectivity should be of a continuous nature. This is one of the major reasons why it is so important to have the performance standards established prior to the evaluation period.

Reliability comes into the picture in terms of consistency in the evaluation process. Although the specific performance standards might vary from year to year, the method of assessing performance should be followed with some consistency. It is also important that all peers be evaluated according to the same process.

Validity is found in the extent to which the final rating reflects the real differences between the actual performance and the standards of performance. This is one of the reasons why it is often most useful to receive input from more than one evaluation source. Of course, this is also closely related to the search for objectivity.

Although the specifics of the process will vary from institution to institution (depending on local needs and requirements), there are certain general steps that are commonly recognized as being appropriate for annual evaluations. Here it is important to note that evaluation is actually a continuous process. It does not begin or stop with the annual review of performance. However, the annual report typically signals the beginning of a formal evaluation that leads to decisions related to the reward system.

1. *Submission of annual report.* The requirements for such a report were discussed with reference to the reporting system. In the interests of objectivity and reliability, it is probably best to have a standard form that can be used by every professional employee in the sport program. This form should be sufficiently flexible to permit inclusion and discussion of extenuating circumstances or unusual achievements or both. The form is submitted to the immediate superior for appropriate processing. Preparation of this report is actually the stage of self-evaluation that was referred to earlier.

2. *Distribution of the report.* This is an optional step in the evaluative process depending on the question of who is to be involved at this level of evaluation. If the program has a personnel or evaluation committee, the report would be referred to that group. It's also possible that the report would be submitted to one or more individuals for preliminary review. If there is no peer assessment, this step would not be included.

3. *Receiving input from other sources.* This also tends to be an optional item although the effort should be made to consider this step. Student evaluations are a prime example of the input that would be received during this phase of the evaluation. Another possibility is to receive feedback from other selected subordinates within the sport program. Sometimes it is also appropriate and useful to receive reports from observers who are external to the program but who are in a position to provide valid comments on one or more aspects of the total performance.

4. *The preliminary assessment or rating.* This step is at the core of the evaluation process. It represents the most concrete attempt to assess the performance of the employee. This initial assessment would be made by either the immediate superior or a personnel committee, depending on local arrangements. It is also tentative in that it is subject to review during the ensuing steps in the complete evaluation process.

Basically, the preliminary evaluation should be aimed at a comparison of results accomplished with desired results. It should also include a consideration of any extenuating circumstances to explain those goals that were not met as well as a notation of accomplishments that exceed the agreed-upon objectives. In most cases, this assessment will also lead to some type of summary judgment about the overall worth of the individual to the program.

Depending on the type of personnel action that is to follow and local requirements, the evaluation may be manifested in any one of several forms. It may be a written, descriptive evaluation. The comments would be directed toward a comparison of perfomance standards with the appraisal reviews. A discussion of critical incidents might also be included in this form of evaluation. In the interest of achieving greater objectivity, it may also be appropriate to utilize a checklist, a rating scale, or some kind of employee comparison system. The latter is most likely to be used in a merit pay situation where it is necessary to discriminate among the various levels of performance. One possibility here is what is known as forced distribution. In that system, the rater distributes employees among a limited number of categories with a specified percent in each category. There may also be a rank-order distribution that is reflected in a numerical rating of all employees in a given unit, based on overall performance in the effort to reach specific objectives. A further refinement is the paired comparison technique. With that, each employee with a given task is paired with every other employee with the same task, and the rater selects the one with the better performance. It should be noted that the disjunctive nature of the enterprise will limit the use of either the rank-order distribution or the paired comparison technique in school or college sport programs. However, either one might be used on a modified basis. Sometimes it is necessary to make comparisons even though it may not seem to be appropriate for the particular situation.

5. *One-on-one interview.* This is an interview that takes place between the immediate supervisor and the employee. In other words, it would be the athletic director meeting with a head coach, the latter meeting with an assistant coach, or the director of the program conferring with a staff assistant. Basically, the interview should focus on a comparison of the employee's self-appraisal with the tentative evaluation that has been prepared either by the supervisor or a peer group. The supervisor should attempt to concentrate on the key points in the performance. This is the primary medium for feedback and reaction from both directions.

6. *Formal submission of the evaluation.* After the conference, the evaluation is formally submitted through the appropriate offices for review with any changes and recommendations for personnel action. For example, an assistant coach's evaluation might be submitted to the head coach and reviewed by the athletic director, the director of the sport program, and the dean of academic affairs. The particular routing will depend on the structure of the institution, but the process is fairly standard.

7. *Follow-up during the year.* Again, it should be noted that evaluation is a continuous process. It does not stop with the submission of the evaluation report. The supervisor should use the report to maintain an ongoing performance file and to

offer constructive criticism throughout the year. This also brings attention to the last component of the controlling function, the reward system.

THE REWARD SYSTEM

The most important thing to keep in mind about the reward system is that it does not represent the end result. First and foremost it is a means in the entire management process. One might be inclined to think of reward only in a more terminal vein as associated with promotion, advancement, or pay raises. Certainly those are important considerations in the reward system. However, even the positive manifestations of reward should serve as stimulants for further improvement in performance. Beyond that, the reward system also includes corrective action and sometimes even necessary disciplinary action. Although reward is the culmination of the controlling process, it flows directly into further thought about planning, organizing, staffing, and directing, as well as the need for continued evaluation. What are some of the key considerations involving the reward system in school and college sport? These are at least 10 in number. Some of the factors are applicable to work in any profession or to the field of education. Others are more direct features of the sport management profession. In any case, they provide the parameters of reward for work performance in school and college sport programs.

Service. This is a reward that stands as a potential for any educator and many professionals in other fields. Yet it is also the reward that is the most abstract and thus, perhaps, the most overlooked. From the perspective of the coach, Fuoss and Troppmann (1981) describe this kind of reward most aptly.

> The self-actualizing coach is likely to find coaching as fulfilling and satisfying as the surgeon who performs a successful operation, or as the lawyer who won a judgment for his client. It is working with young people, watching them grow and mature, and their being better individuals as a result of having "played for you" that makes coaching so rewarding. From a personal standpoint, coaching is satisfying, rewarding, fulfilling, and self-actualizing for the coach (p. 35).

Even though the potential for such reward is generally present in school and college sport, we find great variances in terms of the extent to which it actually materializes and is recognized. Much the same potential should exist for sport instructors and teachers as well as coaches, yet other aspects of the reward system may stand in the way of this becoming a reality. Much of this depends on the orientation and motivation of the individual employee, but beyond that management is the key determinent. This brings us back to a recognition of the unity of the controlling function. It is important to begin with the identification of appropriate performance standards. Then there must be a valid reporting system. After that, the counseling in the evaluation process may be most instrumental in directing the individual toward an appreciation of the service reward.

The extent to which this kind of reward is a reality in school or college sport programs will also depend very much on the nature of the objectives that have been set forth for that program. In general, it would appear that those who coach at the high school level have the best opportunity to experience the satisfaction of contributing to the development of young people. The same kind of reward may be present while working in college programs. However, in many of these programs the potential is reduced through objectives that are aimed at the financial pressure to produce winning teams.

It is quite obvious that the service contribution heads the list of the so-called intrinsic rewards for work in school or college sport. Unfortunately, it is also a reward that cannot be completely programed. To a large extent, the realization of this reward will depend on the motivation of the individual coach, teacher, administrator, or staff member. However, the potential in this area should always loom as an important factor in the controlling process.

Achievement. Having achieved one's objective can be a reward in any context. One of the principal advantages of work in school or college sport is the abundant opportunity to realize such achievement in a concrete setting. The game won, the winning season, the first place finish in the season, and the tournament champion are all direct manifestations of having achieved. The coach is the one employee in school or college sport who has the potential to realize this kind of reward. Unfortunately for him or her, this aspect of reward is also a two-edged sword. With this concrete measurement of achievement goes the accompanying pressure to win. Whether we like it or not, the loss of the "big game" or the losing season is also a form of reward in this setting. Once again this points to the extreme importance of the unity of approach in the entire controlling function.

The picture surrounding the entire sport program is further complicated by the differentiation in achievement potential among other sport management personnel. For the most part, they have neither the advantages nor the disadvantages of the coach. The sport coordinator, sport instructors, business manager, facilities manager, sports information director, and others are working in areas where the achievement (or lack of it) is not as evident. This is one of the reasons why MBO can be a most effective system. It helps to balance the achievement potential for all personnel.

As with the service contribution, the reward of having achieved falls largely into the intrinsic category. However, by contrast with the satisfaction gained from serving others, achievement can also lead to extrinsic rewards. In terms of the controlling function, those who manage school and college programs will have to make some hard decisions regarding the extent to which achievement is to be recognized as an extrinsic factor in the reward system. More about that will be said when we consider the other kinds of rewards, particularly those of a financial nature.

Status. In terms of reward factors, achievement and status are closely related, yet they also are quite separate considerations. One can achieve without attaining significant status. The reverse is also a real possibility. Nevertheless, in many situations there is a positive correlation between achievement and status.

As with achievement, status is also a two-headed consideration for those who work in school and college sport programs. Again, the coach epitomizes both the positive and negative reward factors. Cady (1978) describes the status dilemma of the coach very vividly. "He stands in the eye of the storm: when it blows with him, he is exalted, bestriding the festival, godlike; when it turns and blows the other way, he is strong indeed if it does not tear him to shreds. He becomes, all dimly, the American Vegetation God, watcher of the golden bough, king today, burned tomorrow. We call him, 'coach'" (p. 120).

This matter of status represents a most complicated control factor in the sport programs. It would appear that many of those who seek employment in these programs are initially motivated by the desire to be involved in an activity that is highly visible and has a high degree of popular appeal. Also, the majority of the personnel come from a background wherein they achieved some degree of status as athletes. However, as with achievement, status is not an equallly pervasive reward factor for all sport management personnel. Many of them, particularly the instructors and staff members, work behind the scene. By and large, the coach and the athletic director are the people who could be said to have status. In many cases, the athletic director also attained prior status through his success as a coach. It is fairly easy for either the coach or the A.D. to get "carried away" with the constant reinforcement of status that comes from being successful in the public limelight. At the same time, there is always the equal possibility of suddenly reduced status when the tide turns the other way. The control comes into the picture in the constant need to balance both the internal and external perception regarding status.

Emotional Ambivalence. There is at least one other intrinsic reward in school and college sport that largely involves coaches. In discussing "unique features indigenous to coaching," Fuoss and Troppmann (1981) use the term "emotional ambivalence" (p. 35). They also discuss the emotional drain, "burning out," and the high emotions at games. In a way, the emotional aspect is all part of one picture. It is also related to achievement and status although the emotional component is its own kind of reward factor with both positive and negative dimensions. In terms of emotions, coaching offers its own kind of rewards. The peaks and the valleys, the highs and lows are always present. With that there is the accompanying problem associated with the coach who is removed from coaching or who decides on his or her own account that he or she can no longer meet the emotional demands. On the other side of the coin, the desire to be part of such excitement can be a principal motivating factor for work in this area. In a sense, the emotional involvement is its own kind of reward. The only question is when does the positive quality of exciting work tip in the other direction of excessive emotional pressure. Once again we see the need for a balanced perspective in attempting to control the efforts of those who are on the "firing line" of work in school and college sport.

Financial. One has to begin with the proposition that most people do not seek positions in school or college sport for the potential financial rewards to be derived from such work. If they did, they would certainly be approaching the employment with false expectations. Any misconception is undoubtedly attributed to the notation of the relatively high salaries that are paid to a select group of college football and basketball coaches in addition to added income that these coaches obtain from television shows and other appearances. Obviously, this does not apply to the majority, particularly those who coach or teach at the high school level or both. In general, sport management personnel share the financial limitations that are faced by all educators.

In spite of any limitation, decisions relative to financial remuneration remain the number one extrinsic reward factor in any organization. Any employee knows that attitudes toward salary are always relative to the context of the organization. Employees may also look beyond for points of comparison, but first of all they will look within.

What are the possibilities for a financial reward system for employment in school or college sport programs. Basically, three systems of salary increases are most evident: merit pay, across-the-board increases, and step increases. One might also find any combination of these. In addition, salary increase is usually tied in with advancement or promotion in rank. Some sport programs also have additional stipends for coaching. More about that will be said a little later. Much of what can or cannot be done in terms of financial reward is determined at the institutional level. In recent years, labor unions have also become a key factor in establishing the system. Within some of the larger college sport programs there is more financial autonomy that enables these programs to establish their own financial reward system. At any rate, the pros and cons of the various means of determining financial reward should be considered.

Ideally speaking, all the advantages seem to lie with a merit pay system. The theory behind a merit pay system is hard to refute: personnel are rewarded according to what they have achieved. Difficulties in this system occur only at the practical level in the attempt to measure achievement. What should be the criteria in determining merit pay? The answer to that can be a subject for considerable debate in any program that employs the merit pay system. This again points to the advantages of MBO. At least under that framework one has the opportunity to assess qualitatively and quantitatively the extent to which the individual employee objectives have been reached. The employee is also an integral part of the process in determining those objectives. Therefore, he or she knows what is expected of him or her, and there is prior agreement regarding these expectations. However, even MBO does not provide assurance that merit pay can be implemented without difficulties and limitations. Sometimes it is very difficult to compare performances among various employees, all of whom have been effective in their work. Particularly in sport programs, the disjunctive nature of the tasks may point to difficulties in comparative assessment. Nevertheless, where and when the institutional arrangements permit, some kind of merit pay structure should be given serious consideration as part of the reward system in sport programs.

One of the principal advantages of an across-the-board increase is that it can at least provide partial compensation for a rise in the cost of living. It is often employed with that objective in mind, assuming that all personnel have been basically effective in their performance. Many institutions will also use a combination of the across-the-board and merit pay systems. Obviously, this has certain advantages from both sides. The only real question here is the extent to which the reward should be more directly weighed toward the relative achievement factor.

Some type of step-increase salary system is used in most public schools. It is also found in some colleges and universities. Basically, this is a reward for time in service as well as increased compensation for advanced degree work. The pros and cons of such a system are fairly obvious. It would appear that the rationale is found in the idea that it is often difficult to assess achievement objectively in the educational setting. The across-the-board and step increase is also a common combination. Both of these exist a bit outside the realm of the controlling function per se. Yet they must be taken into account as realistic components of the reward system in many programs.

Another part of the reward system particularly evident in the public schools is that of providing additional compensation for coaching. This kind of arrangement is undesirable for several reasons. First of all, for the most part such compensation is no where nearly commensurate with the work that is involved in these coaching assignments. If there is to be compensation along this line, it should be realistic. Also, in many such cases, those receiving the coaching stipends are physical education teachers who actually put much more time and effort in their coaching than in any instructional responsibility. At the same time they receive a full salary for teaching physical education and a relatively small stipend for coaching. Such an arrangement tends to make a farce out of the whole reward system. Coaching should be recognized as a most integral part of the program. In some cases, even at the high school level, this might mean full-time coaching. In many other situations, there will be a combination teaching-coaching responsibility. But regardless of the split or lack of it, coaching should be built into the position description, and reward is determined accordingly. This is still another reason why it is so important to have an integrated sport management program in the schools and colleges.

Security. Having a relatively secure position is one of the rewards for working in certain organizations. The field of education perhaps heads the list of those occupations that tend to fall into the relatively secure category. The concept of tenure is more or less unique to schools and colleges. In recent years, owing to financial restrictions, there is evidence that tenure does not offer the same kind of security that was evident at one time. Yet one is still in a more protected position by having tenure than if there was no such system.

Those who work in school and college sport programs find themselves in a very complicated situation with respect to tenure. Superficially, one might expect that they stand to benefit from the relative security that is offered by the tenure system in the field of education generally. In some instances and to some extent, this is true. However, again we have to look at the coach to note the uniqueness of the sport situation. There are very few occupations that have less security than that involving coaching. The coach may have tenure in the broadest sense, but there are very few coaches who have tenure in their coaching positions. Schools and colleges should seriously consider the idea of offering tenure to coaches as coaches. This would serve at least two purposes. First, in the interest of the total control factor, it would reduce the pressure on coaches to win at all costs. Second, it would eliminate many of the reassignment problems involving coaches. More about that will be said in the next section of this chapter under reassignment as a reward factor. However, the idea of having the tenured coach is not as simple as it first appears. The physical and emotional demands in coaching are such that many coaches find they cannot measure up to the task for many years. It could well be that any tenure provision would have to be carefully arranged to be contingent upon fulfillment of task demands with appropriate reassignment as an advanced condition.

At any rate, if coaches are truly to be recognized as educators, there should be consistency in the opportunity for tenure. The general topic just prompts further consideration regarding the desirability of tenure in any educational system. As with merit pay, there are many pros and cons with respect to tenure. For the most part, this is an institutional concern that is more or less predetermined by the general modus operandi in the broad field of education. However, in spite of any institutional restraints, it seems apparent that the administrators of school and college sport programs must seek greater consistency in deciding on how tenure will be handled as part of their particular reward system.

Reassignment. Even though we may not customarily think of it in that light, reassignment is also an important consideration in a reward system. It may result from a recognition of a job well done with new opportunites in a new position. Or it may arise from the need for corrective action to stimulate a better performance. In either case, it is part of the reward structure.

Coaching is again in the foreground in terms of reassignment considerations in school and college sport. Many of the reassignments involve coaches who are either completely removed from their coaching responsibilities or assigned to coach another sport. Even though the need for reassignment may be most apparent, two problems are very evident in terms of how this is often handled. Much reassignment takes place after the fact. In other words, the coach is removed from his or her coaching duties, and then the administrator looks around to see where his or her services might be used in the total program. Sometimes this is unavoidable. But again we are reminded of the importance of the annual counseling session or one-on-one interviews during the evaluation process. Every effort should be made to anticipate and prepare for future assignments.

The subject of reassignment also points to the close interdependence among the various managerial functions. In this case, the close connection between effective staffing and appropriate reassignment is most evident. If the coach has been selected only because of strong qualifications in coaching a particular sport, the options are limited when it comes time to exercise control through reassignment. In the very highly competitive programs at the university Division I-A level, such more restricted selection may be necessary in order to obtain the level of competency that is needed for coaching football or basketball. However, administrators must be alerted to future problems related to the reward system when the coach is no longer able or willing to meet the demands of coaching that sport. In the smaller college and high school programs, many of the reassignment problems can be avoided through more careful selection of coaches with qualifications that extend beyond coaching per se.

Additional work. It is well known in many organizations that one of the rewards for a job well done is additional work. There is evidence that frequently those who accomplish the most are either self-motivated or asked to do more as a result of their efforts. Once again, the coach is a classic example of one who experiences this form of reward. In reference to coaching, Fuoss and Troppmann (1981) note that "the work is endless. A recognized coaching cliché is, Coaching is like threading beads on a string with no knot, there is no end to the job!"(p. 40). Earlier in their work, they also point to the additional work demands in reference to John Wooden's reaction at the time of his retirement from coaching.

> John Wooden retired at the termination of the 1975 intercollegiate basketball season after having directed his UCLA Bruins to an unprecedented tenth NCAA national basketball championship in his concluding game as a coach. Wooden reputedly informed his players, "I'm bowing out. I don't want to. I have to" (as reported by Moses, 1975). On another occasion, Wooden was quoted by *The Los Angeles Times,* "They think that when you win a lot that it's easy. The fact is the more you win the harder it is to keep on doing it" (p. 35).

Needless to say, the reward of additional work does not only apply to the winners in sport; the losers can just as easily experience the same demand. Regardless of whether it's winning or losing, it's easy to see why this aspect of the reward system accentuates the significance of the controlling function in school and college sport.

Promotion–Advancement. A realistic appraisal of the promotion–advancement feature of the reward system in school and college sport almost has to begin with the recognition that the opportunities tend to be limited. It is a case of "many are called, but few are chosen." Many assistant coaches never realize their goal of being selected for the head position. Beyond that we need to only note the highly competitive situation in seeking an athletic director's position, particularly at the college level. Even the higher staff positions, such as assistant or associate athletic director, offer limited potential owing to the relatively few programs that have the resources for these positions.

At the college level, the opportunities for promotion are generally tied in with academic rank, the hierarchy of professional status. This also poses certain limitations for those who work in the majority of the college sport programs. The only major exceptions are the appointments in academic programs in sport management . Some colleges also award rank to coaches or sport instructors (or both) who are not directly involved with academic programs. That practice, although possibly defensible, can present certain complications in itself. Generally speaking, promotion in rank results from receipt of the doctorate degree and demonstration of research through publishing. Relatively few coaches hold doctorates. Also, the additional work demands (as noted earlier) are such that the typical coach will not find time for publishing even if he or she is so inclined. This means that a coach has to be evaluated according to a different criterion if academic rank is to be extended to that sector of the professional environment. The situation is further complicated by the fact that academic rank and faculty status also tend to go hand in hand.

What can be done about these limitations in carrying out this aspect of the reward system as part of the controlling function in college sport? The only real answer seems to lie in effective counseling in the evaluation process, which brings attention to the limitations in this area and focuses on other aspects of the complete reward system. One other positive note brings us back to a component of the staffing function, development. Expanding the opportunities for promotion or advancement is one of the principal reasons why development is integral to the complete staffing function.

Firing. In a way, it seems inappropriate to conclude our analysis of the controlling function with the topic of firing. A more diplomatic term, such as dismissal, or release, could have been used. Nevertheless, regardless of what it is called, both management and employees have to face up to the fact that sometimes the reward for subpar results is termination of employment other than through voluntary resignation or retirement. At any rate, it is the last resort. In that respect it is fitting to note it at the end.

As with many of the considerations involving the reward system, the position of the coach with respect to firing is also somewhat unique. It is well known that coaches are high on the list of those groups of individuals who face the real possibility of being fired. Unfortunately, the tendency has been to extend the modus operandi of professional sport, particularly with respect to baseball managers, to the college and school programs. Firing the coach of a professional sport team can be justified because it is well known that he or she was selected for one purpose—to win. This can also be justified with respect to a select number of university sport programs when it has been established at the outset that this is to be the indicator of success for the coach. The problem is found in the commonly accepted idea that the practice of firing the losing coach should be extended to all school and college spectator sport programs. Obviously, much of the pressure in this regard is in an external source. It is at this point that we really see the need for control in school and college sport.

Even when there is apparently just cause for firing a coach, the manner in which it is done should be a prime consideration. Except under the most extenuating circumstances, a coach should not be fired at the school or college level in midseason. This again points to the importance of the annual review of performance as part of the evaluation process. Any deficiencies in performance should be documented in writing at the conclusion of that review. Any coach or other staff member in the sport program should be given at least a one-year warning that the performance must be improved or otherwise he or she may not be reappointed.

Summary

In some respects, the controlling function signals both the end and the beginning. Throughout this book we have noted that there is a certain chronology with respect to planning, organizing, staffing, directing, and controlling. However, it is equally as important to recognize the continuous flow and close connection among all the managerial functions. When we control, we set in motion a whole new series of actions involving planning, organizing, staffing, and directing the program.

 The concept of control is not at all foreign to those who work in school or college sport programs. It is manifested in such considerations as crowd control, eligibility requirements, officiating, control of equipment and facilities, conference regulations, and control of the budget. In this chapter, we have focused attention on the controlling function as it directly relates to those who hold the line and staff positions in the various school and college sport programs. This is based on the assumption that such control is the key to carrying out all aspects of the controlling function in sport. If we are able to provide appropriate performance standards, reporting system, evaluation, and reward systems for these people, there is a good possibility that the other aspects of control can be effectively handled.

 Much of the attention has been directed to the role of the coach in respect to the controlling function. This is not to suggest that the need for control begins or stops with the coach. However, the public visibility and external pressures on the coach offer dramatic evidence of the critical nature of the controlling function in school and college sport. It could be said that the performance standards, reporting system, and evaluative mechanism are built into the very nature of the coach's task before administrators even begin to provide a format for effective control. The coach is judged externally before there is an opportunity for more complete internal assessment. Needless to say, this has a tremendous bearing on the kind of reward system that is operative in school and college sport.

REFERENCES

Cady, Edwin H. *The Big Game*. Knoxville, Tenn. U. of Tennessee Press, 1978.

Deegan, Arthur X., and Fritz, Roger J. *MBO Goes to College*. Clearwater, Fl. Deegan, 1975.

Fuoss, Donald E., and Troppmann, Robert J. *Effective Coaching: A Psychological Approach*. New York. Wiley, 1981.

CHAPTER 7

Sport Management in the Schools and Colleges: In Retrospect

CONCEPTS AND PROBLEMS

Stress on the Integrated Sport Program

Students: The Key Consideration in Any Educational Organization

Basic Distinction Between Athletes and Other Students

No Substitute for the Appropriate Selection of Coaches

Suggestions for Improving the Spectrum of Sport Instruction

Intramural Sport as a Complement to the Instructional Program

Advantages in Having Sport Coordinators

Game Management: A Microcosm of the Total Managerial Concern in School or College Sport

Spectators: The Fourth Component of the Quadrangular Dimension in Sport

Status of Title IX Implementation

The Complex Financial Dimension of School and College Sport Programs

Improving the Quality of Public Relations

The Need to Assess the Relationship Between School and Nonschool Sport Programs

In the preceding chapters we have examined the sport programs in the schools in the context of the five principal managerial functions. This was done under the assumption that the work of professional employees in these programs is largely of a managerial nature. Even though we typically identify various roles such as teaching, coaching, supervising, and administering, these all share the common denominator of being involved with management in some form or another. If one is to understand management, it seems appropriate to begin by noting what one does as a manager. Essentially, a manager plans, organizes, staffs, directs, and controls a program. Thus it is important to analyze in some detail what is involved in carrying out each of these five functions.

The other significant "given" in this book is the unifying concept of sport. Throughout, the approach has been to stress the need for an integrated sport program. Thus, this work is different from most of the previous literature and current practice as it relates to this topic. It is customary to distinguish among physical education, intramural sport, and interscholastic or intercollegiate athletic programs. As a result, we find other texts that are written on the administration of athletics, the administration of physical education and athletics, or the administration of intramural sport programs. In the author's opinion, such divisions have contributed to the organizational confusion that has limited the attainment of the rich potential of a sport management program for consumers and employees. The central thread remains sport, which is really a composite of the various activities that we commonly recognize as being sports. Golf is still golf regardless of the particular manifestation of the activity. It is still necessary to distinguish among the instructional, intramural, and interscholastic or intercollegiate components of the total program, but such distinctions should not be our primary concern. An integrated sport program can do much to facilitate more effective management of personnel, equipment, and facilities.

First we use the functional approach to examine the sport management program. It now seems appropriate to conclude with a somewhat different look at the various managerial concerns in school and college sport. As important as it is to understand what is involved in planning or any other function, we should not leave with the idea that the function is the focus of attention. The managerial functions are merely the facilitating mechanisms in the attempt to offer the most productive program. Most of these concerns have been discussed under the preceding context. Now is a time to pull certain things together and simultaneously take a fresh look at the basic parameters of sport management in the schools and colleges.

STUDENTS

What kind of program is made available to the students? This should be *the* question in any educational organization. When all is said and done, educational institutions exist first and foremost for the purpose of providing a service to students. It is so easy to forget this at a time when schools and colleges have assumed so many roles that extend beyond students per se. All these roles should ultimately demonstrate a contribution to student needs and interests. In Chapter 2, we distinguished between individual objectives and institutional objectives. However, it is important to note that even the institutional objectives are aimed at improving the student status. Even if the principal objective of the sport program is to enhance the image of the school or college, this is done for students past, present, and future.

The fact that the management of the program should be student-oriented is also reinforced through recognition of how sport got into the colleges in the first place.

Cady (1978) makes this point most lucidly in his discussion: "How Did We Get This Way?"

> So, in a burst of chagrin at the shame and confusion of his university after the exposure of cheating in the athletics program, a famous historian wrote me to demand not long ago, "How did we get ths way, anyhow?" If a simple answer existed, of course, there need be no angry question. But you can learn some useful things from a look at the historical paths along which Americans came to get this way . . . . the games which grew into American college sports were indigenous to the student populations because the boys were people in transit, through the colleges, from boy-life to adult-life and brought the games to college with them (pp. 17, 22).

Eventually, the college administrators had to get involved in order to control what had been established by the students. Obviously, the evolution has been one that seems to move the program further and further away from the student body at large. Nevertheless, management is likely to encounter problems if they completely lose sight of the student perspective. This is still another reason why there is strong argument for an integrated sport program that serves the entire student population.

It is true that throughout this book we have focused considerably more attention on athletes, coaches, and spectator sports than on students at large, sport instructors, or intramural supervisors. The only reason for this is that the athlete and the coach provide some of the more visible and dramatic evidence of the principal managerial concerns in sport. Although I think he exaggerates a bit in this regard, Weiss (1969) points to the key role of the athlete in sport: "The athlete is sport incarnated, sport instantiated, sport located for the moment, and by that fact is man himself, incarnated, instantiated, and located." (p. 248). In a way it could be said that the athlete and coach serve as models for the student and instructor in sport. Thus, as noted before, if things are wrong with the athletes and coaches, everything may be wrong with the total sport program.

The real difficulty seems to be in the tendency to overlook the fact that the sport program extends beyond the athlete to mass participation. If that were not the case, one would not note so many examples of inferior instructors and subpar intramural programs. The real key to providing a more viable program for all the students is to be found in the organizing function. The students at large must feel that they have an adequate opportunity to be involved with an organization that epitomizes the action in sport. They cannot be shoved off into the corner in an intramural program that receives scant attention or in a gym class that has the atmosphere of a "glorified recess." Aside from structural considerations, the establishment of appropriate position qualifications also points to the critical nature of the organizing function. We cannot expect that the general student will benefit greatly from a program that is under the direction of an individual who is not qualified by virtue of background and interest. The very nature of the task will make it difficult to find instructors and intramural supervisors who have the committment of coaches, but at least we must seek progress in that direction.

ATHLETES

Before we go any further, it is probably important to clarify exactly what is meant by athletes in this context. The term has been used throughout this book under the assumption that there is a fair amount of consensus as to what distinguishes an athlete from a general sport participant. However, because athletes are here being considered as a separate topic, it seems important to establish more firmly the frame of reference. Basically, a school or college athlete is one who participates in organized interscholastic or intercollegiate sport competition under the direction of a coach. This contrasts an athlete with another student who is an intramural or extramural sport participant or one who receives instruction in a given sport. The most significant aspect of this distinction is that an athlete serves as a representative of his or her school or college regardless of any particular motives for participation. The basic reason for this is that the athlete's performance is available for public examination. Spectator sport is a point of departure. The remaining exposure is provided through media coverage of interscholastic and intercollegiate events, whether or not these are spectator contests as such. The major difference is one involving the degree of exposure.

Why is this an important consideration? Primarily because it indicates the critical nature of the controlling function in the management of athletes. The public visibility creates a situation in which there will always be people outside the program who strive to develop their own reporting system, performance standards, evaluative mechanisms, and reward system for athletes. In short, they want to "get their finger in the pie" particularly in relationship to the controlling components. Financial inducements are a classic case in point as to how the reward system can be used to manipulate the entire program. This shows the need for administrators and coaches to exercise external control in terms of actions taken with respect to athletes. At the same time, it will be difficult to provide that external control unless there is the right kind of internal control in the program.

Internal control reveals the close connection between the controlling function and the planning function as manifested in appropriate policy development. By and large, internal control can be achieved if sound policies have been established and efforts are made to enforce those policies. It begins with the admission of the athlete into the institution and the program and does not cease to be a need until the athlete has received his or her diploma.

The central question surrounding athletes is one involving the extent to which they should be given special attention or privleges as contrasted with the student body at large. The answer to this will largely depend on the level of the institution and the specific program objectives. What is most needed is an elimination of the hypocrisy that has surrounded school and college sport for too many years. We cannot continue with the procedure of presenting the lofty conception of the student-athlete and then, at the same time, continue to offer programs in which the athlete is only a student in a nominal sense. Within recent months, there have been various expressions and interpretations of the problems that confront college sport today. The Sunday, March 21, 1982, edition of *The New York Times* presents a fairly representative statement of the concern.

> Seventeen schools are on the National Collegiate Athletic Association's probation list, equaling the highest number for a single period, "and the list will go higher before it goes lower," according to David Berst, the director of the association's enforement department. At a time when costs are escalating rapidly in college sports, at a time when lucrative television dollars are available for successful football and basketball teams and at a time when increased outside involvement from alumni and boosters have led to excesses and embarrassments in recruiting and, in some cases, outright scandal, educators are being forced to consider whether the atheltic system is out of control.
>
> The violations against the 17 schools range from illegal transportation to illegal entertainment and illegal financial inducements for recruiting prospects . . . .
>
> In addition, other schools are on probation for violations involving forged academic transcripts and unearned credits and administering improper financial aid to athletes . . . .
>
> As many as 35 more schools are under investigation by the N.C.A.A. for possible violations . . . .
>
> "There isn't a meeting that goes by without some discussion of the problems in college athletics," said Dr. Edward J. Bloustein, the president of Rutgers University, who is a member of the board of directors of the American Council on Education and the National Association of State Universities and Land Grant Colleges. It's a little distressing to hear my colleagues say they can't control it and they don't know if they can outvote their coaches with their alumni body." Dr. Bloustein was referring to matters related to the athletic policy within a university (Section 5, p. 1).

Now, of course, it could be argued that the 52 colleges (17 + 35) are not representative of the many colleges throughout the United States. One can undoubtedly identify many college programs in which there are student-athletes in the fuller meaning of that concept. Obviously, the situation at the high school level is also different in many respects. Nevertheless, the collegiate sport powers continue to establish a pattern that points to the overriding and pervasive question about the role of the athlete in any educational institution. Even though the irregularities may be dramatized at the Division I-A level, there is a certain amount of filtering down which affects the conduct of all college and school sport programs.

Getting back to the hypocrisy, what can be done about it? I think that the president of Brown University, Howard R. Swearer, offered a reasonable answer.

The national intercollegiate athletic situation is in considerable flux and, I believe, may have entered a period of rapid transition. Many colleges and universities are facing critical questions that cannot be begged for long.

The driving forces are well known but merit attention anyway, if for no reason than many of us in the older generation may tend to view collegiate sport through the now misty and romantic filter of our undergraduate days. However, the tug of nostalgia should not inhibit us from making a clear assessment of the contemporary scene.

It is important to note that college sports are populated with many kinds of athletes and there are many types of game plans. It would be a mistake to categorize some as right and good and some as wrong and bad. Institutions and leagues are responding differently to powerful forces at work in the society according to their traditions and perceived self-interests—as they should . . . .

The fictions are wearing thin. I, for one, see no harm in associating a professional or semi-professional team with a university; and I see a number of benefits. It would clarify what is now a very murky picture. Athletes should, of course, have the opportunity to take courses and pursue a degree, if they wish; but they would be regarded as athletes first and should be paid accordingly. By so doing, the regulatory and enforcement burden and the temptations for illegal and unethical practices would be dramatically eased. The clear separation between the academic and athletic purposes of the university would be beneficial to both. Who would care if a coach were paid a salary seven times that of the average full professor, so long as the economics of the situation justified it. The ambiguities and stresses which now press on the integrity of the academic programs would be eased.

If the big powers were to choose this course, I think it would benefit all intercollegiate athletics. High school seniors would be given a more clearly defined choice among different kinds of post-secondary athletic experiences. The general public could recognize more clearly the nature of athletic competition in different leagues. The pressures toward "professionalism" on those institutions that chose a different course course might be lessened (Section 5, p. 2).[1]

It is clear that Swearer was advocating a position in which colleges more clearly defined their program objectives and proceeded to offer a sport program that was consistent with those objectives. It can be assumed that, in most cases, colleges should and would opt for a program in which the concept of the scholar-athlete has meaning in the truer sense. Athletes might still be given added attention and have certain privileges, but first and foremost they would be recognized as students. This would also be of assistance in providing a better model for high school athletes, who can also easily forget their identity as students. At the same time, the other kind of model would still be available for those programs and athletes who desire to pursue excellence through sport.

All this brings us back to a recognition of the relative significance of the controlling function with respect to athletes. It also demonstrates the very close con-

[1]*The New York Times,* Sunday, February 21, 1982.

nection between the planning function and the controlling function. The performance standards, reporting system, evaluation, and reward system will be very different if the program is designed to accommodate scholar-athletes or athletes who might also be scholars.

COACHES

When it comes to coaches, there is little doubt as to which of the managerial functions stands out above all the others. Proper staffing is the name of the game. The desired internal control for athletes will not be provided if administrators are negligent in the selection, orientation, training, and development of coaches. This is one of the major reasons the detailed analysis of management training for coaches was included in Chapter 4. However, in the final analysis, there is no substitute for the appropriate selection of coaches. Any orientation, training and development measures are not likely to fall on fertile ground if selection is inappropriate for the particular coaching position. Unfortunately, as noted earlier, there is no magic formula for determining coaching qualifications. The competent coach has a composite of many suitable qualities. Perhaps the best one can do is to note some of the factors that may guide the selection process.

1. Program objectives are the overriding consideration in guiding the selection. The situation here is very much akin to what we noted earlier with respect to athletes. If the program has objectives that are aimed at the scholar-athlete, it is imperative that a coach be selected who is able and willing to make the necessary accommodations in the attempt to meet those objectives. On the other hand, if we follow the Swearer comparison, in certain college programs, the focus may not be on scholars. That would certainly indicate that the ability to recruit would head the list of coaching qualifications in that context. It is time for us to become much more open about our thoughts and actions within this general framework. However, even the latter choice does not mean that everything goes in terms of the recruiting effort. There is still need for control as cited earlier in reference to the ideas of Edwin Cady.

2. General differences in qualifications for high school coaches, as contrasted with college coaches, should also be noted. To a certain extent every coach is a leader, teacher, manager, counselor, trainer, and public relations person. But the teaching and counseling roles are tremendously important at the high school level. For example, Snyder (1980) found that high school coaches are even an important factor in athlete decisions about future educational plans:

> The advice that coaches give their players regarding educational plans beyond high school is positively associated with the players' decisions to attend college. Furthermore, this advice is independent of either parental socioeconomic background or grades. Many players see their coach as influential, but this influence only has a low relationship to educational plans; it is partially a function of the advice given by coaches (p. 199).

Although the college coach also functions very much as a counselor, the role model of the high school coach should be a primary concern in the selection process. It is also important to keep in mind that much of the real teaching in the basics of the sport will occur at that level.

3. The apprenticeship system is integral to the effective preparation of coaches. The art of coaching can only be learned at the scene of the action. Even though coaching minors are desirable—and even coaching majors—they are not a substitute for the apprenticeship. That's the major reason why the internships are so important in these programs. This also conveys an important message for the selection process. Careful attention should be given to the overall performance of a head coach under whom the applicant served as an assistant or intern. There is a strong possibility that a similar modus operandi will be followed by the applicant when he or she is selected for a head position.

4. The overall image projected by the coach should be a principal consideration in all school or college programs regardless of the level. This refers back to Cady's point about "class." The competent coach will have class regardless of how that may be defined. In the selection process, much attention should be directed toward the candidate's presentation of self, including everything that might be involved in that concept. Certainly, poise, communication ability, and appearance are some of the variables to be considered. The importance of this image factor is primarily related to the fact that the coach will always be one of the more visible representatives of the school or college at any level. It just makes sense to select representatives who project favorably for the total program. This is another one of those areas in which all parties concerned need a more honest appraisal of the situation. There is sometimes a tendency to suggest that image really isn't all that important. That may be true of certain professions, but coaching is not among them. Appearance itself may not be the most significant variable, but the total bearing of the coach should be carefully assessed in the selection process.

INSTRUCTION

Throughout the text reference has been made to sport instructors and sport instruction. The terms *sport teachers* or *the teaching of sport* could just as well have been used. In either case, we are referring to the process wherein students learn the skills and knowledge of a given sport. Although more attention has been directed toward the coach than the instructor, this in no way negates the importance of the latter. The relative visibility of coaches and the complexity of the total coaching situation just call for more detailed analysis. We would have to assume that in most programs, particularly the smaller ones, much of the instruction is done by coaches. Of course, the coach also instructs as part of his or her coaching duties, but here we are referring to the teaching of classes apart from the coaching situation.

As one looks over the scope of managerial concerns with respect to instruction, the planning and organizing functions loom as the most critical. In general, what is needed is an overall sensitivity that would bring the instructional area more in line with the attention and quality that are typically found in the coaching situation. It is true that the reward factors will always be more evident in coaching. But this does not mean that there is no room for improvement in the standard of instruction. If schools are unable to offer quality instruction in a given sport, then they should forget about the idea, at least until the proper resources can be provided. Something is amiss as we note the tremendous popularity of private sport clubs and summer sport camps. If the schools were doing the job in this area, the demand would not be nearly as great as is evident at the present time.

The situation is particularly acute at the public school level. There the attainment of quality sport instruction has been severely limited by the inherent deficiencies in the structure of physical education, epitomized by the gym class. The modus operandi is one in which the class comes first; afterwards we will be concerned about the sports to be offered and who is to offer the instruction. This is a classic case of "putting the cart before the horse." As with most everything, there are, of course, exceptions to the general situation. Swimming seems to be one sport wherein we frequently find a quality instructional program in the schools. It could well be that this is out of a matter of necessity due to the inherent safety factor in swimming. At any rate, I offer the following suggestions that would appear to benefit the spectrum of sport instruction in the schools and colleges.

1. The focus on sport instruction should definitely be at the elementary school level. It is well known that the majority of people who acquire a high degree of expertise in a certain sport have had extensive exposure to that sport at an early age. Why not make this opprtunity available to all boys and girls in the school wherever circumstances permit? Such opportunities should not be limited to those children whose parents can afford to send them to a private club for instruction. One also hears considerable criticism about the various community youth sport programs such as Little League baseball, hockey associations, and so on. There is one primary reason why these organizations have such widespread appeal. The needs are not being met in the public school. It is true that in most elementary school programs the children do receive some exposure to various sport skills. Frequently, this is couched within the framework of a movement education experience. Whether it is or isn't, there is seldom what could be called "in-depth" instruction in the sport. The elementary school physical education teacher is also invariably in the position of having to cover several sports regardless of any particular qualifications in most of them. That would be akin to having trombone lessons taught by a piano teacher who had never played the trombone. Evidence shows that sport skills are highly specific to a giveb sport. The instruction should be directed accordingly. More about this will be said later.

2. Thus, sport instruction at the junior high, high school, and college levels should really be viewed as being remedial in nature. Naturally, it would be more remedial as one moves up the educational ladder. In the ideal situation, most of the basic sport instruction would have been received in the elementary school. This may

not be a possibility in some communities owing to limited resources. In such cases, the junior high and even the high school instruction would be much more than remedial in nature. At the college level, the remedial work should clearly focus on the lifetime sports. I see relatively little justification for offering a basketball or softball class at the college level. If a student has not learned to play such a sport by the time he or she enters college, it is relatively unlikely that he or she will ever have much of an experience in that sport.

3. It also seems important to stress a point that was made in Chapter 2. At any level, instruction should only be offered in those sports for which a qualified instructor is available. Naturally, the first determinants are facilities and equipment. A fallacy has been found in the tendency, particularly at the school level, to feel that a physical education teacher is or should be qualified to teach almost any sport. If one were paying an instructor outside the schools for golf lessons, he or she would not expect that the instruction would be given by someone whose expertise is more or less limited to basketball and tennis. Is it not reasonable to expect that taxpayers should receive a comparable return for thier investment in the sport enterprise in the schools? Why should they settle for less just because the instruction is offered in the context of a school system? Even though it is also possible to note deficiencies in this area sometimes, we do not expect that a sport will be coached by someone who does not have in-depth knowledge and skill in that sport. Every effort should be made at least to approximate that standard in the instructional area.

INTRAMURAL SPORT

As used here, the concept of intramural sport refers to that part of the total sport program that offers competitive experiences for the general student body. Essentially, intramural sport offers sport competition for those students who do not qualify for interscholastic or intercollegiate competition or who do not choose to pursue that route in one or more sports. It should be viewed as a complement to the instructional program. Intramural sport is a medium for students to acquire a reasonable degree of skill in those sports in which they have previously received instruction. It is a well-known fact that a sport is really learned only by playing the game. For those who are not involved with interscholastic or intercollegiate competition, intramural sport offers that opportunity.

When one sits back and seriously examines this conception of intramural sport, it's a bit surprising that there is not even more support for this segment of the total program. In a way, it might seem that intramurals would be at the heart of the sport enterprise in the schools. It is true that one finds some exceptionally fine intramural sport programs at the college level, particularly in certain large universities. However, in general, the development of intramural sport in the public schools and small colleges leaves much to be desired. There would appear to be a few basic reasons for this relative deficiency in the realization of the potential for intramural sport.

One of these is, of course, the inevitable comparison with interscholastic or intercollegiate sport. The latter has the visibility. The overall reward factors are much more identifiable in the interscholastic or intercollegiate program. Another factor in the smaller schools is that there may be relatively little need for an intramural program because interscholastic competition is more or less available for all those students who desire to compete on a team. A given student may not be able to make the team of his or her first preference, but some type of interscholastic involvement is generally available. However, that excuse for the lack of a solid intramural progam certainly does not apply to the larger schools and colleges.

It can be said that the structure of physical education has also limited a fuller implementation of the concept of intramural sport. Basically, the financial support has gone to interscholastic or intercollegiate athletics and physical education (gym classes). The irony of the situation is that within the context of physical education we often find a truncated version of intramural sport. In other words, aside from instruction per se, students frequently participate in the various games of sport without the structure and overall advantages of an organized intramural sport program. It is quite depressing to walk by a high school field and find students engaged in a softball game during their gym class. This is a case of being "neither fish nor foul"; the students are not receiving sport instruction, and they do not have the advantages that flow from organized sport competition.

Another common excuse for a subpar intramural program is to suggest that it is a time-facility problem. This argument generally proceeds from the assumption that the period from 8 A.M. to 3:30 P.M. is physical education time and 4 to 6 P.M. is for interscholastic practice sessions. To this is added the further recognition that there generally is a lack of sufficient facilities to permit multiple usage during any given period. There are a couple of fallacies related to that argument. The first is that there is nothing to suggest that intramural sport has to be restricted to the period from 4 to 6 P.M. Monday through Friday. The second is the idea that the period from 8 A.M. to 3:30 P.M. daily is only instructional time. What is needed is a combined schedule for each sport that allots the instructional time and the organized intramural competition time for that sport. This brings us back to a recognition of the advantages in appointing sport coordinators.

SPORT COORDINATORS

Sport coordinators have been referred to at various points in the preceding chapters. The idea of having sport coordinators has been partially implemented in certain colleges. Perhaps the best example is that many programs have an aquatics coordinator. Yet this appears to be another one of those areas in which there is potential for much more extensive development.

In the smaller institutions it is quite likely that the sport coordinator for a given sport and the head coach for that sport will be one and the same person. In other words, that individual will coordinate the instructional, intramural, and interscholastic components of that sport. Within the larger college and university programs it is much more likely that the sport coordinator would only be involved with the instructional and intramural components in those sports that have a heavy responsibility in intercollegiate coaching. In any case, the following are seen as some of the principal advantages in appointing sport coordinators.

1. As noted earlier, this will facilitate the scheduling of instructional time and the time for organized competition. It is assumed that the coordinator would also be scheduling periods of time during which a facility is available for informal participation in that sport. Within some institutions the latter is often referred to as ''free play'' time although the term is a redundancy to say the least. At any rate, the overall schedule for a sport is planned by one person. This will avoid many conflicts.

2. Having a sport coordinator will also contribute significantly to the more effective purchase and care of equipment. It is expected that the coordinator will have in-depth knowledge of the particular equipment needs in the sport. Purchasing arrangments can also be better facilitated. There is also improved accountability for equipment when a coordinator has that responsibility.

3. The sport coordinator can also be an important factor in carrying out the controlling function in an effective manner. The coordinator should have the expertise to establish appropriate performance standards for work in his sport. His or her contribution in evaluation can be equally significant.

4. Appointment of sport coordinators should also facilitate the work in directing the program. This is first of all illustrated by the fact that coordination is one of the integral parts of directing. Beyond that, the implications for delegation and motivation are also clear. The existence of sport coordinators provides a built-in form of delegation. Motivation comes into the picture through the satisfaction that can be gained from the responsibility of developing a sport. Even though there may also be some accompanying pitfalls in terms of the director's need to coordinate the entire program, there are considerable motivational advantages in being able to give individuals their own territory for development.

OFFICIALS

There has been relatively little reference to the topic of officiating in this text. The only reason for this limited attention is found in the fact that many of the decisions involving officials are outside the managerial scope of individual school and college sport programs. For example, Quigley (1982) did a nationwide study of the procedures in the various states for selecting, certifying, and evaluating high school football officials. Although there is considerable variance from state to state, he found that much of the certification and assignment takes place at the state or conference level or both. There are relatively few states in which schools directly contact with officials for assignments. Certainly, within the high schools much of the overall control of officiating takes place at the state level. Among the colleges, conference control of officiating is most significant.

Even though much of this may be outside the local control, obtaining the best qualified officials is obviously one of the priority considerations in school and college sport programs. Orientation and evaluation are two points where schools and colleges can play an active role in improving the quality of officiating. The staff should be thoroughly familiarized with the procedures for obtaining officials and the general regulations for the control of officiating.

Evaluation of officials is a complicated topic. Once again, Quigley found that there is considerable variance in the evaluation of high school football officials. Some states do not require formal evaluations. Others evaluate them only if problems are brought to their attention. Several others evaluate officials only as a basis for making playoff assignments. A few states require an evaluation of each game. The various forms of evaluation also include a spectrum of consideration, including knowledge of the game, control of the game, mechanics, and even appearance. Evaluation may be by former officials, other members of the officiating crew, conference or state association staff, and coaches. The latter are a particular subject of controversy. Some states do not permit coaches to be involved in the evaluative process. On the other hand, other states have a mandatory, postgame evaluation by coaches. Regardless of the variance, it is apparent that some form of evaluation of officials is extremely important. On the other side of the coin, it is equally as important that the officials have the opportunity to evaluate the schools and colleges with respect to the contests at which they officiate. In general, the entire topic of officiating points to the importance of the controlling function in school and college sport. The official is an integral component of the universal quadrangular dimension involving the athlete, coach, spectator, and officials in the game of sport. Within that complicated context, much of the direct control resides with the official. However, the ability of the official to control the game will also depend on many other variables. This brings us back to a recognition of the relative importance of effective game management in the sport setting.

GAME MANAGEMENT

As was noted earlier in the text, game management can actually be viewed as a microcosm of the total managerial concern in school or college sport. In the management of the game we find direct evidence of the degree of effectiveness in carrying out the planning, organizing, staffing, directing, and controlling functions. Success in game management will go a long way in reflecting positively on the conduct of the entire sport program. In terms of external evaluation, game management is the most apparent consideration.

Two components of the planning function stand out with respect to game management. The first of these is forecasting. Administrators and coaches should attempt to foresee any special circumstances that are likely to surround the game ahead. Any number of possibilities may exist. There may be need for additional security owing to an anticipated overflow crowd, the existence of previous disturbances, or other extenuating circumstances. The weather prediction may point to the need for alteranative sites or changes in the modus operandi for the game. Forecasting in game management also extends to travel plans. It may be necessary to make last-minute adjustments. There may be special circumstances that involve the next opponent, whether away or at home. Regardless of the particular details, effective game management begins by careful consideration of what can be projected in terms of the next contest, one at a time.

The other key dimension in the planning component of game management is in the procedural area. Basically, procedures are needed to cover all or most of the following areas.

1. Facility preparation, maintenance, and control.
2. Equipment distribution and control.
3. Ticket distribution and control.
4. Security.
5. Parking.
6. Scoreboard usage.
7. Locker room for visiting team.
8. Use of PA system.
9. Treatment of injuries.
10. Scorebooks.
11. Provisions for officials.
12. Provisions for media.
13. Cash accountability for ticket sales.
14. Halftime entertainment.
15. Concessions.

The extent to which any of the above are applicable to a particular school or college sport contest will, of course, vary depending on the size of the prgram, the nature of the sport, and the level of competition. Certainly, in college spectator sport all these would be important planning factors. Surely there are aspects of game management procedures that are also not covered by the preceding listing. But, in general, these provide the parameters for procedural planning for the game.

In the case of game management, procedural planning leads directly into the organizing function. It would seem that the key component here is one involving the delineation of relationships. Generally speaking, game management proceeds quite smoothly if there is specific accountability for the various checklist items. By contrast, if there is more than one person responsible for a given task, confusion is likely to result. As was noted earlier, it is usually advantageous to have one person who has overall responsibility for the management of the game or contest.

The staffing function in game management points directly at the relative importance of the training component. People reallly only learn game management by doing it. There is no substitute for experienced scorers, equipment managers, security personnel, and so on. Consequently, there has to be ample opportunity for apprenticeship work by students and others who aspire to ultimately take on greater responsibility in the well-managed game. "Working in the trenches" is germane to the staffing function in game management.

When it comes to directing, effective game management is really a clear manifestation of all the components that are involved in directing a program. However, among these, coordination is the most demonstrable evidence that the job is being done. This ties in very closely with the careful delineation of relationships in carrying out the staffing function. Obviously, proper delegation is also a key factor in facilitating the coordination. The management of differences enters the picture when we note the varying circumstances surrounding the different sports. From one standpoint, it might be said that game management is not game management. Each sport has its own special set of circumstances that more or less dictate what has to be done in preparing for and conducting the contest. The comparison between the popular spectator sports and those that are more generally restricted to participants is the most obvious contrast. However, that is not the only point of difference. As an example, the equipment needs in gymnastics present unique features in terms of preparation and control. In other words, the management of a gymnastics meet offers some different features from manageing a soccer game. Again, the need for coordination looms in the foreground.

Among all the managerial functions, controlling is the one that offers the most obvious representation in game management. All the components of control are built into the very nature of the game or contest. The reporting system is automatic—what happens in the context of the game and what surrounds the game? Ther performance standards are established through recognition of what transpired in previous games. The evaluation is public, including several dimensions and involving officials, coaches, and spectators. The reward system is manifested not only in games won and lost but also in having taken part in a well-played and managed contest or in one that falls short of that goal. Needless to say, if there is a lack of control, game management will be a prime indicator.

SPECTATORS

One would err in writing a book about sport management in the schools and colleges without making at least some reference to the fourth component of the quadrangular dimension in sport—the spectator. Interestingly, not much is written or even said about spectators aside from promotion (much of which is aimed at attracting spectators) and crowd control. Part of this may be attributed to the fact that spectators are the one component that is the least integral part of many sport contests. However, that situation is offset by the qualifier that the relative importance of the spectator is directly dependent on the objectives that have been established for the program. Most of the possible institutional objectives that were discussed in the second chapter are clearly tied in with the spectator component. Whether this is viewed as being right or wrong, it is also a reality that a considerable segment of the sport enterprise in American schools and colleges involves the spectator dimension. Therefore, the topic deserves a bit more analysis, as such.

The planning and control functions are the key considerations in terms of the spectator situation from the management perspective. A good place to begin is to take note of Novak's distinction between a fan and a spectator. According to him, a fan is not a mere spoectator; a fan is one who really identifies with the team or players (or both) and who really cares about what happens on the playing field. A fan may also be entertained, but he or she does not attend the sport contest only for that purpose.

The implications of this distinction are rather apparent for school and college sport programs. By and large the promotional efforts should be directed toward those potential spectators who are also potential fans. Schools and colleges are not first and foremost in the entertainment business. Entertainment may be a by-product of the activity, but that is different from setting it forth as the raison d'être for the program. On the other side of the coin, it is also true that the establishment of a strong fan following is not without its pitfalls. Many of the control problems in school and college sport may be attributed to fans who get carried away in their enthusiasm and emotional support for the team. For instance, many of the recruiting violations could be traced back to alumni and other fan pressure to win at all costs. It is also very true that a fair amount of the abuse thrown at officials may be attributed to the overzealous fan. All that merely points to the equal importance of the controlling function.

At the same time, it is necessary to take into account the fact that many of the crowd control problems also stem from spectators who are obviously there for reasons other than the contest itself; they are not fans in the true sense. There will always be some problems of this type. From the standpoint of planning promotions and controlling the crowd situation, it makes sense to take all steps necessary to focus the attention on potential spectators who will also be fans. Students and alumni (as well, of course, parents) offer the best potential for identification with the team or players or both. Within recent years, particularly in certain parts of the country, there has been some evidence that student support for interscholastic and intercollegiate spectator sport is not what is was at one time. It is encouraging to note that the student spirit may be revived. Actions taken by students at Indiana University present a case in point.

> But there's another potentially important source of promotion power sitting right under the AD's nose, often in tens of thousands. It's known as the student body.

Probably the foremost example of how students can get involved in the promotion of intercollegiate sports is found in Bloomington, Indiana; where nearly 400 Indiana University students belong to the highly successful Student Athletic Board (SAB).

The SAB, which bills itself as "the Spirit Behind IU Athletics," is a well-organized, extremely active group dedicated to "raising enthusiasm at all IU athletic events" . . . .

"At IU, we really feel that student apathy is a thing of the past," says SAB President Cathy Reinman, a senior in English and Forensic Studies. "You just don't see it here" (pp. 9–10).[2]

From a longitudinal perspective, it is also important to keep in mind that the students are the alumni of the future. Those who manage school and college sport programs are constantly faced with the challenge of obtaining better institutional support for their programs. The potentially richest source of support will be alumni who have been fans since their college days. Naturally, particularly in the larger university programs, the total marketing effort will be directed toward the vast array of spectators, whatever might motivate them to attend the game. But the development of a strong fan following, bulwarked by students and alumni, looms as the integral consideration in an assessment of the spectator dimension in school and college sport.

TITLE IX

During the past 10 years, Title IX perhaps represents the number one topic for consideration by those people who have the responsibility for administering school or college sport programs. It could be argued that finances are always the leading topic, but even the financial situation cannot be isolated from Title IX concerns. It is true that current financial pressures are not only related to Title IX, but the latter is also a major factor in the school and college sport budgets.

Two articles that appeared in *The NCAA News* of July 14 and July 28, 1982, provide a rather complete analysis of the status of Title IX in relationship to sport programs at the time of this writing. The articles are reprints of a speech given by William D. Kramer to the College Sports Information Directors of America on June 29, 1982. Kramer represents the NCAA's legal firm, Squire, Sanders, & Dempsey, of Washington, D.C.. His speech was entitled "Is Title IX a Dead Issue?" Although it is difficult to predict what further developments will have taken place by the time this book is in print, several observations made by Kramer are worthy of note.

His overall conclusion is that Title IX is far from being dead, but the impact has mellowed. The influence of Title IX, particularly in athletics, has been extensive, continues to be extensive, and will continue to proceed in that direction. What

[2]*Athletic Purchasing and Facilities,* November 1980.

has subsided is the controversy that ensued through the initial reactions to Title IX. Kramer (July 14, 1982) cited a report that was issued by the National Advisory Council on Women's Educational Programs in the fall of 1981.

> Athletics is far from the sole focus of Title IX, but it is the area with the most visible and dramatic changes. Requirements for equality of opportunity have led to increased numbers of sports being offered to women in high school and in two- and four-year colleges, many more female athletes and growing public attention to women's athletics. The vast differences between the budgets for men's and women's university athletic programs are shrinking: Athletic scholarships are helping women as well as men to obtain a college education (p. 1).

From a management perspective, it is probably most significant to note the five ways in which Title IX has diminished as an issue according to Kramer. (July 14, 1982).

1. The turmoil surrounding Title IX is no longer nearly as evident as it was in the past few years.
2. The media are now focusing less attention on the topic. The focus has shifted to the actual participation of women athletes and away from the debate of Title IX as a concept.
3. It is no longer much of a legislative matter. That is, there are fewer pending bills related to Title IX. From a legal standpoint what remains is the litigation, which one hopes will resolve some important questions.
4. The federal government is no longer so actively involved in intervening in the affairs of the educational institutions.
5. The colleges have demonstrated significant progress in responding to Title IX. "In 1966–67, fewer than 16,000 women participated in intercollegiate sports at NCAA member-institutions—about 10 percent of all student-athletes. By 1971–72, prior to the enactment of Title IX, this number had increased to nearly, 32,000. By 1980–81, there were nearly 72,000 female participants in intercollegiate athletics at NCAA member institutions—nearly 30 percent of all student-athletes" (p. 3).

It seems reasonable to conclude that the changes brought about by Title IX and any accompanying social developments are now an established fact. The initial adjustment has been made. As we look ahead, the hope is that the focus will continue to shift more and more from mere compliance to efforts to improve the *quality* of participation for women athletes.

PERSONS WITH HANDICAPPED CONDITIONS

A topic that has not been discussed in the previous chapters is persons with handicapped conditions. The primary reason for the omission was that we assumed that what was said about the management of programs for the mass of participants also applies to the handicapped. However, as with Title IX, the topic of individuals with handicapped conditions is too significant in contemporary sport programs to ignore some of the key factors to be considered by those who have the managerial responsibiltiy.

As is true of Title IX, legislation has also been the pivotal factor in bringing about significant changes in opportunities for the handicapped. Thus, compliance also is a critical concern in this area. A key piece of legislation is the Rehabilitation Act of 1973. Section 504 of that act requires that newly constructed or renovated buildings that provide federally funded services to the public must include access for the handicapped. The funding may be in whole or in part. Almost every school or college has some form of federal funding. Consequently, Section 504 is generally applicable to all schools and colleges. Every educational program receiving federal aid must assess its programs to determine if they are accessible to the handicapped and must make any necessary adjustments if there is a lack of accessibility. This does not mean that every part of every building has to be accessible. Rather, the requirement is met if a given program, as a whole, is accessible to all students.

Thus, compliance for a sport program does not mean all students must have access to a particular sport. What it does mean is that all students must have access to sport participation in some form or another. The most general application is in the areas of locker rooms and showers. Needless to say, beyond compliance per se, everly effort should be made to broaden the scope of sport participation for individuals with handicapped conditions. The planning function becomes the key component in this regard. Also, the entire matter of handicapped individuals again points to the advantages of offering an integrated sport program that stresses the participation of all students in the common denominator of sport. Bronzan (August 1980) offers a succinct statement of the current position that undergirds planning for handicapped students.

> Until recently, whenever schools made any provisions for handicapped students, the usual approach was to provide them with separate facilities, programs, and leaders. Fortunately, the current practice and procedure is to encourage the handicapped to participate in the mainstream whenever possible. Only when absolutely necessary and to the benefit of the handicapped is special consideration provided. And, when the latter is deemed appropriate, these activities are coeducational (p. 12).

Administrators of school and college sport programs can benefit most by knowing who can be contacted for specific information about what can be done to meet the access challenge for their program. There are numerous sources of such information. The following are among the more useful possibilities.

1. The Accessibility Information Center at the National Center for a Barrier Free Environment, Suite 1006, 1140 Connecticut Avenue, N.W., Washington, D.C. The center operates a toll-free hotline at (800) 424–2809.

2. The Center for Education for Nontraditional Students, Inc. (CENTS), has an Access Awareness staff, which will travel to a campus to conduct workshops designed to meet specific needs. The workshops are offered free to faculty, administrators, and staff of postsecondary institutions. For information, contact the Community Outreach Specialist, CENTS, 3130 Grimes Avenue N., Robbinsdale, Minn. 55422. Phone: (612) 588–5141.

FINANCE

If one were to identify the single topic that is most pervasive in school and college sport programs, it would have to be finance. It could easily be argued that this is the number one topic within almost any organization because financial support is essential to an organization's establishment and development. The business world speaks for itself. However, anyone working in an educational institution can also readily attest to the importance of adequate financial support. So, why should finance be a particularly acute concern in school and college sport? The answer can be found largely in the multifaceted nature of a sport program's involvement with finances in some form or another. Each of the following considerations points to a financial dimension that has to be addressed in the management of a school or college sport program.

Facilities

The relatively unique dependence on adequate facilities in the realm of sport is most apparent. Personnel is still the number one variable. But, aside from that, no other factor will have as much effect as the facility on the quality of the program. The same degree of importance of facilities is not found in most of the other programs that are offered by educational institutions. Adequate laboratories are probably the other major exception. Even though there may be a desire for better classrooms, the quality of the program is not as directly affected as that of a sport program with a subpar facility. This situation has to be coupled with the facts that facilities represent the major capital outlay expenditure and sport facilities rank high among such expenditures. The entire restriction is further heightened by two other considerations. Many school and college administrators (as well as faculty) are not necessarily convinced that sport facilities should receive a top priority in the total capital outlay for facilities. Also, there is a general tendency to associate sport facilities only with spectator sport involving a relatively few participants. The net effect of all this is that the planning strategy becomes most critical in this area. To be more specific, it is the strategy for financing the facilities. All possible sources of funding should be considered. They are likely to include the following.

- Institutional funds that are either directly appropriated by the state or district or come from student tuition in the case of private schools.
- Revenue from ticket sales.
- Alumni support.
- Booster Club support extending beyond alumni involvement.
- Funds amortized by student fees.
- Appropriated funds for joint use of instructional facilities.
- Institutional business enterprises.
- Banks or other commercial lending sources.
- Revenue from public use of facilities.
- Special fund-raising drives.

In most cases, the specific funding strategy will involve a combination selected from the preceding sources. Exactly what the combination should be is obviously something to be determined after a careful analysis of the local situation and variables. It is very clear that the first listed source, institutional funding from appropriations or tuition, is not likely to be a viable source for many schools and colleges in the current economic climate. Selection from the remaining possibilities depends greatly on the objectives that have been established for the total sport program. That is the key. It will be difficult to gain support for a proposed facility addition or renovation if there is little evidence of a correlation between stated facility needs, program objectives, and the actual conduct of the program.

Equipment.

Next to facilities, equipment also has to rank as one of the leading financial concerns in the sport enterprise. As with facilities, the right kind of equipment is also indispensable to the quality program. There is little doubt that the principal consideration is to purchase safe equipment to reduce or prevent injuries. Beyond that, the quality of the program is invariably related to the quality of the equipment. The key factor in this area is to establish a successful relationship between the sport program and more than one supplier. Sport coordinators and coaches should play an important role in planning for the purchase of equipment because they are the people who are in the best position to know the equipment demands and peculiarities for their given sport. In general, obtaining high quality equipment usually means purchasing the name brands. However, the entire equipment business is in the midst of extensive change in two opposite directions. In some sports, such as football, product liability lawsuits are forcing equipment manufacturers to get out of that business. On the other side of the spectrum, we find an explosion of manufacturers in other kinds of equipment. Shoes are perhaps the most notable example. Those who manage programs that supply shoes for athletes would do well to consult a podiatrist who specializes in the treatment of athletes. Aside from shoes, it seems reasonable to suggest that one should not offer the sport or supply the equipment if high-quality, safe equipment cannot be provided. This, of ocurse, does not preclude the possibility of assessing a "user" fee in those sport programs, particularly school sport, where there is a lack of sufficient resources to meet all the equipment needs. More about that will be said a little later.

Tickets

The fact that most school and college sport programs are involved with the ticket business also adds to their relatively unique financial position among other units in the educational setting. The performing arts are perhaps the only other unit that even approximates this situation. Also, of course, with respect to the Division I football and basketball programs, it is more than just another financial factor; tickets are integral to the total financial picture.

In terms of financial planning, all schools and colleges face two basic questions with respect to interscholastic or intercollegiate sport contests: (1) should admission be charged? (2) what should be the cost for admission? It should be rather apparent that the first question can best be answered after a consideration of the objectives for a specific sport program. The second question is more complex. There is no magic formula for determining ticket prices. Broyles and Hay (1979) discuss the "pricing strategy for products and services" (p. 193). They probably come about as close as one can get to identifying a ticket-pricing strategy. In essence, the choice revolves around the competition for the product or service, however one wishes to classify an athletic contest. This may be either direct competition with other athletic events or indirect competition with the broader entertainment environment. Whether to price above, at, or below the market will depend on an accurate assessment of that competitive situation. General and specific locations are thus key factors in the pricing decisions. For example, school and colleges in the larger cities typically face a highly competitive market in terms of both direct and indirect competition.

Aside from the basic questions, the entire ticket structure is complicated by a number of other decisions that have to be made relative to season tickets, reserved tickets, faculty and staff discounts and prices, students discounts or admission with activity cards, complimentary passes, and so forth. By and large, program objectives and the assessment of the market will be the basis of the specific decisions.

Blaum (1982) surveyed a number of Division I, II, and III colleges in regard to student ticket procedures for intercollegiate football and basketball. As one would expect, he found considerable difference between Division II and III colleges on the one hand and Division I schools on the other hand. For the most part, the allotment of student tickets in Division II and III programs is almost entirely unlimited owing to the smaller student enrollments and the relatively less demand for attending. However, even among 17 Division I institutions included in his survey there is considerable variance in terms of the student allotment. For example, one university with a student enrollment of 32,000 allots 19,600 tickets in a football stadium that seats 83,000 people. Another university with almost the identical enrollment has an unlimited student allotment for a stadium that seats 52,000. The answer in attempting to explain this difference has to be found in an assessment of the market conditions and program objectives. The analysis of the basketball ticket allotment at these same 17 universities reveals a simialr variance. One university, with a student enrollment of 18,600 allots 3000 student tickets in an arena that seats 16,600. Another, with an enrollment of 32,000, allots 3900 tickets in an area that seats 7200.

The Blaum study also reveals some variance in terms of the distribution of the student ticket revenue within the university. In 14 of the Division I universities, the student ticket revenue is retained within the athletic department. The other 3 universities absorb the revenue in the general university budget. Among 11 Division II institutions surveyed, 6 retain the student ticket revenue in the athletic department, 3 place the revenue in the college budget, and 2 have the revenue distributed to the student government association. As would be expected, the tendency to put student ticket revenue in the general college budget is more evident at the Division III level. Among 11 colleges surveyed, 9 of them follow this budgeting arrangement whereas 2 colleges retain the revenue within the athletic department.

Even though the Blaum study is but a very limited example of the total picture involving collegiate football and basketball tickets, it points to the complexity and variance regarding tickets in the total financial picture. Program objectives, general location of the institution, and specific location of the institution are certainly important factors in discussions regarding pricing and distribution of tickets among students, faculty, booster club members, and the general public. Needless to say, the entire ticket situation requires regular and consistent analysis.

Travel

It would also be difficult to overlook the significance of travel in the total financial picture surrounding school and college sport. Even though students from other school and college programs also travel at institutional expense, the porportion of funds spent for sport team travel is exceedingly high. It is estimated that about 75 percent of the typical high school sport budget, exclusive of salaries, is allotted for travel. The reasons for this are so obvious that they need not be mentioned. Regardless of the reasons, the impact of travel in the unique financial situation in school and college sport is a fact.

By and large, the topic of travel merely heightens the significance of the planning function in school and college sport. I think that Broyles and Hay (1979) exaggerate considerably when they curtly dismiss the topic of travel with these matter-of-fact statements: "Most successful teams try to have their members ready to play, both physically and mentally, before each game. Administrators insist on traveling first class. Not only is travel planned, but also first-class meals and lodging are usually arranged for team members. Anything less than first-class travel is usually considered a negative factor in determining a team's ability to win. Therefore, a team's travel policy is to go first class with plenty of time to spare'' (pp. 199–200). Surely their comments must be aimed primarily, if not only, at Division I football and basketball in the universities. Naturally, everyone would like to travel first class. Coaches and athletes would be the last ones to argue against that proposition. It's also quite likely that there may be a positive correlation between first-class accommodations and team success. However, it is ridiculous to suggest that administrators insist on traveling first class. The coaches may feel that their teams should always travel first class. But the administrators are faced with the reality of high travel costs in a restricted budget.

All of this again brings us back to the importance of developing travel plans that are consistent with program objectives. If it can be demonstrated that there is a high correlation between first-class travel and team success and if program objectives are largely geared at team success, then logic tells us that the travel budget has to be a top priority. However, many school and college sport programs are more likely to arrive at the conclusion that some travel restrictions have to be made in order to reach other priorities in terms of the total program objectives.

User Fees

The subject of travel also points to another financial dimension that is currently receiving considerable attention in sport programs, particularly those at the high school level. Recognition of the importance of adequate funds for travel has forced administrators to seek additional sources of revenue for this area. Support for equipment needs fall much into the same category. One possibility is to assess the student or the parent a set fee for participation in each sport. For example, in the high school sport program there might be an across-the-board assessment of $30 for each interscholastic participant in each sport. There could also be a variable schedule of user fees among the sports, taking into account that some teams are required to travel much more than others and that equipment costs are relatively much higher in some sports. Such a fee is based on the concept of pay as you go or pay as you play. This type of concept is also somewhat unique to sport in the public education sector although there are precedents in terms of assessing students for field trips or establishing laboratory fees for certain classes.

There seem to be two principal concerns that surround the idea of assessing a user fee for participation in interscholastic sport. The first of these concerns is largely internally based. Administrators, coaches, and other supporters of the athletic program tend to be apprehensive that the user fee will be viewed as a substitute for public funding from the school board or legislature. It is, of course, true that a user fee will not begin to cover all program costs.

The second concern is expressed from a more external perspective. It revolves around the thought that the fee is in conflict with the tradition of a ''free'' public education for all youth. The question is repeatedly raised as to what happens to those students whose family cannot afford to pay the fee, particularly those families who have several children engaged in a number of sports. However, where the fee has been implemented, allowances are made for students who would otherwise be excluded from participation for financial reasons. The "free lunch" program in the school serves as a precedent in this regard.

The user fee also has legal implications. Maria Dennison, a legislative consultant for the Sporting Goods Manufacturers Association, presented this aspect in the May 1982 issue of *Athletic Purchasing and Facilities*. She noted that the legality of participation fees was being challenged in Iowa, Wisconsin, and Michigan. On the other hand, any challenge in this regard also raises the question as to whether extracurricular activities are basic to the free education concept in American schools. In California, the State Superior Court ruled in favor of the fee when a suit was brought against the Santa Barbara school board. Dennison also noted regional differences in terms of attitudes toward the implementation of such fees.

> In a survey of states throughout the country, "pay for play" programs were found to be most prevalent in California and Massachusetts, where propositions 13 and 2½ have taken their toll. In the Northeast, schools in Connecticut, Pennsylvania, Maine, Rhode Island, and Maryland have also implemented participation fee initiatives, after great debate, and the continued resistance of some coaches, student government representatives, parents, and teachers. In each case, however, "pay for play" programns were seen to be working well, except where families had several children engaged in a number of activities (p. 26).

By contrast, in the South there has been less demand for a user fee because the need has not been as evident owing to very active booster clubs and generally stronger community support for interscholastic sport. As has already been noted, the legal concern seems to be a significant consideration in the Midwest.

It is difficult to predict at this time to what extent the user fee or "pay as you play" concept will be further developed nationwide. Some of the legal interpretations may ultimately tell the story. In the meantime, the basic idea seems to make considerable sense. There is every reason to believe that the general financial pinch in educational programs will be with us for some time. The user fee may be one legitimate way to help preserve many aspects of an interscholastic sport program, which is held in high regard by many people. Why penalize the elderly, the poor, and other detached public citizens by having them contribute excessively through taxes for the support of programs that by and large benefit others?

Television

At the college level, there is no other area in which the financial impact is being as heavily felt today as that involving television, including cablevision. Changes are taking place so rapidly that anything written about the topic is out of date almost as quickly as it appears in print. For example, at this writing, those who work in or closely follow college sport have been electrified to learn of the "NCAA cartel decision.'' By the time this book is printed, the decision might be reversed. On the other hand, it could also be that the decision has been sustained and the effect is already being felt. Perhaps a better possibility is that the battle will continue to be waged and the final answer remains in doubt. At any rate, the financial implications are worthy of note regardless of the eventual outcome.

A UPI article of September 16, 1982, spread the news that is currently raising the eyebrows in college sport..

> Calling the NCAA a "classical cartel," a federal judge Wednesday ruled the organization has no business regulating college football telecasts and struck down its $280.6 million agreement with three television networks.
>
> U.S. District Judge Juan Burciaga rule the telecasts are "the property of the institutions participating in the game" and "that right may be sold or assigned by those institutions at their discretion." . . .
>
> Burciaga's ruling throws out a four-year agreement totaling $280.6 million that went into effect this fall involving the NCAA, ABC, CBS, and the Turner Broadcast System. . . .
>
> The opinion said the NCAA produced "artificially high" and low prices for broadcasts, maintained mechanisms for punishing members who threatened to violate its rules and took a "sizeable cut" of revenues for itself.
>
> The landmark ruling was the result of a challenge to the NCAA contract filed last year on behalf of the Univeristy of Oklahoma Board of Regents and the University of Georgia Athletic Association.
>
> An appeal of the ruling by the NCAA is expected. . . .
>
> The two schools contended the NCAA's television broadcast policies violate anti-trust statutes because they forced schools from negotiating broadcast fees separately.
>
> The schools contended the NCAA policies were designed to "fix prices and restrict output," that they constituted a "group boycott" and left the NCAA with "monopoly power" over television rights.
>
> Burciaga agreed, saying the NCAA's broadcast policies violated two portions of the Sherman Anti-Trust Act, and granted a permanent injunction that forbids the NCAA from entering into any broadcast arrangement on behalf of its members (p. 45).[3]

It is clear that the financial welfare of the vast majority of college sport progams is dependent on NCAA support. If the NCAA is unsuccessful in its appeal of the Burciaga decision, the possibilities for major change in the financial situation and subsequent structure of college sport are immense.

As noted earlier, the entire mattter is in such a state of flux that the reader of this book may already have witnessed considerable change. The best we can do is conjecture. It would appear that the major college football powers are headed for a

[3]Reported in *The Morning Union* (Springfield, Mass.) September 16, 1982.

split from the NCAA that would enable these institutions to negotiate their independent television contracts. Should that happen, the financial base of the NCAA operation would be severely reduced, and most of the college sport programs would be directly affected. On the other hand, maybe the NCAA will be able to make adjustments to permit that organization to carry on business more or less as usual. At any rate, television represents one of the most unique features of a contemporary college sport program. It is a feature that is unmatched in the total collegiate environment.

Scholarships and Financial Aid

There is at least one other concern at the college level that has to be addressed if one is to begin to understand the complicated, financial dimension of the sport program. Basically, the concern centers around the criteria to be employed in awarding financial aid to athletes. Should aid be given in the form of scholarships that recognize achievement aside from any financial need? The term *scholarship* usually implies award for academic achievement. Thus, in recent years it has been more common to identify grants-in-aid in the athletic context. But whether they are called scholarships or grants-in-aid, there remains considerable disagreement as to whether financial aid should be awarded on the basis of need only. As recently as a few years ago, the NCAA members were one vote short of restricting grants-in-aid to students who demonstrated need. Those who oppose the need-only criterion are frequently inclined to point out that there are all kinds of interpretations as to what constitutes need and that institutions merely manipulate the need criterion to fit their own purposes in obtaining the athletes whom they desire for the program.

Then, of course, more recently there is also the question involving the awarding of athletic scholarships or grants-in-aid to women. This is partially governed by Title IX, but questions still remain. It appears that many women would prefer a more restricted scholarship approach, but they also seek greater equity between men and women in this regard. Parkhouse and Lapin (1980) note the divergence in opinion.

> Of the women athletic directors responding to a survey conducted by the authors 28 percent prefer to see scholarships given out based on need, 30 percent favor ability alone, and 31 percent back combining need and ability. Four percent specify need first and ability second, seven percent say need and adademic achievement (p. 108).

The entire situation surrounding financial aid for athletes seems to point to one need: consistency. To begin with, there is a need for consistency between the objectives of the program and the awarding of scholarships or grants-in-aid. If the program is aimed at enhancing the image of the college through high-level spectator sport, then grants-in-aid without consideration of need seem to be entirely in order. There should be an accompanying financial consistency. It is assumed that such a program will also have to spend considerably more money on the recruiting effort and that there will be sufficient gate and television revenue to finance the recruiting and the grants-in-aid. On the other hand, if the program is not directed toward the above set of considerations, there is little reason for believing that athletic scholarships should be awarded on any basis other than the demonstrated need factor. In this regard, there should also be consistency between men and women. The argument is sometimes used that athletic scholarships should be awarded for ability only because there are some academic-scholarships that are awarded according to the ability criterion. That argument really doesn't hold up when one considers the realtively small number of academic scholarships in comparison to extensive financial outlays in athletic grants-in-aid.

Greater consistency in the awarding of scholarships should assist many colleges in getting out of the gray area in the conduct of their sport programs. The financial implications of existing in the gray area are very evident. If a program has an extensive outlay of funds in athletic grants-in-aid (and the accompanying recruiting expenses), it is difficult to justify and even operate such a program when ther is insufficient gate receipt and television revenue to warrant the expense. Any college might still choose to award athletic scholarships on a need basis, but that is a different story. Financial aid for needy students is a generally accepted premise in contemporary educational institutions. If a sport program is working completely in an educational framework, athletic scholarships are a logical extension of academic scholarships. By the same token, athletic grants-in-aid for athletic ability only go hand in hand with revenue-producing spectator sport. Consistency in the scholarship area would force many more colleges either to "fish or cut bait" in the direction of their sport programs.

PUBLIC RELATIONS

Next to finance, public relations may well be the most pervasive concern in a school or college sport program. It is also obvious that the two topics are more or less inseparable because adequate financial support is usually dependent on effective public relations. At the same time it also seems safe to say that publicatons relations is probably one of the most misunderstood, and consequently abused, concepts. There is a general tendency to associate public relations only with publicity. That is certainly an integral component of public relations, but the dimensions of a complete and effective public relations program extend far beyond publicity per se. Bronzan (1971) notes that the term is used in various senses. However, he places some restrictions on the term and, at the same time, offers an appropriatre frame of reference for public relations in school and college sport.

> Confusion and perplexity can be minimized if the term is restricted to describing the planned effort to influence opinion through acceptable performance and two-way communication between the sender and receiver. Public relations includes both performance and communications used to form profitable relationships with the public.

A common error is to use the term public relations to define some of its functional roles such as publicity, press-agentry, and institutional advertising. These roles, however important, do not comprise the whole of public relations. Actually these functional roles are in reality mere tools of public relations, not its equivalent (p. 218).

Bronzan's conception of public relations can be used to note several points that would assist in increasing the quality of public relations in school and college sport.

1. Schools and colleges should do a better job of communicating their objectives for the total sport program. At the same time there should be greater consistency between the stated program objectives and the actual conduct of the program. Much of the public recognition of school and college sport will only be in the form of identifying with winning teams. As important as that may be, particularly in certain contexts, the communication is tenuous if it is rooted only in the concept of winning.

2. Everyone employed in the school or college sport program should be viewed as a public relations agent, and every employee should accept that responsibility. The highly visible nature of a sport program is a fact of life. It is difficult to provide effective communication if the coaches, instructors, sports information director, and others are conveying mixed signals. As valuable as it might be to have a sport promotion director, public relations is not a one-person job.

3. There is no substitute for a quality program. That is the initial point of recognition for any public relations expert. Every program has its strengths and weaknesses. The media will be quick to note both, particularly in terms of the more visible sports. Sport program personnel must do whatever they can to disseminate information on the strengths within the total program.

4. The receiver noted in Bronzan's definition is indeed a diversified receiver in school and college sport. It is not only the media and those reached by the media. The receiver or multifaceted public includes students, staff, faculty, administrators, trustees or school board members, alumni, donors, government officials, parents, and the community at large. The public relations thrust should be directed to provide effective communication with all those groups in addition to any media releases. This includes the receipt of information from these groups as well as the dissemenation of applicable information to each group.

5. There should be some kind of continuity in the public relations approach. It appears that too often the public relations direction is a reflection of crisis management. Although there is also a need to communicate the changes that are taking place within the program, the public must also be able to appreciate those enduring elements that provide a consistent sense of direction in the development of the total program. In other words, an effective public relations program will reflect a basic stability while still being able to cope with needed change.

6. In the final analysis, students and alumni are the most effective public relations agents. Therefore, it is particularly critical that these constituencies understand the program objectives and that they have experiences that will enable them to support the various components of the program.

SCHOOL AND NONSCHOOL SPORT PROGRAMS

This is a topic that has been more or less lurking beneath the surface throughout the discussion in this book. Clearly the focus has been on the management of an integrated sport program in the schools and colleges. However, the public school sport situation must also be assessed within the broader context of the total community sport program. The overall fragmentation of the sport enterprise is very evident after one examines the sport structure within a typical commmunity. To begin with, of course, there is the basic distinction between sport programs in the private sector as contrasted with those programs offered by public agencies. Our primary concern here is not with the sport services offered by private or commercial agencies. The commercial sport ventures are merely a reflection of the American way in business. Private or commercial sport offers an important supplement to public sponsorship. The only real link with the schools might be when the school system contracts for certain specialized sport services offered by a commercial agency. For example, the school might set up a program whereby students, on a volunteer, user-fee basis, are bused to a ski resort in the vicinity for skiing instruction.

The principal area for examination is the total sector of publicly financed sport wherein we find both school and nonschool sport programs. Most communities, including many small towns, have two sport programs that operate completely separately from one another; the physical education departments of local school systems and local recreation departments. To a great extent, the services offered by these two entities complement one another. However, because these two systems have developed independently of one another, they have frequently spawned overlapping services while some areas of need in the sport realm are not met.

The overlapping of services often results in conflicts over facilities use, program delivery, and funding. The emergence of legislation such as Proposition 13 in California and Proposition 2 ½ in Massachusetts has made this problem especially acute. In general, the lmitations on revenue access have adversely affected sport program delivery. At the same time, local sport program planning nationwide has suffered from the absence of a systematic analysis of local needs and how available resources and programs do or do not meet these needs. There is little evidence of the relationships among the local sport programs for youth and the degree of involvement in these programs. The various programs have often developed in a haphazard manner, based commonly on the existence of a vocal constituency or the predilection of a sport administrator.

At least one study has focused considerable attention on the nature and extent of involvement in youth sport programs. It was a study initiated by the State Legislature of Michigan in 1975 (Seefeldt, Gilliam, Blievernicht, and Bruce, 1978). However, that study was aimed primarily at an assessment of the participant involvement and attitudes toward the participation. There is still a need for more extensive investigation as to how the various programs are organized and how they relate to the school structure. Following are some of the areas that should be explored in those communities that offer both school and nonschool sport programs, publicly funded.

1. *Sports offered*. Exactly what sports are offered for the different age groups in the various communities? Which of these sports are being offered by both school and nonschool agencies? Are they being offered for the same age grouping? Are they being offered during the same time span? What are the participant figures for each sport (school and nonschool), including distribution among boys and girls?

2. *Finances*. What are the budget amounts for the various sport programs, including community recreation sport, interscholastic sport, intramural sport, and physical education classes? Within each context, what are the sources of financial support? For each program, what are the percentages of support from local taxation, parental support (through user fees), booster club support, and other sources of support?

3. *Facilities*. Which of the sport facilities in the community are currently jointly used by the school and the community recreation program? Which sport facilities are used only by the school? Which sport facilities are used only by the community recreation programs? What is the extent of duplication of facilities? Does either program utilize any private facilities? If so, what are the cost factors involved?

4. *Personnel*. What is the number of full- and part-time community recreation personnel who work in sport programs? What is their current salary allocation? What is the number of full- and part-time physical education instructors in the schools? What is their salary allocation? In addition to physical education instructors, how many coaches are employed in the school program? What is the total allocation for coaches' salaries? What is the salary allocation for an athletic director? For a director of physical education? Is this a combined position or two separate positions? What other staff positions and salaries are part of the total personnel structure?

All these questions represent territory for which most communities and states now lack composite information. In many cases, the answers will not be easily obtained. However, we cannot begin to bring about improvement in the school and nonschool sport programs unless we have some sort of picture as to what is involved in the management of the diverse agencies which are offering those programs.

Seefeldt (1982) addressed the overriding question surrounding the total sport program within any community: "Can School, Non-School Sports Work Toward Common Goals?" His conclusion seems to be that this will be most difficult if the situation continues to exist in the present pattern.

In today's economy, the ultimate determination of whether physical education or sport programs in the elementary school survive seems destined to be made on a cost-benefit basis. Since public school sports offerings below age 14 are relatively few, the emerging conflict seems to center on physical education versus agency-sponsored sports programs.

Although these two programs have been operating in the same communities without either open competition or cooperation for years, why is coexistence suddenly an issue? Again, the decisions seem to revolve around the delivery of desirable services for the smallest expenditure of public funds.

If decisions about community support for physical education or agency-sponsored sports programs are to be made on a cost-benefit basis, the evidence seems to favor the agency-sponsored sports. Actions taken during the past several years by parents, school administrators and boards of education reflect this trend.

However, in their haste to reduce the costs of programs, many administrators and boards of education may have eliminated or reduced the offerings in physical education without considering the consequences of such actions. Aside from the proposition that some physical education programs may not be worthy of support, there are many direct and subtle tactics that have rendered many of these programs ineffective.

For example, how many teachers in other subject areas would purport to achieve significant improvement in skills if they only met with their students for two one-half hour periods per week for a total of 36 hours during the school year? Yet, this is the customary lot of the physical education teacher.

Conversely, youth sports coaches may interact with their athletes 10 or more hours each week, over seasons extending 12 or more weeks.

Other factors that favor the coach-athlete rather than the teacher-student interaction are the teaching ratios of adults to students, motivation and goals of the learners, range in skill level among the learners and the scope of the content to be taught.

The problems in physical education programs are frequently compounded when the content is taught by teachers with no special education or interest in the area. It is not surprising that decision makers have abdicated to agencies these programs of physical activity that were once the responsibility of the public schools (p. 12).

By and large, Seefeldt's diagnosis of the problems that are involved in this school and nonschool sport complexity is accurate. However, it would appear that his proposed solution is quite different from that advocated in this book. Later in the article Seefeldt states: ''Physical education teachers must redefine their objectives to focus on health-related physical fitness and mastery of fundamental motor patterns and motor skills. Concentration on objectives that can be achieved, rather than exposure to activities in which mastery is impossible, would do much to reestablish the credibility that physical education programs seem to have lost in the last two decades'' (p. 14). Implicit in his suggestion is the idea that sport programs would become more or less the province of nonschool agencies. He is certainly right in his conclusion that the schools have been negligent in the attempt to offer meaningful sport programs for youth below the high school level. However, the solution is not to move the school out of the sport picture at the elementary and junior high levels because this would probably only add to certain current problems.

One has to begin with the recognition that the most viable sport program for youth at the present time is the interscholastic sport program. At the same time the greatest deficiencies are found in sport programs in the schools for children below age 14. Also, we have the accompanying problems that many people are critical of the nonschool sport programs because of the lack of efffective leadership, coaching, and teaching that is sometimes evident in these programs. If there is a problem here, moving the sport program completely away from the schools at the elementary and junior high levels will only serve to compound that problem further. What we really need is a concerted effort to improve the quality and extent of the instructional and intramural components of the total sport program in the public schools so that they are at least somewhere near the quality of the interscholastic component in many high schools. We need an integrated community sport program in grades K–12.

Physical education teachers must redefine their objectives to focus on health-related physical fitness and mastery of fundamental motor patterns—that is, exercise science. Many physical educators currently do their work within that framework. That is a legitimate and significant area of professional work that is also receiving considerable public and private support outside the school system. The status of this work within the school could be enhanced considerably by establishing a separate exercise science component that in most cases would probably be organized as part of the broader health program.

However, not all physical educators wish to or should go in the direction indicated by Seefeldt. Basically, those are the sport people who have seen their areaa succeed relatively well in the interscholastic context but who have been restricted in the development of instructional and intramural sport at all levels owing to the nature of physical education on the one hand and widespread support for nonschool sports on the other side of the ledger. This is the group that should be out front in developing the sport management profession within the context of the school system.

Even if they might agree, the skeptics are saying that these ideas will never come to fruition. .They will quickly point to the pragmatics of the situation and suggest that politics and existing organizational arrangements will preclude the shift from nonschool to school sport at all age levels. They will note that leaders in community recreation and other nonschool sport agencies are not about to surrender their domain to professional sport personnel in the schools. They may be right, but it certainly is worth a try. Right now the schools have an advantage with their well-established interscholastic sport programs. Does it really make much sense to have nonschool sport programs prerparing the youth for later participation in interscholastic sport? Any preparation is undoubtedly better than none, but if we really believe in the educational value of a sport program, then we should be consistent in organizing and carrying out such a program. Probably most parents would not want to have their children prepared in other subject matter areas outside the schools in ages 5 to 14 so that they could then pursue these subjects in the schools at the high school level. In essence, what it amounts to is that we either get about the business of offering a viable, integrated sport program in the schools or have the schools remove themselves from the sport enterprise altogether. However, the latter choice is not likely to materialize because Americans long ago made the decision that they like the mix of sport and education. The way things are now we seem to be caught between two worlds with some clear disadvantages for both sides. Worse than that, it is ultimately the youth who are handicapped by the lack of development of an integrated sport program.

Getting back to the skeptics, the first thing we need is a clearer picture of the total parameters involving the existing sport structure within the various communities. That is why we have a need for the kind of studies that were suggested earlier. When we have more specific, composite information about the sports, finances, facilities, and personnel involved in both the school and nonschool sectors, we will be in a better position to determine what should be done and what can be done to improve the communitywide sport services for youth. It could well be that the conclusions drawn from the situation will point to the need to retain many of the nonschool sport programs as significant extensions of the sport program in the public schools. But certainly we need a picture of how each sport can be managed from a community perspective rather than from the present condition of continued fragmentation and lack of coordinated planning.

Where this is considered feasible, it would make sense to have a community sport director, who would hold a school position. Establishing this as a school position is again consistent with the American integration of sport and education. Reporting to the director would be a sport coordinator for each sport of significance in that community. What is of significance may be in doubt, but the reference is to those sports that typically comprise the offerings of an interscholastic sport program. These sport coordinators would also hold school positions. As an example, a given community might have a baseball coordinator among other possibilities. In the relatively smaller communities, that coordinator might also be the head baseball coach in the high school. At any rate, the coordinator would be ultimately responsible for the entire baseball program in the community. Personnel, finances, facilites, and equipment for baseball would all be managed under his or her direction. In terms of the nonschool components, the Little League, Babe Ruth League, and American Legion ball might continue to operate, but the integration would be with the school and the higher-level management at the community level would emanate from the school. Under such an arrangement, there would be considerable potential for having a baseball program that is well planned, organized, staffed, directed, and controlled. Basically, this would facilitate the achievement of unity of purpose. Similar examples could be cited for other sports in the community.

When all is said and done, the topic of school and nonschool sport points to a couple of basic questions that should be of concern in any community. What is the complete status of existing programs? Once that is determined, what can be done to produce more effective delivery of sport services within this dual context?

REFERENCES
Amdur, Neil. "Problems are Mounting in N.C.A.A." *The New York Times*. March 21, 1982, Section 5, p. 1.

Blaum, Eugenme J. "Student Ticket Procedures for Intercollegiate Football and Basketball for selected Division I, II and III Colleges and Universities." Unpublished paper, 1982.

Bronzan, Robert T. "A Comprehensive Guide to Planning Facilities for the Handicapped." *Athletic Purchasing and Facilities*.e Vol. 4, No. 8, August 1980, pp. 12–14.

———. "Public Relations." In *Administration of Athletics in Colleges and Universities*. Edward S. Steitz (ed.). Washington, D.C. National Education Association, 1971.

Broyles, J. Frank, and Hay, Robert D. *Administration of Athletic Programs: A Managerial Approach*. Englewood Cliffs, N.J. Prentice-Hall, 1979.

Cady, Edwin H. *The Big Game*. Knoxville, Tenn. U. of Tennessee Press, 1978.

Dennison, Maria. "What Will "Pay for Play" do to School Sports?" *Athletic Purchasing and Facilities*. Vol. 6, No. 5, May 1982, pp. 1, 3.

Kramer, William D. "NCAA Attorney Discusses Changes in Title IX." Speech reprinted in *NCAA News*. July 28, 1982, p. 3.

———. "Title IX Not a Dead Issue, But It's Mellowing." Speech reprinted in *NCAA News*. July 14, 1982, pp. ?.

Parkhouse, Bonnie L., and Lapin, Jackie. *The Woman in Athletic Administration*. Santa Monica, Calif. Goodyear, 1980.

Quigley, Michael. "A Study in Stripes." Unpublished paper, 1982.

Seefeldt, Vern. "Can School, Non-School Sports Work Toward Common Goals?" *Athletics Purchasing and Facilities*. Vol. 6, No. 9, September 1982, p. 10–14.

———, Gilliam, Thomas, Blievernicht, David, and Bruce, Russell. "Scope of Youth Sports Programs in the State of Michigan." in *Psychological Perspectives in Youth Sports*. Frank L. Small and Ronald E. Smith (eds.). New York. Wiley, 1978, pp. 17–67.

Snyder, Edlon E. "High School Athletes and Their Coaches: Educational Plans and Advice." In *Sport and American Society: Selected Readings*. George H. Sage (comp.) Reading, Mass. Addison-Wesley, 1980.

Swearer, Howard R. "An Ivy League President Looks at College Sports." *The New York Times*. February 21, 1982, Section 5, p. 2.

"Tapping Student Spirit at Indiana University." *Athletic Purchasing and Facilities*. Vol. 4, No. 11, November 1980, pp. 9–12.

United Press International News Service. "Judge Blasts NCAA, Colleges Get TV Rights." Reported in Springfield, Mass. *The Morning Union*, September 16, 1982, p. 45.

Weiss, Paul. *Sport: A Philosphic Inquiry*. Carbondale and Edwardsville, Ill. Southern Illinois U. P., 1969.

Academic Programs in Sport Management

CONCEPTS AND PROBLEMS

Importance of the Organizational Structure for a Sport Management Program
Obtaining Qualified Faculty
Degree Level?
Relative Importance of Admissions Criteria and Procedures
Developing an Appropriate Curriculum
No Substitute for the Internship
The Program of Study Extends Beyond the Classroom

At various points, we have referred to academic programs in sport management. Thus, it seems appropriate to examine this developing area in detail. A few programs of this type have been in existence for soem time. However, in the past few years we have witnessed a considerable expansion of programs in sport management or sport administration or at least steps in that direction. It is estimated that there are now about 75 such programs on the North American continent, and the number is increasing each year. There is little doubt that this is the way to go in terms of the most appropriate preparation for those who aspire to managerial positions in sport. The only surprising thing is that it took so long for people to recognize the need for this kind of program development. At the same time one has to be cautious about assessing the progress in this direction because, like any newly developed field, it is evident that there are programs and then there are programs. Many of the sport management programs are still very much in the genesis stage and are barely distinguishable from the traditional physical education program. For example, an institution does not really have an academic program in sport management by offering a single course with that title. Therefore, let us examine some of the key considerations in the development of a full-fledged academic program in sport management.

ORGANIZATIONAL STRUCTURE

It is safe to say at the outset that for the most part sport management is not a primary administrative unit in the colleges or universities at the present time. In other words, we have a number of sport management programs but generally do not find departments, divisions, schools, or colleges of sport management. From our perspective it would certainly seem desirable to have at least departments of sport management, but in the meantime we have to work within the context of existing structures.

An examination of such structures reveals that there are two logical possibilities for an administrative framework for the development of a sport management program. One is a department or school of physical education, and the other is a department or school of business administration or management. Ideally, the latter would seem like the most appropriate choice. However, we also have to realize that relatively few departments or schools of business administration have shown any interest in developing a sport management program to date. That more or less leaves physical education as the administrative base for a sport management program, at least until the program can achieve a more independent status.

As long as an academic program in sport management remains in the context of a larger physical education unit, the organization of the sport management program within the broader unit is also extremely important. Every effort should be made to establish some form of semi-independent status for the sport management program. The independence would be particularly evident in the freedom to develop a curriculum and a total course of study that are most appropriate for the professional preparation of students in sport management. This is almost impossible to achieve if students are shackled by traditional physical education requirements.

FACULTY

If a sport management program originates within the context of physical education, it is reasonable to assume that the initial faculty are likely to be restricted to those who come from the physical education background. As a matter of fact, as we look at existing programs, it is apparent that there usually are one or two physical educators who take the leadership in developing a sport management program within the various physical education units. They may teach one or two sport management courses and then "farm out" the students to selected other disciplines and professional schools across campus. For example, it is customary for many of these students to take course work offered by faculty in business administration, economics, communication studies, and related fields. That is a step in the right direction, but it is only a step.

For continued progress in the development of an effective academic program in sport management, it is necessary to have a nucleus of faculty whose interest and expertise are clearly in this area. This goal can be approached from at least three directions. One is to have the physical educators "retool" to be able to offer courses, arrange internships, and generally guide a total program of study that is applicable to sport management. The key here is the real committment on the part of the physical educators to move in that direction. A second possibility is to attempt to recruit faculty from other applicable disciplines or professional fields. For example, the fields of business administration or management, economics, political science, computer science, law, and communications studies represent potential sources for such recruitment. The important point here, of course, is that possible candidates must have a strong background and interest in sport in order to be able and willing to make the transition. This can also be a limited recruitment area owing to the highly competitive market in some of these fields. In other words, it may be difficult to attract a professor from the field of business administration because of the number of placement opportunities and the competitive salary range in that field. Nevertheless, the record shows that well-qualified faculty in sport management can be obtained from such sources, and efforts should continue in that direction.

The third potential source of faculty may offer the best hope in the long run. This is to recruit faculty who have completed a Ph.D. program in sport management. Such programs are very few in number at present and are also still in the early stages of development. Yet well-qualified graduates from solid programs in this area should be in the best position really to contribute to the advancement of other academic programs in sport management that offer the bachelor's or master's degree or both in sport management. The University of Massachusetts at Amherst can be noted as one source that currently has the resources to prepare Ph.D. students in sport management.

BACHELOR'S DEGREE OR MASTER'S DEGREE PROGRAM OR BOTH

Most institutions that decide to embark on academic preparation in sport management will have to make a basic choice as to whether they will develop an undergraduate program or a graduate program. In some cases, the decision will be to develop the program at both levels. However, it is clear that this requires a fair amount of institutional support in terms of faculty positions and other forms of financial support for programs at both levels. Also, some colleges may only be in the position to offer bachelor's degree work.

I think that those who have worked with both B.S. and M.S. programs in sport management would confirm that each has its advantages and disadvantages. Perhaps the principal advantage of the B.S. program is that during four years of work students are able to take many more courses that are applicable to their future workout in the sport enterprise. This situation may be accompanied by the limitation that many of these students will lack the more well-rounded, general education that can be noted among a large number of the M.S. students. Also the bachelor's degree students face certain limitations in terms of internship opportunities and immediate placement. This is particularly true of those who aspire to work in college sport.

The major advantage of an M.S. program is probably found in the potentially rich pool of applicants for such degree work in sport management. Basically, this exists owing to the large number of college athletes who major in various fields. They have a strong background and interest in sport, but for one or many reasons they chose to pursue an undergraduate major outside this area. Thus, they tend to offer a rich combination of solid academic preparation and extensive sport background. Of course, another clear advantage of the M.S. program over the B.S. program is that it provides the entry-level degree work for most sport management positions in the colleges. The principal disadvantage of the M.S. program is related to a time factor. Students normally pursue this degree with two or three semesters of course work prior to the internship. They come from a variety of undergraduate backgrounds and have a limited amount of time to be directly exposed to sport management preparation. This may mean that some of these students develop relatively little identification with the fuller intent of an academic program in sport management. They might view the M.S. program as being only a transitory measure in gaining entry to the sport world. Yet there are also M.S. students in sport management who acquire a deeper appreciaton of the field after this relatively brief exposure. Usually, the key is to be found in the selection process for master's degree students.

In the final analysis, it seems that there is a most legitimate place for either bachelor's degree work or master's degree work or both in sport management. Each institution considering such a program will have to make the choice based on available resources and the potential pool of applicants for either degree.

ADMISSIONS

It is difficult to overestimate the relative importance of admissions criteria and procedures for any academic program. In the case of a sport management program, any general concern about admissions is legitimate for at least two reasons. First of all, such a program is likely to attract a large number of applicants in comparison to the space available (admissions quota) in most situations. This may be largely attributed to the dual appeal found both in the concept of sport and that of management. Also, it is rather apparent that much of the future success in sport management positions is dependent on qualifications that extend beyond the academic dimension per se. To be more specific, the nature of the previous sport involvement is often a most significant contributory factor to future success.

For these reasons, those who develop academic programs in sport management must give particularly close attention to admissions criteria and procedures. Having said that, this is not always as simple as it first appears. Some of the undergraduate programs will be restricted by institutional procedures wherein a given program has virtually no control over the admissions process. In other words, under such an arrangement, a program might have to accept a student who declares sport management as his or her major. However, even in those situations much attention should be directed toward counseling or advising student out of sport management if they do not appear to have the qualifications that generally contribute to success in the field.

Regardless of any admissions restraints, a required interview stands near the top of the list in terms of desirable admissions procedures. There should always be an effort to determine the fit among the applicant's background, the applicant's career aspirations, and the projected opportunities in that career field. For the most part, the degree of fit can only be determined through an interview. Prior to the interview, it is also helpful to consider a written statement from the applicant in which he or she addresses the background qualifications in relationship to the career aspiration.

Those programs that have direct control of admissions should, of course, not limit their decisions to the interview. It is always necessary to obtain a composite picture involving high school standing or undergraduate grade point average, standardized test scores, and letters of recommendation. In terms of standardized test scores, the Graduate Management Admissions Test (GMAT) is recommended for master's degree programs. Owing to the fact that is is a program in sport management, it makes sense to utilize the one standardized test that is designed in that direction. Although letters of recommendation tend to be somewhat limited in their usefulness, it is generally beneficial to obtain letters from two different kinds of sources: those who are able to assess the applicant's academic ability and those who have information on the nature of the applicant's sport involvement.

In general, it seems safe to say that it is important to have definite criteria for admission while maintaining sufficient flexibility to consider the total profile of the applicant. A slightly deficient grade point average may be offset by relatively high test scores. The interview may reveal unusually strong potential in certain areas. The letters of recommendation may point to a unique qualification. Admissions is always a complicated matter, and sport management admissions only reinforce that fact. Sport management is very much a "people-oriented" profession. The selection process must be aimed at total assessment to meet the qualifications for this line of professional work.

THE CURRICULUM

Most of the existing curricula in sport management are still very much in the earlier stages of development. Typically, the pattern has been to have students take a few sport management courses, a few sport theory courses, and some courses in a department or school of business administration. The latter is still a very worthwhile source of curricular support, but every effort should be made to enhance the sport management curriculum per se. Experience to date shows that the following topics represent some of the more applicable content in designing a sport management curriculum.

Sport Business and Finance

Sport Promotion and Public Relations (Marketing)

Policy Development in Sport

Sport and the Law

Leadership in Sport Organizations

Sport Facilities Management

Labor Relations in Sport

The Athletic Director: A Managerial Analysis

Professional Sport: A Managerial Analysis

Those topics certainly do not represent the scope or potential for developing an appropriate sport management curriculum. But at least they are some of the more up-front considerations in the management of the sport enterprise.

Much, of course, also depends on whether one is considering an undergraduate or graduate curriculum. There is obviously considerable more latitude in framing a four-year undergraduate cuirriculum. At least a quarter of that curriculum should be structured around general education, distribution, or core requirements at the college or university level. Undergraduate sport management majors can also benefit from a solid background in the theory of sport (i.e., courses in the economics, history, philosophy, sociology, and psychology of sport). In those institutions that have a department or school of business adminsitration, every effort should also be made to provide a distribution of business administration courses for the sport management majors. Either prior to or shortly after entry to the program, the sport management student should take an overview course under the title of "Introduction to Sport Management" or a similar title. The primary purpose of such a course would be twofold: to examine the scope of the sport enterprise and to provide the parameters of management within that setting.

In many respects, a master's degree curriculum is much more difficult to construct. This is primarily because these students generally only take about 8 to 10 courses during their total program of study. Moreover, many come from very diverse academic backgrounds. Part of this divergence may be accommodated through one overview course that provides the orientation to sport management. The need for the policy development course is also quite apparent at this level. Beyond that, perhaps the most appropriate approach is to have students select courses from the topics given earlier that seem to be most in line with their specific career plans.

THE INTERNSHIP

Almost anyone who has ever taught in an academic program in sport management or who is an alumnus of such a program will tell you that there is no substitute for the internship. I suspect this may also be true of certain other fields, for instance, medicine. At any rate, there is little doubt about the thought that much of the direct expertise in sport management can only be learned on the job. This in no way negates the importance of the earlier curricular pursuits. The courses provide the theoretical temper for what is to follow in the applied arena of the internship. From the student's perspective, an internship may offer another distinct advantage. It often leads directly to a full-time position or provides the experience and contacts to gain entry into other positions.

A few conditions are essential in the establishment of solid internship arrangements. The relative value of the internship is so much dependent on the role and attitude of the sponsor in the sport organization. The sponsor must be a person who understands the nature of a viable internship and who is in a position to facilitate that goal. If an intern is viewed only as "cheap labor," the internship falls far short of the ideal. Fortunately, our experience has been that there are a rapidly increasing number of sport organizations that are sensitive to the requirements for an effective internship.

Internship arrangements require very close coordination among the student, the adviser, and the sponsor in the sport organization. Within the academic program the adviser plays a key role because he or she can gradually accumulate a base of information about potential internship sites. Continued contact with alumni from the sport management program can also facilitate the development of that source of information. The adviser also plays an important role in recommending prospective interns who meet the qualifications that are being sought by the particular organization in the field.

It is important for each academic program in sport management to develop an internship contract that is signed by the intern, the sponsor, and the adviser. The contract should include a statement about the duration of the internship and any provisions for financial support through a stipend, meals, lodging, and so on. Internships should be at least one semester in length. This fits in best with the academic schedule, and it is rather unlikely that the needs can be met in a shorter period of time. Sometimes it is mutually beneficial for both the student and the organization to arrange internships that extend to one or two years.

A standard evaluation form should also be used to assess the student's work during the internship. This is particularly important in many situations where internships are arranged on a nationwide basis or within a large region of the country. The only direct assessment will be that of the sponsor, and the written evaluation provides at least some documentation of how well the student functioned in the internship situation. It can also be most beneficial to have the intern submit a final report at the completion of the internship. This might include a weekly diary of experiences as well as commentary on significant field experiences in sport management that can be accumulated as part of an information system for research and discussion with future sport management students.

AN INTEGRATED AND TOTAL PROGRAM OF STUDY

The discussion of internships also brings attention to a final point that is integral to a successful academic program in sport management. Although the courses provide the basis for study, they are but a part of the total picture in really being prepared for a sport management position. There is a need for each student to get involved in a more integrated and total manner that extends beyond the classroom as such. What are some of the added dimensions that can contribute toward that goal?

One possibility is what can be called the pre-internship, mini-internship, or prefield experiences. Essentially what this involves is that the student volunteers his or her services to work with some facet of a sport organization while engaged in the regular curricular pursuits. This might mean working with the athletic department's ticket manager or sports information director. In other cases, it might be coaching a junior high school team or serving as an assistant for a high school team. Various possibilities exist: the important thing is that the student somehow or other gets involved with the actual conduct of one or more dimensions of the sport enterprise. This kind of arrangement is generally more easily facilitated with master's degree students than with undergraduate because the latter are often participating as college athletes while pursuing their degree work. The combination of taking a full-course load and being a member of a college team may leave little time for other prefield experiences. Of course, the athletic experience in itself can be viewed as being the most valuable preparation for future work in sport management. On the other hand, there is an equal need to provide in-service experiences for those undergraduate sport management majors who are not members of collegiate teams.

Appropriately selected and carefully planned guest lectures can also contribute significantly to total program development. There are a number of leaders in the various segments of the sport enterprise who have much to offer in this regard. Students stand to benefit potentially from such lectures in at least two ways. The first hand experience of the lecturers offers a valuable complement to the regular curricular content. Probably what is even more important, the lectures (with accompanying arrangements) may provide the contacts that are so significant in the network of sport organizations. Sometimes the contact with a sport leader may be the initial step in sponsorship.

The total experience of the sport management student may be further enriched by guiding him or her in some form of field research. This may or may not be directly related to a course. Regardless of the particular format, the field research should lead to the development of a sport management paper that can serve as a documentation of the student's substantive inquiry into the field. When properly conceived and presented, it can measurably enhance the credential profile of the student who is looking for the leading edge in the competitive market of sport management positions. Ideally, the field research will provide the link between the course work and the operation of the sport enterprise. It is at this point that we particularly see the potential for an integrated academic program. Thus, there is also hope that academic programs in sport management, in turn, will show the way for an integrated sport management program in the schools and colleges.

INDEX

Date Due

DATE			
MAR 2 4 1987			
DEC 1 1 1990			